TERMINAL CONFERENCE

July 1945

PAPERS
AND
MINUTES OF MEETINGS
TERMINAL CONFERENCE

EDITED AND PUBLISHED BY THE

OFFICE, U. S. SECRETARY
OF THE COMBINED CHIEFS OF STAFF
1945

Published by Books Express Publishing
Copyright © Books Express, 2011
ISBN 978-1-780394-03-9

Books Express publications are available from all good retail and online booksellers. For publishing proposals and direct ordering please contact us at: info@books-express.com

TOP SECRET

TABLE OF CONTENTS

PAPERS

C.C.S.		PAGE
462/25	Staff Conversations with Portugal . . . . *(Memorandum by the United States Chiefs of Staff)*	1
462/26	Staff Conversations with Portugal . . . . *(Memorandum by the British Chiefs of Staff)*	5
643/3	Estimate of the Enemy Situation (as of 6 July 1945) . . . *(Report by the Combined Intelligence Committee)*	7
679/6	Disposition of Captured German Passenger Ships . . . . *(Memorandum by the United States Chiefs of Staff)*	45
679/7	British Troopship Employment in U.S. Trans-Atlantic Programs, First Half of 1946 . . . . *(Memorandum by the United States Chiefs of Staff)*	49
679/8	Employment of Captured Enemy Ocean-Going Passenger Shipping and British Troopship Employment in U.S. Trans-Atlantic Programs in the First Half of 1946 . . . . . . *(Memorandum by the British Chiefs of Staff)*	51
679/9	Employment of Captured Enemy Ocean-Going Passenger Shipping and British Troopship Employment in U.S. Trans-Atlantic Programs in the First Half of 1946 . . . . . . *(Memorandum by the United States Chiefs of Staff)*	53
706/11	Disposal of Enemy War Matériel in Germany and Austria *(Report by the Combined Administrative Committee)*	55
706/14 TERMINAL	Disposal of Enemy War Matériel in Germany and Austria *(Memorandum by the United States Chiefs of Staff)*	63
842	French and Dutch Participation in the War Against Japan *(Memorandum by the Representatives of the British Chiefs of Staff)*	67

i

TOP SECRET

TABLE OF CONTENTS

PAPERS

C.C.S.		PAGE
842/1	French and Dutch Participation in the War Against Japan *(Memorandum by the United States Chiefs of Staff)*	71
842/2	French and Dutch Participation in the War Against Japan *(Memorandum by the United States Chiefs of Staff)*	73
866	Future of Allied Force Headquarters, Mediterranean *(Memorandum by the Representatives of the British Chiefs of Staff)*	75
866/1	Future of Allied Force Headquarters, Mediterranean *(Memorandum by the United States Chiefs of Staff)*	77
866/2	Future of Allied Force Headquarters, Mediterranean *(Memorandum by the Representatives of the British Chiefs of Staff)*	79
877	Basic Objectives, Strategy, and Policies *(Memorandum by the United States Chiefs of Staff)*	81
877/1	Basic Objectives, Strategy, and Policies *(Memorandum by the Representatives of the British Chiefs of Staff)*	85
877/2	Basic Objectives, Strategy, and Policies *(Memorandum by the United States Chiefs of Staff)*	87
877/4	Basic Objectives, Strategy, and Policies *(Memorandum by the British Chiefs of Staff)*	89
877/5	Basic Objectives, Strategy, and Policies *(Memorandum by the United States Chiefs of Staff)*	95

TOP SECRET

TABLE OF CONTENTS

PAPERS

C.C.S.		PAGE
880	Agenda for the Next United States-British Staff Conference *(Memorandum by the Representatives of the British Chiefs of Staff)*	101
880/1	Agenda for the Next United States-British Staff Conference *(Memorandum by the Representatives of the British Chiefs of Staff)*	105
880/2	Agenda for Military Staff Conferences *(Memorandum by the United States Chiefs of Staff)*	107
880/3	Size of Military Staffs for TERMINAL *(Memorandum by the United States Chiefs of Staff)*	113
880/4	Development of Operations in the Pacific *(Memorandum by the United States Chiefs of Staff)*	117
880/5	Agenda for Military Staff Conferences *(Memorandum by the Representatives of the British Chiefs of Staff)*	109
880/6	Size of Military Staffs for TERMINAL *(Memorandum by the Representatives of the British Chiefs of Staff)*	115
880/7	Agenda for the Forthcoming Conference *(Memorandum by the United States Chiefs of Staff)*	111
880/8	Planning Date for the End of Organized Resistance by Japan *(Memorandum by the United States Chiefs of Staff)*	121
880/9	Program and Procedure for the Conference *(Memorandum by the British Chiefs of Staff)*	123

TOP SECRET

TABLE OF CONTENTS

PAPERS

C.C.S.		PAGE
880/10	Program and Procedure for the Conference *(Memorandum by the United States Chiefs of Staff)*	127
884	Information for the Russians Concerning the Japanese War *(Memorandum by the Representatives of the British Chiefs of Staff)*	129
884/1	Information for the Russians Concerning the Japanese War *(Memorandum by the United States Chiefs of Staff)*	131
884/2	Information for the Russians Concerning the Japanese War *(Memorandum by the British Chiefs of Staff)*	133
889	British Contribution to the Final Phase of the War Against Japan *(Memorandum by the Representatives of the British Chiefs of Staff)*	135
889/1	British Participation in the War Against Japan *(Memorandum by the United States Chiefs of Staff)*	139
889/2	British Participation in the War Against Japan *(Memorandum by the United States Chiefs of Staff)*	141
889/3	British Participation in the War Against Japan *(Memorandum by the United States Chiefs of Staff)*	145
890	Control and Command in the War Against Japan *(Memorandum by the Representatives of the British Chiefs of Staff)*	147
890/1	Control and Command in the War Against Japan *(Memorandum by the United States Chiefs of Staff)*	153

TOP SECRET

TABLE OF CONTENTS

PAPERS

C.C.S.		PAGE
890/2	Control and Command in the War Against Japan *(Memorandum by the British Chiefs of Staff)*	157
890/3	Command in Indo-China *(Memorandum by the British Chiefs of Staff)*	159
891	Combined Chiefs of Staff Machinery After the War with Japan *(Memorandum by the British Chiefs of Staff)*	161
891/1	Combined Chiefs of Staff Machinery After the War with Japan *(Memorandum by the United States Chiefs of Staff)*	165
892	Progress Report on Operations in the Southeast Asia Command *(Report by the Supreme Allied Commander, Southeast Asia)*	167
892/2	Directive to the Supreme Allied Commander, Southeast Asia *(Note by the Secretaries)*	175
893	General Progress Report on Recent Operations in the Pacific *(Memorandum by the United States Chiefs of Staff)*	181
893/1	Progress Report on Operations in China, April 1944 through June 1945 *(Memorandum by the United States Chiefs of Staff)*	191
894	Report on Army Air Operations in the War Against Japan *(Memorandum by the United States Chiefs of Staff)*	205

TOP SECRET

TABLE OF CONTENTS

PAPERS

C.C.S.		PAGE
895	Participation of Two French Colonial Infantry Divisions in Far Eastern Operations . . . . *(Memorandum by the United States Chiefs of Staff)*	217
895/1	Participation of Two French Colonial Infantry Divisions in Far Eastern Operations . . . . *(Memorandum by the British Chiefs of Staff)*	223
895/2	Participation of Two French Colonial Infantry Divisions in Far Eastern Operations . . . . *(Memorandum by the United States Chiefs of Staff)*	225
896	Internationalization of the Danube River . . . . *(Memorandum by the United States Chiefs of Staff)*	227
896/1	Internationalization of the Danube River . . . . *(Memorandum by the British Chiefs of Staff)*	233
897	Provision of Personnel Shipping for the Requirements of Allied Governments . . . . *(Report by the Combined Military Transportation Committee in consultation with the Combined Shipping Adjustment Board)*	235
897/1	Provision of Personnel Shipping for the Requirements of Allied Governments . . . . *(Note by the Secretaries)*	243
900/3	Report to the President and Prime Minister . . . . . . *(Note by the Secretaries)*	247

TOP SECRET

TABLE OF CONTENTS

MINUTES OF MEETINGS
TERMINAL CONFERENCE

	PAGE
C.C.S. 193d Meeting	269

    Program and Procedure for the Conference

    Estimate of the Enemy Situation

    Progress Reports on Operations in the Pacific and Southeast Asia Command

    Development of Operations in the Pacific

    Report on Army Air Operations in the War Against Japan

C.C.S. 194th Meeting	273

    British Participation in the War Against Japan

C.C.S. 195th Meeting	279

    French and Dutch Participation in the War Against Japan

    Staff Conversations with Portugal

    Southeast Asia and Southwest Pacific Area

    Control and Command in the War Against Japan

C.C.S. 196th Meeting	285

    Participation of Two French Colonial Infantry Divisions in Far Eastern Operations

    Combined Chiefs of Staff Machinery After the War with Japan

    Information for the Russians Concerning the Japanese War

    Planning Date for the End of Organized Resistance by Japan

    Appointment of Colonel Douglas to Allied Commission in Italy

TOP SECRET

TABLE OF CONTENTS

MINUTES OF MEETINGS

TERMINAL CONFERENCE

	PAGE
C.C.S. 197th Meeting	291

    Directive to the Supreme Allied Commander, Southeast Asia

    Disposal of Enemy War Matériel in Germany and Austria

C.C.S. 198th Meeting	295

    Basic Objectives, Strategy, and Policies

    British Troopship Employment in the U.S. Trans-Atlantic Programs, First Half of 1946

    Disposition of Captured German Passenger Ships

C.C.S. 199th Meeting	299

    Employment of Captured Enemy Ocean-Going Passenger Shipping and British Troopship Employment in U.S. Trans-Atlantic Programs in the First Half of 1946

    Provision of Personnel Ships for the Requirements of Allied Governments

    Command in French Indo-China

    Report to the President and Prime Minister

    Control of Allied Naval Units other than U.S. at Present Under Command of Seventh U.S. Fleet

C.C.S. 200th Meeting	303

    200th Meeting of the Combined Chiefs of Staff

    Operations in Southeast Asia Command

TOP SECRET

TABLE OF CONTENTS

MINUTES OF TERMINAL PLENARY MEETING

	PAGE
Plenary Meeting between the United States and Great Britain . . .	307

    Basic Objectives, Strategy, and Policies

    Provision of Supplies and Equipment to Great Britain

    Equipment and Supplies for Forces of Occupation other than American

    United Kingdom Import Program

    British Participation in the War Against Japan

TOP SECRET

TABLE OF CONTENTS

MINUTES OF TERMINAL
TRIPARTITE MILITARY MEETING

	PAGE
Tripartite Military Meeting	313

    Intentions and Plans of the U.S.S.R. with Reference to the Japanese

    Japanese Lines of Communication with Manchuria

    Strength and Distribution of the Japanese Forces

    Employment of U.S. Troops Redeployed from the European Theater

    Operations of the U.S. Naval Forces in the War Against Japan

    Operations of the U.S. Army Air Forces in the War Against Japan

    Operations to Increase Movement of Supplies into China

    Operations to Maintain a Line of Communications via the North Pacific

    Operations in Southeast Asia

TOP SECRET

TABLE OF CONTENTS

MINUTES OF MEETING

U.S.-U.S.S.R. CHIEFS OF STAFF

PAGE

Meeting of the Chiefs of Staff of the United States and of the Soviet Union 325

    Establishment of Radio Stations for Transmitting Weather Data

    U.S.-U.S.S.R. Zones of Naval and Air Operations in the Sea of Japan

    U.S.-U.S.S.R. Zones of Air Operations in Korea and Manchuria

    Establishment of Liaison Groups between the American and Soviet Commanders in the Far East

    Emergency Port and Airfield Facilities

    Line of Communications from Kyushu to Vladivostok

    Weekly Report of Operations

INDEX 339

TOP SECRET

C.C.S. 462/25
C.C.S. 462/26

STAFF CONVERSATIONS WITH PORTUGAL

References:

CCS 195th Meeting, Item 3
CCS 900/3, paragraph 17

    C.C.S. 462/25, a memorandum by the United States Chiefs of Staff, dated 16 July 1945, and C.C.S. 462/26, a memorandum by the British Chiefs of Staff, dated 18 July, were considered by the Combined Chiefs of Staff in their 195th Meeting (18 July). The Combined Chiefs of Staff approved the letter to the Department of State and Foreign Office in the Enclosure to C.C.S. 462/25, as amended by C.C.S. 462/26.

TOP SECRET

C.C.S. 462/25 16 July 1945

COMBINED CHIEFS OF STAFF

STAFF CONVERSATIONS WITH PORTUGAL

Reference:

CCS 462 Series

Memorandum by the United States Chiefs of Staff

1. The report by the Combined Administrative Committee in consultation with the Combined Staff Planners in C.C.S. 462/19* on the report of the Anglo-American Military Mission (C.C.S. 462/15*) relative to proposals for Portuguese participation in Allied operations for the recapture of Timor was submitted to the Combined Chiefs of Staff on 3 January 1945. This report recommended that a letter be dispatched to the Department of State and Foreign Office setting forth the conclusions of the Combined Chiefs of Staff on the staff conversations with the Portuguese. Action on C.C.S. 462/19 has been deferred at the request of the British Chiefs of Staff. As a result the Department of State and Foreign Office have not as yet been advised of the conclusions of the Combined Chiefs of Staff on the staff conferences held with the Portuguese although these conversations were held some nine months ago. The Department of State is pressing the United States Chiefs of Staff for information regarding the details of the plan for Portuguese participation in any operations directed toward liberation of Timor.

2. The United States Chiefs of Staff understand that the British Chiefs of Staff's delay in acting on C.C.S. 462/19 is due to lack of information from Australia on that country's ability to provide accommodations for the Portuguese contingent. The end of the war in Europe makes out of date the draft letter to the Department of State and Foreign Office contained in Appendix "A" of C.C.S. 462/19 in two particulars. The United States Chiefs of Staff have therefore revised the letter to the Department of State and Foreign Office contained in Appendix "A" to C.C.S. 462/19 along broader lines. It is recommended that the Combined Chiefs of Staff approve the enclosed letter to the Department of State and Foreign Office. In view of the urgency of the matter, the United States Chiefs of Staff would appreciate prompt consideration of this paper by the British Chiefs of Staff.

---

* Not published herein.

TOP SECRET

ENCLOSURE

DRAFT

LETTER TO THE DEPARTMENT OF STATE AND FOREIGN OFFICE

The Combined Chiefs of Staff on 2 September 1944 appointed an Anglo-American Military Mission to enter into conversations with Portuguese military authorities to discuss Portuguese proposals for participation in such operations as may be conducted eventually to expel the Japanese from Portuguese Timor. The Combined Chiefs of Staff have arrived at the following conclusions on the report of this mission:—

a. The Combined Chiefs of Staff are agreed on the acceptance of Portuguese assistance in such operations as may be conducted eventually to expel the Japanese from Portuguese Timor. While they have made no agreement with the Portuguese military authorities as to the direct use of Portuguese forces, they have recognized the possibility of such use and agreed that plans will be worked out as a result of the studies conducted in staff conversations in Lisbon.

b. As between the two military forces offered by Portugal (a regimental combat team of 4,000 or a battalion combat team of 2,200, both including 400 native troops), the larger force is acceptable and can be trained in the theater.

c. The air component offered by Portugal should under no circumstances be included in the acceptance of the Portuguese offer in view of the small number of planes available and the state of the training of the pilots, mechanics, and radio specialists.

d. There is no objection from the military viewpoint to Portugal receiving munitions when they can be spared but negotiation as to the basis for transfer is an action to be taken on a governmental level.

e. The Combined Chiefs of Staff in accepting Portuguese participation do not intend to enter into a commitment for the retaking of Portuguese Timor. Neither is acceptance to be construed as a commitment to use Portuguese troops in any other area.

f. Military operations against Portuguese Timor must for the present await the completion of operations against higher priority Japanese-held objectives. The Combined Chiefs of Staff will notify the Portuguese military

TOP SECRET

authorities of impending operations against Portuguese Timor in time for them to prepare their troops for participation therein. Details as to the assembly, shipment, training, and equipping of the Portuguese force will be decided by the Combined Chiefs of Staff at the appropriate time.

The Combined Chiefs of Staff have no objection to the disclosure of any of the above information to the Portuguese if the Department of State or Foreign Office deem it necessary in diplomatic conversations. The participation of Portuguese forces in the liberation of Portuguese Timor is considered of little importance in the war against Japan.

TOP SECRET

C.C.S. 462/26   18 July 1945

COMBINED CHIEFS OF STAFF

STAFF CONVERSATIONS WITH PORTUGAL

Memorandum by the British Chiefs of Staff

1. We have considered the memorandum (C.C.S. 462/25) by the United States Chiefs of Staff and are in general agreement with the draft letter to the Department of State and Foreign Office attached as the Enclosure thereto.

2. We propose, however, two minor amendments as follows:—

a. In subparagraph *b.* of the proposed letter, it is stated that "the larger force is acceptable and can be trained in the theater." The situation in this respect is that the Australian authorities have informed us that they cannot accept any Portuguese force. An inquiry has now been addressed to the Commander in Chief, Ceylon, asking him whether he can accept the Portuguese and, if so, the size of force he can accommodate, pointing out that we prefer the larger force.

No reply has yet been received. We cannot, therefore, be certain which of the two forces we can accept or where the training area will be.

We, therefore, propose that subparagraph *b.* of the draft letter should read as follows:—

"As between the two military forces offered by Portugal (a regimental combat team of 4,000 or a battalion combat team of 2,200, both including 400 native troops), the larger force is likely to be the more acceptable. Steps are being taken to allocate a suitable training area."

b. We suggest that the last sentence of the draft letter may be interpreted as failing to give due weight to the political desirability of Portuguese participation in the liberation of Timor.

We propose that the sentence should read:—

"The participation of Portuguese forces in the liberation of Portuguese Timor is considered of little <u>military</u> importance in the war against Japan."

TOP SECRET

3. Subject to the above amendments, we recommend that the Combined Chiefs of Staff approve the despatch of the letter to the Department of State and the Foreign Office as proposed in C.C.S. 462/25.

SECRET

C.C.S. 643/3

ESTIMATE OF THE ENEMY SITUATION
(as of 6 July 1945)

References:

CCS 880, paragraph 1 (1)
CCS 193d Meeting, Item 2

The Combined Chiefs of Staff took note of C.C.S. 643/3 in their 193d Meeting (16 July).

SECRET

C.C.S. 643/3　　　　　　　　　　　　　　　　　　　　　　8 July 1945

COMBINED CHIEFS OF STAFF

ESTIMATE OF THE ENEMY SITUATION
(as of 6 July 1945)

Note by the Secretaries

The enclosed report prepared by the Combined Intelligence Committee in reference to paragraph 1 (1) of C.C.S. 880 as directed by the Combined Chiefs of Staff is submitted for consideration.

A. J. McFARLAND,
A. T. CORNWALL-JONES,
Combined Secretariat.

SECRET

INDEX TO C.C.S. 643/3

ESTIMATE OF THE ENEMY SITUATION
(as of 6 July 1945)

	PAGE
The Problem	
1. To Estimate the Japanese Situation and Intentions	12
Summary	
2. Over-All Situation	12
3. Economic Situation	13
4. Armed Forces	
a. Ground	14
b. Air	14
c. Naval	15
5. Defense of Japan	15
6. Korea, Manchuria, and North China	16
7. Central and South China and Formosa	16
8. Southern Areas	16
9. Pacific Islands	16
10. Political Situation	17
Conclusions	
11. Probable Military Strategy	17
12. Probable Political Strategy	18
13. Possibility of Surrender	18
Appendix "A"—Economic Situation	
1. General	20
2. Transportation	
a. Shipping	20
b. Railroads	21
c. Roads	21

SECRET

PAGE

3. Industry
   a. General 21
   b. Shipbuilding 22
   c. Armaments 22
   d. Aircraft 22
   e. Electronics 22
   f. Steel 23
   g. Aluminum 23
   h. Non-ferrous Metals 23
   i. Chemicals and Fertilizer 23
4. Petroleum Products
   a. Aviation Fuel 23
   b. Lubricating Oils 24
   c. Other Petroleum Products 24
5. Coal 24
6. Food 24
7. Manpower 25
8. Civilian Supply 25
9. Regional Economic Administration 25

Appendix "B"—Armed Forces

Ground Forces
1. Japanese 27
2. Puppets 27
3. National Volunteer Army 27

Air Forces
4. Aircraft Strength
   a. General 28
   b. Production 29
   c. Wastage 29
   d. Future Combat Aircraft Strength 29
   e. Trainers 29

SECRET

	PAGE
5. Deployment	29
6. Capabilities	30

Naval Forces

7. Strength	30
Map—Japanese Armed Forces—Ground	32

Appendix "C"—Capabilities and Intentions for the Defense of Japan Proper

1. Present Strength and Dispositions	
a. Ground	33
b. Air	33
c. Naval	33
2. Capabilities	33
3. Intentions	34

Appendix "D"—Military Situation, Capabilities, and Intentions in Korea, Manchuria, and North China ... 36

Appendix "E"—Military Situation, Capabilities, and Intentions in Central and South China and Formosa ... 37

Appendix "F"—Situation, Capabilities, and Intentions in the Southern Areas ... 38

Appendix "G"—Situation in the Pacific Islands ... 40

Appendix "H"—Political Situation

1. General Situation	41
2. Internal Political Situation	41
3. Foreign Policy	42
4. Possibility of Surrender	43

SECRET

ENCLOSURE

ESTIMATE OF THE ENEMY SITUATION
(as of 6 July 1945)

Report by the Combined Intelligence Committee

THE PROBLEM

1. To estimate the Japanese situation and intentions.

SUMMARY

2. *Over-All Situation.* Recent advances in the western Pacific, culminating in the capture of Okinawa, provide the Allies with bases from which effective air attacks can be directed against all important areas under Japanese control. Furthermore, the Allies are now in possession of potential forward bases for an invasion of the Japanese home islands, Korea, or the central China coast. Air bases in the interior of China are being recaptured and may be more fully utilized. In addition, increasing Soviet forces in the Maritime Provinces and along the Amur River threaten Manchuria and the areas bordering the Japan Sea.

On the continent the Japanese are now forced to depend upon inadequate and vulnerable land communications. Japan's seaborne communications with all areas south of the Yangtze River have been practically severed. Sea traffic between Japan proper and ports from Shanghai northward to southern Korea is limited to hazardous runs along the Korean and North China coasts. Even the relatively short shipping routes across the Sea of Japan and the Tsushima Straits are increasingly menaced by Allied mining, aerial, and submarine activities.

The southern areas are not only cut off from the home islands, but the Japanese find it increasingly difficult to maintain communications between the various territories in the south which are still in their possession.

Sea and air operations have virtually destroyed the capability of the Japanese naval and air forces for other than suicide operations against our forces. Blockade, and air attacks on productive capacity and concentrated reserves of matériel, are seriously impairing remaining Japanese defensive capabilities. The incendiary bombing attack of Japanese cities has had a profound psychological and economic effect on the Japanese. The complete destruction of major areas in all of the important war production centers is placing a tremendous strain upon residual economy, substituting appreciably for the lack of high combat expenditures and producing a chaotic condition in administration and control, which will greatly accelerate the effects of subsequent all-out attacks upon transportation. On the other hand, stocks of ammunition and ammunition production facilities still require intensive and extremely heavy attacks to produce any shortage significant to the interests of invasion and occupation.

3. *Economic Situation. (Appendix "A")*. The Japanese economic position has deteriorated greatly. The resources of the Outer Zone are no longer available. Transportation between the complementary parts of the Inner Zone* (food and raw materials from North China, Manchuria, and Korea in return for finished products of the islands of Japan) has been seriously curtailed during the last few months, owing to the shortage of shipping (now only 1,300,000 gross registered tons of operable ships over 1,000 tons), Allied submarine and mining activities, and aerial bombardment. Thus, heavy industry in Japan is currently able to produce only at rates far below the capacity of existing plant facilities. For example, although peak production of steel in the islands of Japan has never exceeded 6,000,000 metric tons, current production is only at the rate of 3,500,000 tons. Production of aluminum, chemicals, and fertilizers is also hampered by the transportation difficulties.

Increasingly heavy air attacks, supplementing continued and intensified blockade, are seriously reducing Japan's residual production. The output of end products has been substantially lowered. Recent aircraft production is estimated at 1,200-1,500 combat planes monthly, as compared with a peak production of 2,300 reached late in 1944. The Japanese are so short of aviation fuel that orthodox air operations of a sustained nature in any significant force are improbable, although sufficient gasoline will be available to meet their capabilities for all-out suicide attacks. The electronics industry is not able to provide the armed forces with adequate supplies of radar or of radio and sound equipment. On the other hand, reserves of ordnance, other than heavier types of equipment, are believed to be large.

Manpower is not in general a limiting factor on either Japanese production or the size of her army. Bombing of industrial facilities in urban areas has led to workers being released to agriculture.

---
* Japan proper, Korea, Manchuria, North China, and Karafuto (Sakhalin).

There is increasing evidence of Japanese concern with regard to the food situation in Japan proper. Only slight decreases in over-all food supplies are, however, anticipated during 1945, although urban dwellers may be seriously affected by disturbances in distribution and losses of stocks resulting from air attacks. More acute is the shortage of consumer goods, the supply of which has been inadequate and which has been aggravated by the current bombings. Partly with an eye to an impending disruption of transport, the Japanese have set up eight regional administrations, each possessing sweeping powers to perform as well as possible in case of emergency.

4. *Armed Forces. (Appendix "B")*.

a. Ground. The ground component of the Japanese armed forces remains Japan's greatest military asset. There are at present some 110 infantry and four armored divisions in the Japanese Army with a total strength of about 4,600,000 men. They are disposed as shown in the map attached to Appendix "B." This force will probably be increased by about 30 divisions by the end of the year; some of these new units may be in existence at present. About 1,000,000 men, however, are now for all practical purposes isolated from the Japanese Inner Zone. The remainder, some 95 divisions (over 4,000,000 men), will be disposed in the main Japanese islands, Korea, Manchuria, and in China north of the Yangtze.

In addition to their regular ground forces, the Japanese have some 300,000 Manchurian and 900,000 Chinese puppet troops of questionable combat value, but capable of guarding lines of communications and performing service duties. Some defections among the Chinese puppets will occur as operations progress. There will probably be a considerable reduction in their strength by the end of 1945.

b. Air. Until September 1944, the Japanese air forces steadily increased in size. Since that time they have suffered a substantial reduction in strength. The total strength of combat aircraft assigned to both tactical and training units has been reduced from 8,200 as of 1 September 1944 to about 5,000 as of late June 1945. Thus the availability of combat aircraft has been already lowered during this period by about 40 percent. As a result of the greatly expanded Allied air action against Japan, the Japanese aircraft industry, as well as airfield installations, supplies, and repair facilities will suffer greatly during the next few months.

The Japanese believe their maximum air capability to be in the employment of suicide tactics, directed primarily against ships. Currently the Japanese High Command is doing everything possible to improve the training, planning, and accomplishment of suicide air missions. Apparently they have decided to sacrifice future air potential in favor of maximum employment of all available aircraft and pilots to meet any actual invasion. Great numbers of trainer-type aircraft are being equipped for suicide missions and pilot trainees are being assigned to suicide units.

The current trend of deployment, which we expect will continue, indicates that the Japanese will in the near future have over 90 percent of their entire air strength concentrated in the main Japanese islands, Korea, Manchuria, and North China.

c. Naval. The Japanese Navy has been reduced in size to about the equivalent of one small and unbalanced task force. With the exception of two damaged cruisers, one destroyer, and some submarines in the Singapore area, remaining battleships, carriers, and cruisers appear to be immobilized in home waters. Their main capability and probable employment hereafter will be in suicide attacks by a small task force, and harassing and suicide operations by small surface craft and submarine attacks. Extensive mine fields probably exist in the vicinity of important harbors and other strategic areas around the homeland.

5. *Defense of Japan. (Appendix "C").* The defense of the main islands of Japan is receiving and will continue to receive the primary attention of the Japanese.

We estimate that by late 1945 there will be available in the Japanese home islands and their outposts in the Ryukyus, Izu-Bonins, and Kuriles more than 35 active divisions and 14 depot divisions, which, plus army troops, will total over 2,000,000 men. The Japanese also will continue development of the "National Volunteer Army" and may form combat home defense units to supplement their regular armed forces. Fanatical resistance will be offered in the defense of any of the home islands. The Japanese would commit all ground forces they could sustain in action in the defense of Kyushu and that part of Honshu which includes the Kanto Plain, Nagoya, and Osaka areas, while considerably weaker defense would be expected in other parts of Honshu, Shikoku, and Hokkaido for both logistical and strategical reasons.

We believe that in the defense of any one of the main Japanese islands, except possibly Hokkaido, the Japanese would commit against us, primarily in suicide operations, all available aircraft, either in tactical or training units. Such attacks would be continued to the limit of their capability without regard for conservation of air strength for any possible later need.

SECRET

Remaining Japanese naval units would be also sacrificed to the limit of their capability in the all-out effort to repel our invasion of any one of the main Japanese islands.

6. *Korea, Manchuria, and North China. (Appendix "D")*. The Japanese ground forces in this area now total over 1,200,000 men (24 active divisions and 5 depot divisions). In anticipation of a possible Soviet entry into the war, these forces will be further increased by withdrawals from Central and South China, and we believe they might have about 1,500,000 men, including more than 40 divisions, in this area by the end of the year. In so far as they are able to do so, the Japanese are preparing for an independent defense of Manchuria, Korea, and North China, and it is unlikely that any substantial reinforcements or supplies will be sent hereafter to this area from Japan proper. We believe that in the event of war with the U.S.S.R., opposition to the Soviets would be left primarily to the Japanese ground forces and that Japan would continue to commit the great bulk of its air strength against us in defense of the home islands.

7. *Central and South China and Formosa. (Appendix "E")*. The Japanese now have about 650,000 men (20 divisions) in Central and South China and another 190,000 men (5 divisions) in Formosa. However, the rapid advance of Allied forces in the Pacific, the interdiction of Japan's shipping routes, apprehension regarding the entry of the U.S.S.R. into the war, and the growing threat of Allied invasion of the east China Coast are forcing the Japanese to shift strength in China northward. We believe that the Japanese are prepared, if circumstances necessitate, to abandon all holdings in China south of the Yellow River, leaving a force of about 125,000, including four divisions in the Canton-Hong Kong area, and a force of 160,000, including six divisions in the Shanghai-Nanking area to deny them to the Allies. Japanese forces in Formosa are cut off and will remain substantially unchanged in numbers.

8. *Southern Areas. (Appendix "F")*. The Japanese in the southern areas (over 600,000 men) have been cut off from the home islands and will receive no further reinforcement or supply. We believe that they will form a perimeter of defense running generally through southeast Burma, Thailand, Malaya, Sumatra, Java, Borneo, and French Indo-China. Island areas outside this perimeter will be defended by local garrisons. Redistribution of forces within the area will be difficult owing to Allied action and to the very limited transportation facilities. No offensive capability exists, but defense will be determined on the part of local ground forces, using the resources initially available to them.

9. *Pacific Islands. (Appendix "G")*. Japanese ground forces cut off in the Pacific islands (the Mandates, Solomons, Bismarcks, New Guinea, and the

Philippines), amounting to about 300,000 men, have no offensive capabilities, but will hold out to the maximum extent of their ability.

10. *Political Situation. (Appendix "H").* The political situation in Japan is dominated by the progressive deterioration of the military situation. The Japanese Diet has now practically legislated itself out of existence and the Government has assumed sweeping powers that enable it to rule by decree. The Government thus hopes to be in a position to act without fear of major opposition, whether it should determine to continue the war to the bitter end or to seek peace.

The Japanese still find unconditional surrender unacceptable, but they are becoming increasingly desirous of a compromise. Fully aware of the growing weakness of Japan's position, her leaders will make desperate attempts to keep the Soviet Union at least neutral, to sow civil strife in China, and to win the support of conquered peoples. In their present dilemma they are playing for time in the hope that Allied war weariness, jealousies, and conflicts of aims, or some "miracle," will present a method of extricating them from their admitted critical situation.

CONCLUSIONS

11. *Probable Military Strategy.* The primary preoccupation of the Japanese High Command at present is the defense of the home islands, especially Kyushu and Honshu. For this defense they may dispose by the end of 1945 more than 35 active divisions plus 14 depot divisions, which, with army troops, will total over 2,000,000 men. Except possibly in the case of Hokkaido, all available aircraft will be employed in the defense of the home islands, mainly in suicide operations. Their air effort might amount initially to 400-500 sorties of combat-type aircraft and 200-300 sorties of trainer-type aircraft during any 24-hour period; this effort will, however, decline rapidly. Similarly all remaining naval units will be employed in suicide operations in defense of the homeland.

The secondary preoccupation of the Japanese is to build up their forces in Manchuria, Korea, and North China against the Soviet threat. There they might dispose up to 40 divisions, totalling about 1,500,000 men, by December of this year. Reinforcements will come from Central and South China. They are unlikely to make a strong air effort in defense of Manchuria at the expense of the defense of Japan. If circumstances require it, the Japanese are prepared to abandon all of China south of the general line Tungkuan-Kaifeng-Nanking-Hangchow, except for the Canton-Hong Kong pocket, which they will hold with a strong garrison.

SECRET

All other areas will be regarded as of minor importance only. They will not be reinforced from the Inner Zone, but their garrisons will be ordered to resist to the last in order to contain Allied forces which might otherwise be used against Japan, and in order to deny to the Allies strategic materials and bases in their areas. Strategy in these outlying areas will, therefore, be designed to keep Japanese forces in being rather than to defend particular objectives to the last or to undertake more than, at the most, local counteroffensives.

12. *Probable Political Strategy.* In general, Japan will use all political means for avoiding complete defeat or unconditional surrender. During the next few months the future political strategy of the Government will exhibit the following aims: To,

a. Continue and even increase its attempts to secure complete political unity within the Empire, possibly through personal rule, real or apparent, of the Emperor.

b. Attempt to foster a belief among Japan's enemies that the war will prove costly and long drawn out if the United Nations insist on fighting until the complete conquest of Japan.

c. Make desperate efforts to persuade the U.S.S.R. to continue her neutrality, if necessary by offering important territorial or other concessions, while at the same time making every effort to sow discord between the Americans and British on one side and the Russians on the other. As the situation deteriorates still further, Japan may even make a serious attempt to use the U.S.S.R. as a mediator in ending the war.

d. Put out intermittent peace feelers, in an effort to bring the war to an acceptable end, to weaken the determination of the United Nations to fight to the bitter end, or to create inter-Allied dissension.

e. Take all possible advantage of estranged relations between the Communists and Kuomintang factions in China.

13. *Possibility of Surrender.* The Japanese ruling groups are aware of the desperate military situation and are increasingly desirous of a compromise peace, but still find unconditional surrender unacceptable. The basic policy of the present government is to fight as long and as desperately as possible in the hope of avoiding complete defeat and of acquiring a better bargaining position in a negotiated peace. Japanese leaders are now playing for time in the hope that Allied war weariness, Allied disunity, or some "miracle," will present an opportunity to arrange a compromise peace.

We believe that a considerable portion of the Japanese population now consider absolute military defeat to be probable. The increasing effects of sea blockade and cumulative devastation wrought by strategic bombing, which has already rendered millions homeless and has destroyed from 25 to 50 percent of the built-up area of Japan's most important cities, should make this realization increasingly general. An entry of the Soviet Union into the war would finally convince the Japanese of the inevitability of complete defeat. Although individual Japanese willingly sacrifice themselves in the service of the nation, we doubt that the nation as a whole is predisposed toward national suicide. Rather, the Japanese as a nation have a strong concept of national survival, regardless of the fate of individuals. They would probably prefer national survival, even through surrender, to virtual extinction.

The Japanese believe, however, that unconditional surrender would be the equivalent of national extinction. There are as yet no indications that the Japanese are ready to accept such terms. The ideas of foreign occupation of the Japanese homeland, foreign custody of the person of the Emperor, and the loss of prestige entailed by the acceptance of "unconditional surrender" are most revolting to the Japanese. To avoid these conditions, if possible, and, in any event, to insure survival of the institution of the Emperor, the Japanese might well be willing to withdraw from all the territory they have seized on the Asiatic continent and in the southern Pacific, and even to agree to the independence of Korea and to the practical disarmament of their military forces.

A conditional surrender by the Japanese Government along the lines stated above might be offered by them at any time from now until the time of the complete destruction of all Japanese power of resistance.

Since the Japanese Army is the principal repository of the Japanese military tradition it follows that the army leaders must, with a sufficient degree of unanimity, acknowledge defeat before Japan can be induced to surrender. This might be brought about either by the defeat of the main Japanese armies in the Inner Zone or through a desire on the part of the army leaders to salvage something from the wreck with a view to maintaining military tradition. For a surrender to be acceptable to the Japanese Army, it would be necessary for the military leaders to believe that it would not entail discrediting warrior tradition and that it would permit the ultimate resurgence of a military Japan.

APPENDIX "A"

ECONOMIC SITUATION

1. *General.* The Japanese economic position has deteriorated considerably during the past year. Important raw materials from the southern areas, such as non-ferrous metals, high grade iron ore, bauxite, oil, and rubber are no longer available. The severe cut in the size of the Japanese merchant marine, rail transportation difficulties on the continent, and continuing direct attacks against Japanese industrial facilities and urban areas by United States bombers have reduced the war potential of the Inner Zone substantially below the levels of a year ago.

The Inner Zone itself is no longer an economic entity. The hazards to enemy shipping in the Sea of Japan, particularly in the Tsushima and Korean Straits area by Allied air and submarine attacks and the mining of the coastal waters has seriously disrupted movements of essential supplies across this last remaining lifeline between Japan proper and the continent. The shortage of minesweepers and escorts for convoys further restricts the use of these remaining shipping lanes and causes additional deterioration of the Japanese economic situation.

2. *Transportation.*

a. Shipping. Deterioration of the Japanese shipping position begun in 1943 and accelerated during 1944 continues to be one of the principal factors affecting Japan's industrial effort. Heavy losses already sustained by Japan's merchant fleet, as well as current Allied naval and air operations against the remainder of this fleet, prevent Japan from utilizing to the full extent even the resources of the Inner Zone in spite of fairly short hauls and less vulnerable routes. Despite capture of some 700,000 tons of foreign ships and an increased 1944 rate of shipbuilding, Japan's pre-war merchant tonnage of some 6,000,000 tons* of steel ships of 1,000 tons and over has been reduced to an estimated operable 1,300,000 tons including a large tonnage of tankers. There are, in addition, a large number of smaller ships available. The need for the convoy system and the mining of the coastal waters further limits the efficient employment of the reduced shipping which is available.

The present major demands on Japanese shipping are for the movement of coal, pig iron, iron ore, aluminous shale, salt, and foodstuffs from the

---

* Figures are in gross registered tons.

continent; coal, lumber, and pulp from Karafuto; coal and other commodities between points in Japan proper; commodities between points on the continent; and troops and military supplies throughout the area.

b. Railroads. The railways in Japan, supplemented by coastal shipping, are currently capable of carrying the essential industrial and military freight. Air attacks to date probably have not seriously impaired rail operations.

The system of rail lines, however, is relatively vulnerable to attack by air. Steep grades and numerous tunnels, bridges, and retaining walls are characteristic features of all the lines. Vulnerable bottlenecks exist at the rail tunnel between Honshu and Kyushu and the rail ferries connecting Honshu with Hokkaido and with Shikoku.

The decline in their merchant fleet has forced the Japanese to rely, for the major portion of their imports of continental materials, upon the railways leading from North China and Manchuria to the Korean ports facing Japan. Because of the limited capacity of those lines and of operating difficulties which have been encountered, the Japanese have been able to import much less of those materials than have been available at the points of production.

c. Roads. The road systems of Japan and of other Inner Zone areas are not very highly developed and consist of a few trunk gravel-surfaced roads connecting the main cities and a number of rather poorly constructed and maintained connecting roads. Long distance truck transport is of little importance, and trucks have been used mainly for local distribution. There is a shortage of trucks, fuel, servicing facilities, and repair parts.

3. *Industry.*

a. General. Because of the shortage of merchant shipping and the interdiction of transport routes, the islands of Japan are being cut off from the continental areas. The continental areas and the islands of Japan are economically complementary to each other, the former supplying Japan with raw materials and food, and the latter supplying the continent with finished products. Raw materials are being accumulated on the continent for which there is insufficient processing capacity, while Japanese processing equipment is becoming increasingly idle as stock piles decrease. Lowered war production in the Inner Zone as a whole has resulted.

The Japanese have received assistance from the Germans in the form of techniques, devices, and weapons, the employment of which might have a bearing on the war in the Pacific. Among the most important items

Appendix "A"

are electronics, ordnance, rockets, guided missiles, submarines, aircraft, and jet propulsion. Japanese capability to utilize this assistance effectively, however, is limited.

b. Shipbuilding. We believe that the rate of construction of merchant ships of 1,000 gross registered tons and over, which reached an average of 100,000 tons per month in 1944 has declined in recent months to about 75,000 tons and will decline progressively from now on.

c. Armaments.

(1) *Ordnance.* We estimate that the manufacture of weapons in the Inner Zone for ground troops had produced large reserves of light weapons by 1 July 1945. Reserves of divisional weapons will be sufficient to equip more than 30 new divisions, except for modern field artillery. Additional reserves of 1,000,000 rifles, 10,000 light machine guns, and 2,000 anti-tank guns are believed to be available. No appreciable reserve of tanks or of certain important heavy artillery weapons is believed to exist.

(2) *Ammunition.* We believe that the Japanese have accumulated in the islands of Japan a substantial stock of small arms ammunition. There are indications, however, that artillery ammunition is in tight supply and that practice ammunition has been curtailed. Recently there has been emphasis on anti-aircraft ammunition production at the expense of other types.

Depending on the number of divisions involved and the severity of the fighting, the Japanese have adequate supplies of ground ammunition to resist invasion for many months.

d. Aircraft. Aircraft production has declined from a peak of about 2,300 planes per month as of the end of 1944 to a recent production of 1,200 to 1,500 aircraft per month. Bombing of aircraft assembly and engine plants and the subsidiary industries accounts for much of the decline, but an important temporary contributing factor was the dispersal of plants in the early part of 1945. As a result of dispersal, it is unlikely that production can be reduced much below its present rate by precision attacks on the factories alone. Attacks on industrial areas and transportation will have a considerable indirect effect on the aircraft industry, however, and it is possible that four or five months of such attacks will reduce Japanese aircraft production to about 1,000 planes a month.

e. Electronics. The Japanese electronics industry is not able to provide the armed forces with adequate supplies of radar, or of radio and sonic equipment, despite the high priority given the industry.

Appendix "A"

f. Steel. The islands of Japan have plant facilities for producing over 10,000,000 tons of steel ingots annually, but neither before nor during the war has production exceeded 6,000,000 metric tons. Imports of iron ore have been declining progressively since early in the war and coal imports have been declining since at least the beginning of 1944. Domestic production of iron ore in Japan is estimated, at a maximum, at one million tons per year of iron content. An additional 2,500,000 tons of iron content are available on the continent. Some of it is being sent to Japan as pig iron and steel, but little is currently being shipped as iron ore. Scrap iron and scrap steel, domestic iron ore, and estimated imports are sufficient to support an annual steel production of not more than 3,500,000 tons. There are probably no shortages of ferro-alloys at this reduced rate of production. Inadequate supplies of steel are believed already to have curtailed the production of armaments. As Japan is thought to have no substantial stocks of crude or rolled steel, further decline in steel production would be reflected in additional curtailment in armament output, in shipbuilding, and in railroad and industrial maintenance.

g. Aluminum. The aluminum industry in the home islands is almost wholly dependent on imports of aluminous ores from the continent. We believe that there is no substantial stock pile of such ores in Japan. Plant capacity of the home islands is estimated at about 150,000 metric tons annually although production during the fiscal year beginning 1 April 1944 probably did not exceed 130,000 tons. Current production is estimated at about 75,000 tons annually. In addition, about 35,000 tons are now being produced in Korea and Manchuria, some of which is shipped to Japan. This is enough aluminum for production of airplanes at about or slightly above present rates. The blockade will eventually affect Japan's ability to import aluminum, but in view of the small tonnage involved, and the high priority given to shipments, it will be some time before this factor makes itself felt.

h. Non-Ferrous Metals. It is unlikely that supplies of copper, lead, zinc, and other metals will constitute critically limiting factors in the reduced Japanese economy.

i. Chemicals and Fertilizers. The home islands' production of major basic chemicals and fertilizers, alkalis (soda ash, caustic soda), phosphates, sulphate of ammonia, nitric and sulphuric acids, is hampered by shortages of salt (imported from North China and Manchuria), coal, other raw materials, and power.

4. *Petroleum Products.*

a. Aviation Fuel. The Japanese are believed to be short of aviation fuel. Inner Zone stocks are now estimated at about 1,350,000 barrels, and Inner

SECRET

Zone production of aviation gasoline and alcohol available for aircraft use (measured in terms of gasoline equipment) is about 125,000 barrels a month. With such small amounts of fuel available, the Japanese air forces have been forced to reduce consumption to far below their 1944 monthly average, estimated at about 600,000 barrels. Training and transport operations are already considerably affected by the shortage. We believe that aviation fuel will be the limiting factor in orthodox but not in suicide combat operations. Combat efficiency will be lowered by inadequacy in training and shortages at individual bases may interfere more and more frequently with the execution of planned operations.

b. Lubricating Oils. There is a shortage of lubricating oils produced from petroleum. As a result, substitutes have been used, apparently on an increasing scale. In particular, castor oil has been used in aircraft engines, with some loss in efficiency.

c. Other Petroleum Products. Japan's stocks of fuel and diesel oil are believed to be sufficient to last for not more than a year at estimated consumption rates.

5. *Coal.* Production in Japan has been declining for some time and at present may not exceed 40,000,000 metric tons annually as compared with a wartime peak of 50,000,000 tons. We estimate that during the year ending 31 March 1945 Japan imported from the continent and Karafuto about 5,000,000 tons. As a result of shipping shortages, imports of coal during the year ending 31 March 1946 may not exceed 2,500,000 tons. The coal shortage, particularly in suitable coking coals, is affecting production in basic war industries.

6. *Food.* Japan normally produces roughly 85 percent of her food supply. The bulk of the Japanese diet is provided by the staple ration. This ration, supplied originally in rice and currently by a combination of rice and rice substitutes (other grains and potatoes), requires annually some 11,000,000 net metric tons, after deduction of seed, milling loss, and non-food use. Japan's 1944 rice crop and 1945 winter grain crop, both somewhat below normal, are expected to supply roughly 9,000,000 tons net, in edible form, after deduction of waste and non-food uses. Domestic potato production and imports of Korean rice and Manchurian cereals will probably be sufficient to supply the balance of the staple requirement until the rice harvest beginning in November 1945. If not, the Japanese can draw upon their rice stock pile, estimated roughly at 2,000,000 tons. A shortage of foodstuffs is being experienced in the urban areas due mainly to distribution difficulties and the probability that government stocks and hoarded supplies have been partially destroyed by air raids.

Appendix "A"

The staple ration is deficient in proteins and protective elements, which are supplied in the Japanese diet by fish, soy beans, and vegetables. The fish catch has been reduced possibly by 50 percent since 1939, thereby increasing the importance in the diet of the protein supplied by soy beans. (Supply of soy beans, approximately 70 percent of which are imported from Manchuria and Korea, is believed to have been maintained at or above pre-war levels.) Supplies of vegetables have probably continued close to pre-war levels. However, inefficient distribution causes recurring shortages of supplementary food in urban areas.

7. *Manpower.* There has long been a shortage of technicians and skilled workers in Japan, but manpower is not, in general, a limiting factor on either Japanese production or the size of the armed forces. Induction of additional men into the armed forces during 1945 will be offset partly by normal additions to the labor forces and by further employment of women and children and partly by a decrease in the demand for industrial labor as a result of the decline in industrial activity. In fact, industrial workers in bombed-out urban areas are being released to agriculture.

8. *Civilian Supply.* Lack of raw materials since early in the war has severely curtailed civilian supplies, particularly of clothing. The position has steadily deteriorated throughout the war. Recently, because of the impossibility of obtaining appreciable supplies of cotton, wool, and materials for synthetic fibers from the continent, and the effect of bombing of the industrial centers and of communications, the situation has become greatly aggravated. The supply of consumer goods is entirely inadequate to meet the needs of the population, particularly now, when so many have been bombed out of their homes and have presumably lost their belongings. Owing in part to the consumer goods shortage, there is an increasing threat of inflation.

9. *Regional Economic Administration.* A regional administration of Japan was set up in mid-June by the "Extraordinary War Measures Bill" which provided, in the case of an emergency, for the delegation of unlimited powers to Superintendents-General of eight regional administrations. Coupled with this new administrative structure, the Army, the Navy, the banks, and the large Japanese business concerns set up corresponding administrative districts. The Japanese administration has for decades been centralized in Tokyo. The present regional decentralization is occasioned not only by the fear that the transportation and communication links within Japan may be destroyed, but also that Tokyo, the nerve center, may be made completely ineffective. The Japanese are endeavoring to make these regions as self-sufficient as possible. A broad survey of the population and the average rice crop of each district shows

Appendix "A"

SECRET

that only one district has a large surplus, two are very seriously deficient and the remaining five are borderline cases. Though simple equipment for resistance forces may be stocked or manufactured in the districts, complex war materials cannot be produced in each of these regions adequately for a long period of defense.

SECRET

APPENDIX "B"

ARMED FORCES

GROUND FORCES (See attached map.)

1. *Japanese.* The ground strength of the Japanese armed forces remains formidable. Including air and naval ground elements as well as the Army, it totals some 4,600,000 men. We believe there are some 110 infantry and 4 armored divisions in the Japanese Army; 30 or more additional divisions will have been formed by the end of the year, of which about half will have been formed by conversion of existing units. Some of these may be in existence now.

Japanese ground strength in or able to be withdrawn into the Inner Zone now amounts to some 3,300,000 men, including approximately 60 divisions. By the end of the year ground strength in the Inner Zone may amount to over 4,000,000 men, including up to 95 divisions.

The firepower of Japanese ground units is less than that of comparable Allied units, and in general their equipment is not up to Allied standards. The Japanese ground forces are particularly deficient in heavy weapons, motor transport, and armor (only four armored divisions have been identified). They are generally well trained, but there have been some instances of troops being committed to combat before the completion of their basic training. Such troops and relatively untrained service personnel are normally employed in combat in the latter stages of losing campaigns, as on Okinawa. The morale of the ground forces remains high, but some deterioration from previous standards is evident.

2. *Puppets.* In addition to the above, the Japanese maintain some 300,000 Manchurian and 900,000 Chinese puppet troops of doubtful quality and loyalty. They are used primarily to guard communications and perform service duties, and to lesser extent in combat against the Chinese. Their effectiveness will be considerably reduced as the Japanese withdraw from large areas of China.

3. *National Volunteer Army.* The Japanese are exerting strenuous efforts to create an effective home guard in anticipation of invasion. Below is listed the available manpower of military age (17-44) in Japan proper by military districts. Logistical difficulties and the purpose of their employment would preclude the use of any substantial numbers outside their own areas.

Appendix "B"

SECRET

Available Manpower (17-44)

Northern (Hokkaido)	493,000
Northeastern	927,400
Eastern	3,265,800
East Central	1,260,700
Central (Kinki)	2,059,400
West Central (Chugoku)	772,400
Shikoku	408,500
Western (Kyushu)	1,409,100
	10,596,300

Of these some 8,800,000 are thought to be physically fit according to Japanese standards and could be made available for military service. We believe that as much as 40 percent of this total (3,520,000) are reservists. In areas under attack elements of the National Volunteer Army would be called out for guard and labor purposes and eventually for combat to the extent of their limited capabilities. A reserve of more than 1,000,000 rifles is believed to be available for this purpose.

AIR FORCES

4. *Aircraft Strength.*

   a. General. Until September 1944, the Japanese air forces steadily increased in size. Since then they have suffered heavy losses, and their combat aircraft strength has been reduced 40 percent, as appears from the following table:

	Tactical Units	*Training Units*	*Total*
1 September 1944 (Beginning of air attacks on the Philippines)	6,200	2,000	8,200
18 March 1945 (Ryukyus Campaign)	4,300	2,200	6,500
26 June 1945	3,800	1,200	5,000

Except for planes undergoing repairs or modification in depots or in transit to units, the Japanese have no reserves behind their present unit strength of 5,000 combat aircraft.

Appendix "B"

SECRET

b. Production. The Japanese aircraft industry has been heavily damaged by VLR and carrier attacks. Factories which once accounted for 45 percent of aircraft assembly and 70 percent of aircraft engine production have been virtually destroyed. Nevertheless, by dispersing their facilities, the Japanese have been able to maintain production during the past few months at a rate ranging between 1,250 and 1,500 combat planes a month. There is still a number of large factories producing both airframes and engines, and attacks on these plants should further reduce production. However, new plants replacing bombed-out factories will be so widely dispersed that substantial recovery over a long period of time cannot be prevented by precision attacks on factories alone. Attacks on urban industrial areas and transportation facilities will have a considerable indirect effect on future aircraft production, and it is possible that four or five months of such attacks will reduce Japan's aircraft production to about 1,000 planes a month.

c. Wastage. Since 1 September 1944, Japanese combat and non-combat losses have averaged more than 2,300 planes a month. This figure includes heavy losses on the ground in the Philippines and in the large-scale suicide attacks of the Ryukyus campaign. Recently the Japanese have been able to limit their losses on the ground by improved dispersal facilities and by flying reconnaissance planes, bombers, and occasionally even fighters away from Allied strikes. Moreover, now that Okinawa is secured, the scale of suicide attacks in this area will probably decline. In these circumstances it is probable that Japanese losses in the next few months will be below the monthly average given above.

d. Future Combat Aircraft Strength. Taking all factors into consideration, we believe that Japanese combat air strength will continue to decline, and in the absence of an invasion would not exceed 3,000 on 1 January 1946. Thereafter production will probably shrink.

e. Trainers. In addition to combat aircraft, the Japanese now possess about 6,000 trainers, many of which have been specially equipped for suicide attacks. Trainer production is not large, and Allied attacks on training fields during the next few months should bring about a substantial reduction in trainer strength.

5. *Deployment.* Since the beginning of the Ryukyus campaign, air strength has been moved to Japan and Korea from other areas, and this trend probably will continue. In the near future over 90 percent of the Japanese air forces will be concentrated in the main Japanese islands, Korea, Manchuria, and North China. Japanese combat aircraft strength in all other areas will steadily deteriorate as a result of attrition or withdrawals and the lack of replacements.

Appendix "B"

SECRET

6. *Capabilities*. The capability of the Japanese air forces to operate effectively against us in either defensive or offensive warfare carried out along orthodox lines has been very greatly reduced. The Japanese themselves appreciate this fact and have concentrated their attention upon suicide tactics as the most successful method of attack with the planes and pilots at their disposal. While they will continue some training and tactical operations along orthodox lines, such orthodox employment will be intended primarily to supplement and facilitate suicide missions. Currently, the Japanese High Command is doing everything possible to improve the training, planning, and accomplishment of suicide air missions.

The Japanese apparently have decided to sacrifice future air potential in favor of maximum employment of all available aircraft and pilots, whether in training or tactical units, against Allied invasion of the home islands. Great numbers of trainer-type aircraft are being equipped for suicide missions and pilot trainees are being assigned to suicide units.

Allocation of aviation gasoline for training purposes has been drastically reduced, and there is accumulating evidence of an actual shortage of aviation gasoline. However, except for distributional difficulties, it seems probable that the Japanese air forces will be able to conserve sufficient gasoline for a short-lived all-out air effort against the initial invasion of the home islands.

The Japanese are believed capable of developing a jet-propelled plane which could operate as an orthodox fighter or bomber, but not in sufficient quantity to be of serious consequence. They are attempting to develop a variety of jet-driven suicide devices, however, and the Baka, a small rocket-driven, pilot-controlled aircraft launched from a medium bomber, has already made its appearance. The Baka has not been employed in sufficient numbers to permit an appraisal of its effectiveness, but its further development, the use of the German V-1 with a suicide pilot, and the appearance of other jet-driven suicide devices are possibilities.

NAVAL FORCES

7. *Strength*. As a result of the losses sustained during three and one-half years of war, Japanese naval strength has been reduced to virtual impotency in the face of Allied naval power. In addition Japan possesses no capability for any substantial recovery.

Appendix "B"

The present strength of the Japanese Navy is believed not to exceed:—

2 Battleships	4 Heavy cruisers
2 Battleship-Aircraft carriers	2 Light cruisers
4 Aircraft carriers (large)	42 Destroyers
3 Aircraft carriers (small)	57 Submarines
2 Aircraft carriers (escort)	

All of this strength is in home waters with the exception of two damaged heavy cruisers and a very small number of destroyers and submarines in southern areas.

The naval force listed above would appear to have considerable potential, but its capabilities are weakened by the following factors: (1) the limited sphere of operations permits the more effective use of aircraft from land bases rather than from carriers, and the carriers become a net liability to protect; (2) two damaged heavy cruisers are in the Singapore area and their ability to return to Japan proper is most problematical; (3) there is a serious lack of escorts due to the shortage of heavy destroyers (1,600-2,300 tons) and the relative ineffectiveness of the more numerous smaller destroyers (1,000 tons); (4) most major enemy naval bases are within range of Allied land or carrier-based aircraft which might possibly force naval units based therein to seek refuge in the Sea of Japan. While the Japanese possess an appreciable number of submarines, their threat to Allied naval forces cannot be considered serious in view of their ineffectiveness during the past.

The Japanese are primarily engaged in the construction of small ships, such as destroyers, submarines, escort craft, midget submarines, one-man torpedoes, suicide and small combatant surface craft.

We believe that when Allied positions in the Ryukyus are consolidated, Japanese lines of communications from Japan proper to all outside areas except those to the continent across the Sea of Japan will be severed. Japanese destroyers, minesweepers, and other small escort craft will concentrate on the task of protecting shipping on these remaining lifelines to the continent. However, they are already inadequate for this purpose, and this shortage will become more acute in the face of increasing Allied mining, air, and submarine attacks. This situation would be further aggravated should the U.S.S.R. enter the war.

The main offensive capability and the most likely employment of the Japanese Navy from now on will be in suicide attacks by a small task force, harassing and suicide operations by smaller surface craft and submarine attacks. Extensive mine fields probably exist in the vicinity of harbors and other strategic areas around the homeland.

Appendix "B"

SECRET

ANNEX TO APPENDIX "B"

MAP OF WESTERN PACIFIC AREA

JAPANESE ARMED FORCES—GROUND

18 June 1945

Annex to Appendix "B"

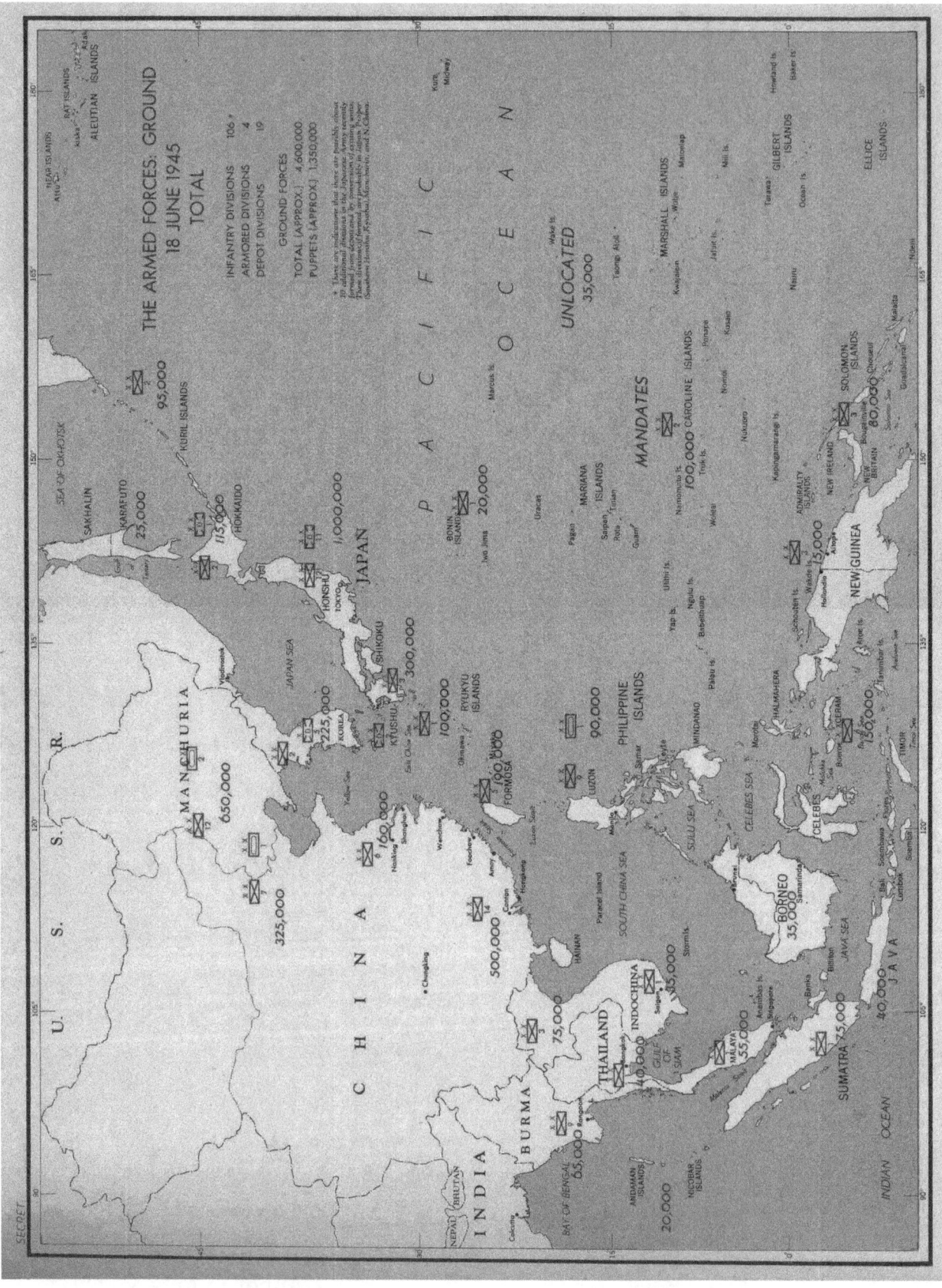

SECRET

APPENDIX "C"

CAPABILITIES AND INTENTIONS
FOR THE DEFENSE OF JAPAN PROPER

1. *Present Strength and Dispositions.*

   a. Ground. Present Japanese ground strength in the home islands and their island outposts (Ryukyus, Izus, Kuriles, and Karafuto) is estimated at 1,600,000 men, including some 21 active and 14 depot divisions. Additional divisions are probably in the process of formation, and some of these may already be in existence.

   By the end of 1945 this strength could be built up to over 2,000,000 men, including more than 35 active divisions and 14 depot divisions. The increase would result largely from the mobilization of local manpower, since substantial reinforcement from the continent will not be feasible.

   b. Air. At present there are approximately 5,000 combat aircraft assigned to tactical and training units, and of this number about 4,000 are located in Japan proper and Korea. In addition to these combat aircraft the Japanese have about 6,000 trainer-type aircraft. Although large numbers of these trainers are based outside of Japan proper, it is possible that within a short time several thousand will be equipped for carrying bombs and made available for suicide operations in the defense of the home islands.

   c. Naval. Practically all of the remaining Japanese naval forces, as set forth in Appendix "B," are now located and will continue to be based in home waters.

2. *Capabilities.* Japan's ability to defend the home islands against amphibious assault has been seriously impaired by the virtual neutralization of her navy, the deterioration of her air forces, the disruption of her communications with the continent and southern areas, and the heavy bomb damage suffered by her industrial facilities. She is incapable of remedying these conditions, which will progressively worsen. She retains, however, the advantages of an air force suicidally dangerous while it lasts, formidable ground forces, peculiarly difficult terrain, and a fanatically loyal population.

   Japanese naval forces in home waters will have only the capability of harassing and suicide attacks mainly by small surface craft and submarines. Extensive mine fields probably exist in the vicinity of important harbors and in other strategic areas around the homeland.

Appendix "C"

SECRET

Prior to the time when landing operations are undertaken against any part of Japan proper, local and adjacent airfields should be largely neutralized and the effectiveness of enemy air operations from nearby bases should be considerably reduced by our pre-invasion air attacks. However, a very large number of airfields will be within easy range and one-way suicide sorties could be flown against us directly from distant bases. We believe that low serviceability and other factors would probably prevent the enemy from launching against Allied invasion forces more than 400 to 500 sorties of combat-type aircraft and 200 to 300 sorties of trainer-type aircraft during any 24-hour period. Such an all-out effort could not be maintained, but recurring attacks of this nature may be expected on a progressively decreasing scale, following intervals of recuperation. The employment of Baka bombs will be limited by their dependence upon suitable launching aircraft and orthodox air cover. This threat might be greatly increased if the Japanese devise a satisfactory ground-launching device for this type of weapon. Favored by the proximity of hills and land masses, the maximum air capability of the Japanese would be mass suicide operations at night or under conditions of poor visibility. The Japanese air forces will have very low capabilities in opposing Allied air operations and they will not be able to give effective direct support to Japanese ground troops.

Against an invasion of Kyushu or Honshu, the Japanese ground forces would exert maximum resistance. Various factors would limit the number of divisions which could be sustained in simultaneous front-line action in any one area to 20 or less. An invasion of Shikoku or Hokkaido would elicit a considerably weaker reaction since these areas are less vital strategically, and also because of the logistical difficulties inherent in an attempt to reinforce and supply over water in the face of overwhelming air and naval superiority.

3. *Intentions*. Preparation to resist invasion of the home islands is Japan's overriding strategic purpose. In the time remaining every effort will be made to improve coastal defenses in threatened areas, to build up defensive forces, and to develop such auxiliary services as the National Volunteer Army. Efforts to effect administrative decentralization will also be pressed, so that any isolated area may be able to carry on with the greatest possible degree of self-sufficiency. Psychological preparation for invasion will also be stressed.

The principal concentrations of defensive ground strength will probably be in the Kyushu, Nagoya-Hamamatsu, and Kanto Plain areas.

The Japanese would defend tenaciously their remaining island outposts. Against any invasion of the home islands, with the possible exception of

Appendix "C"

SECRET

Hokkaido, they would commit all available air and naval strength. The Japanese would commit all ground forces that could be sustained in action in the defense of Kyushu and that part of Honshu which includes the Kanto Plain, Nagoya, and Osaka areas. Considerably weaker defense would be encountered in other parts of Honshu, Shikoku, and Hokkaido because of logistical and strategical reasons.

Appendix "C"

SECRET

APPENDIX "D"

MILITARY SITUATION, CAPABILITIES, AND INTENTIONS IN KOREA, MANCHURIA, AND NORTH CHINA

Present Japanese ground strength in Manchuria, Korea, and North China is estimated at 1,200,000 men, including some 24 active and 5 depot divisions. This strength is disposed as shown in the map attached to Appendix "B." Until early in 1944 the Japanese maintained intact their forces in Manchuria (the Kwantung Army). Since then, however, they have withdrawn most of the original divisions of that army, replacing them with newly formed units. Increasing apprehension of Soviet entry into the war is now causing them to reinforce this area from Central and South China, and by the end of the year their strength in North China, Manchuria, and Korea may increase to 1,500,000 men, including more than 40 divisions. Since substantial support from Japan proper can no longer be expected, the area will be organized for independent defense. We anticipate that strong concentrations will be maintained in eastern Manchuria to threaten Vladivostok, in central Manchuria and in North China to meet possible Soviet attacks from the northwest, and in Korea to guard against amphibious invasion and as a reserve.

At the present time the Japanese have based in Korea 550 combat aircraft and in Manchuria and North China about 400 combat aircraft. We believe, however, that air strength in Korea is and will continue to be mainly concerned with the defense against Allied forces in the Pacific. If, at some later date, the U.S.S.R. should enter the war, we believe that the Japanese would continue to commit the bulk of their air strength for the defense of Japan proper and southern Korea, leaving opposition to the U.S.S.R. primarily to their ground forces.

Appendix "D"

SECRET

APPENDIX "E"

MILITARY SITUATION, CAPABILITIES, AND INTENTIONS IN CENTRAL AND SOUTH CHINA AND FORMOSA

The Japanese now have about 650,000 men, including 20 divisions, in Central and South China, and another 190,000 men, including five divisions, in Formosa. Formosa is already cut off; Japanese strength there will remain unchanged. On the continent, however, Japanese strength is being redisposed northward and eastward as a result of increasing apprehension of Soviet entry into the war and of Allied landings from the East China Sea. We believe some 10 divisions will be so redisposed. It is probable that the coast between Ningpo and the Shantung Peninsula will be reinforced, and that a strategic reserve of some six divisions will be maintained in the Nanking area to meet an amphibious attack or to move north in the event of Soviet entry into the war. We anticipate that, until either of these events occurs, the Japanese will endeavor to keep open the line of the Hankow-Canton railway, and that, when forced to abandon it, they will leave some 125,000 men, including four divisions, to hold the Canton-Hong Kong area as long as possible.

If circumstances require it, the Japanese are prepared to abandon all of China south of the general line Tungkuan-Kaifeng-Nanking-Hangchow, except for the Canton-Hong Kong pocket.

Hereafter the Japanese will offer very little air and only negligible naval opposition in any of these areas.

Appendix "E"

SECRET

APPENDIX "F"

SITUATION, CAPABILITIES, AND INTENTIONS
IN THE SOUTHERN AREAS

The southern areas are cut off from Japan and soon will be incapable of significant mutual support. The air and naval strength remaining there is strategically negligible. The defense of each area therefore depends upon local ground forces and locally available supplies and reserve stocks.

The present disposition of Japanese ground strength in the southern areas is estimated to be as follows:—

Northern Indo-China	75,000
Southern Indo-China	35,000
Burma-Thailand	105,000
Andamans-Nicobars	20,000
Malaya	55,000
Sumatra	75,000
Java	40,000
Borneo	35,000
Celebes, Halmahera, Dutch New Guinea, Banda Sea area	150,000
Northeastern New Guinea	15,000
TOTAL	605,000

Units in these areas are already generally below strength. Areas east of the Celebes are generally inadequately supplied with munitions and rations. To the west of these areas there are stocks of munitions and rations, and there are some facilities for manufacturing small arms and ammunition. Shipping and rail facilities will be inadequate to distribute to best advantage the supplies that exist.

The Japanese are endeavoring to redispose their strength within the southern areas in order to reinforce the Malaya Peninsula, the Tenasserim Coast, and Thailand. They will be restricted in their accomplishment of significant redispositions because of Allied action and lack of adequate transportation.

Appendix "F"

SECRET

Japanese air capabilities in the southern areas are limited to reconnaissance, weak interception, and small-scale suicide attacks. The naval forces remaining there can accomplish no more than nuisance attacks. Ground force capabilities are limited to a predominantly static defense of occupied localities. The Japanese will, however, defend such areas with determination, in order to inflict attrition, contain Allied forces and deny them to the Allies. Resistance in the South is unlikely to cease as long as resistance continues in the North.

Appendix "F"

SECRET

APPENDIX "G"

SITUATION IN THE PACIFIC ISLANDS

Some 270,000 Japanese troops are now isolated in the Pacific islands, as follows:—

Bismarcks – Solomons	80,000
Japanese Mandates	100,000
Bonins	20,000
Philippines	70,000

No element of these forces has any capability other than that for a desperate, last-ditch defense of the area it occupies.

SECRET

APPENDIX "H"

POLITICAL SITUATION

1. *General Situation.* The political situation in Japan is dominated by the progressive deterioration of the military situation, particularly in the last few months. Japan's political isolation resulting from the collapse of Germany, the loss of Okinawa, and the great and growing destruction in Japan proper by air attacks, have convinced the Japanese by and large that victory for them is impossible. Consequently the present Government's internal and external policy can only be one of desperate defense. To some this may mean a fight to obtain the best possible terms in a negotiated peace; to others it expresses a natural instinct to fight on regardless of the consequences. The theme of internal policy is national unity, and in its name further drastic measures have recently been taken to make the Central Government as far as possible thoroughly representative of the whole nation, to strengthen its powers even further, and thence, as it were, to devolve upon local authority an unprecedented degree of administrative power for dealing with emergency conditions.

2. *Internal Political Situation.* The real government of Japan is the invisible one, and we do not know what shifts of power have taken place behind the scene. It must be assumed, however, that main, effective control still lies essentially with military elements, if only because the army remains Japan's greatest asset.

With this important reservation it should be noted that positions in the visible Cabinet are held less and less by known military extremists, and progressively more by representatives of the Court, big business, conservative bureaucracy and moderate army and navy leadership. The Suzuki Cabinet is typical in this respect and in its effort to maintain popularity by close identification with the Throne and by inclusion of members of diverse political groups. Undoubtedly such a government is less unpopular than overt military dictatorship; undoubtedly also the government is of a kind which might be expected to entertain ideas of a compromise peace, although very likely on a basis which would make no appeal at all to Japan's enemies. To some degree its views might be made to prevail on the military extremists outside the Government, against whom the powers conferred on the Government by the "Emergency Wartime Measures Law" could be used, but the invisible government referred to above must be expected to have its say before any decision is taken. In this connection the appointment of a strong Home Minister with a number of assistants possessing a reputation for ruthlessness indicates

Appendix "H"

SECRET

intention on part of the Government to keep the internal situation firmly in hand.

Whatever views the Suzuki Government or individual members of it may hold about the possibilities of compromise, there can be no doubt that the Government is doing everything to ensure a desperate defense of the homeland, if no other way out of the crisis shows itself. Recent indications are the continued emphasis on the organization of the National Volunteer Army and the really radical effort towards decentralization of authority. The latter by giving unprecedented powers to specially constituted local authorities, provides against administrative breakdowns should Tokyo, the administrative capital of a hitherto strongly centralized country, be overrun by an invading force or communications between one part of the country and another be cut. Decentralization provides also against a transport and supplies breakdown by contemplating a great degree of local self-sufficiency in food and munitions. The Government has taken to itself other practically unlimited powers over manpower and property and this program is calculated, no doubt, not only to raise fighting efficiency to its maximum but also to impress Japan's enemies with the likely cost of an invasion of the home islands.

3. *Foreign Policy*. Undoubtedly the chief aims of Japanese foreign policy are to keep the Soviets out of the war and to drive a wedge between the western Allies and the U.S.S.R. This is attested by the extremely friendly tone of the Japanese press and radio towards the U.S.S.R. The latter nevertheless continues to be a source of anxiety and foreboding.

The re-appointment of Togo, former Ambassador to Moscow and reputedly friendly to the U.S.S.R., to the post of Foreign Minister which he held at the time of Pearl Harbor suggests, however, that despite realistic appraisal of the meaning of Soviet denunciation on 5 April 1945 of the Russo-Japanese neutrality pact, Japan still hopes to propitiate the U.S.S.R. The abandonment of former Foreign Minister Shigemitsu in favor of Togo might be held to mean the abandonment of any real hope of a compromise peace with the United States and Britain, but this presumption perhaps goes too far.

Other aspects of Japanese policy are to keep alive Kuomintang-Communist discord in China, and if possible to precipitate a civil war.

At the same time the Japanese are making strenuous efforts to keep their puppet regimes in Southeast Asia, Manchuria, and Nanking under control and otherwise to secure greater cooperation from Japan's subject peoples. Propaganda about the erstwhile Greater East Asia Co-Prosperity scheme has

Appendix "H"

SECRET

quietly subsided and is in abeyance, with some tacit admissions that the scheme has failed for the present. Despite Japanese promises of "independence" and various political concessions there is unrest in all Japanese-controlled areas, and the Japanese may well be obliged to increase their repressive measures.

During the next few months the future political strategy of the Government will exhibit the following aims:—

a. Continue and even increase its attempts to secure complete political unity within the Empire, possibly through personal rule, real or apparent, by the Emperor.

b. Attempt to foster a belief among Japan's enemies that the war will prove costly and long drawn out if the United Nations insist on fighting until the complete conquest of Japan.

c. Make desperate efforts to persuade the U.S.S.R. to continue her neutrality, if necessary by offering important territorial or other concessions, while at the same time making every effort to sow discord between the Americans and British on one side and the Russians on the other. As the situation deteriorates still further, Japan may even make a serious attempt to use the U.S.S.R. as a mediator in ending the war.

d. Put out intermittent peace feelers, in an effort to bring the war to an acceptable end, to weaken the determination of the United Nations to fight to the bitter end, or to create inter-Allied dissension.

e. Take all possible advantage of estranged relations between the Communists and the Kuomintang factions in China.

4. *Possibility of Surrender.* The Japanese ruling groups are aware of the desperate military situation and are increasingly desirous of a compromise peace, but still find "unconditional surrender" unacceptable. Indeed the formal acceptance of "unconditional surrender" by Japanese constituted authority must be deemed basically unlikely, since the term probably implies to the Japanese mind the overthrow of the Emperor and the position of the Imperial House, the extinction of the Japanese traditions and of the Japanese way of life, and the abolition of the Japanese constitution.

These fundamental psychological objections to formal "unconditional surrender" as interpreted by the Japanese are so strong that not even blockade and strategic bombing on the present scale are likely to bring it about. The basic policy of the present Government is to fight as long and as desperately as possible to avoid complete defeat and in order to acquire a better bargaining

Appendix "H"

position in a negotiated peace. Japanese leaders are now playing for time in the hope that Allied war weariness, Allied disunity, or some "miracle" will present an opportunity to avoid final defeat and arrange a compromise peace.

As regards the Japanese people as a whole, we believe that a considerable portion of them now consider absolute defeat to be probable. The increasing effects of sea blockade and cumulative devastation wrought by strategic bombing should make this realization increasingly general. An entry of the Soviet Union into the war would finally convince the Japanese of the inevitability of complete defeat. Although individual Japanese willingly sacrifice themselves in the service of the nation, we doubt that the nation as a whole is predisposed toward national suicide. Rather, the Japanese as a nation have a strong concept of national survival, regardless of the fate of individuals. When confronted with the absolute impossibility of avoiding complete defeat, they would probably prefer national survival, even through surrender, to virtual extinction.

The Japanese believe, however, that unconditional surrender would be the equivalent of national extinction. There are as yet no indications that the Japanese are ready to accept such terms. The ideas of foreign occupation of the Japanese homeland, foreign custody of the person of the Emperor, and the loss of prestige entailed by the acceptance of "unconditional surrender" are most revolting to the Japanese. To avoid these conditions, if possible, and, in any event, to insure survival of the institution of the Emperor, the Japanese might well be willing to withdraw from all the territory they have seized on the Asiatic continent and in the southern Pacific, and even to agree to the independence of Korea and to the practical disarmament of their military forces.

A conditional surrender by the Japanese Government along the lines stated above might be offered by them at any time from now until the time of the complete destruction of all Japanese power of resistance.

Since the Japanese Army is the principal repository of the Japanese military tradition it follows that the army leaders must, with a sufficient degree of unanimity, acknowledge defeat before Japan can be induced to surrender. This might be brought about either by the defeat of the main Japanese armies in the Inner Zone or through a desire on the part of the army leaders to salvage something from the wreck with a view to maintaining military tradition. For a surrender to be acceptable to the Japanese Army, it would be necessary for the military leaders to believe that it would not entail discrediting warrior tradition and that it would permit the ultimate resurgence of a military Japan.

Appendix "H"

TOP SECRET

C.C.S. 679/6
C.C.S. 679/7
C.C.S. 679/8
C.C.S. 679/9

EMPLOYMENT OF CAPTURED ENEMY OCEAN-GOING PASSENGER SHIPPING AND BRITISH TROOPSHIP EMPLOYMENT IN U.S. TRANS-ATLANTIC PROGRAMS IN THE FIRST HALF OF 1946

References:

CCS 198th Meeting, Items 3 & 4
CCS 199th Meeting, Item 2
CCS 900/3, paragraph 20

C.C.S. 679/6 (18 July 1945) and C.C.S. 679/7 (19 July) circulated memoranda by the United States Chiefs of Staff. C.C.S. 679/8 (22 July), the reply of the British Chiefs of Staff and C.C.S. 679/9 (23 July), the United States Chiefs of Staff proposed modifications thereof, were considered by the Combined Chiefs of Staff in their 199th Meeting (23 July).

THE COMBINED CHIEFS OF STAFF:—

a. Agreed to allocate the total lift of the seven ships listed in C.C.S. 679/6 for United States employment up to 31 December 1945.

b. Took note that the United States Chiefs of Staff would allocate to the United Kingdom a lift of 16,000 during the remainder of 1945 for the movement of Canadians.

c. Directed the Combined Military Transportation Committee, in collaboration with the Combined Shipping Adjustment Board, to submit by 15 September 1945 a report, on the lines of C.C.S. 679/1, of the combined requirements and combined resources (including captured enemy trooplift) for the first half of 1946, the study to cover the recommendation in paragraph 7 of C.C.S. 679/7 and the employment during the first half of 1946 of the seven ships listed in C.C.S. 679/6.

TOP SECRET

C.C.S. 679/6   18 July 1945

COMBINED CHIEFS OF STAFF

DISPOSITION OF CAPTURED GERMAN PASSENGER SHIPS

Memorandum by the United States Chiefs of Staff

1. The United States Chiefs of Staff have indicated in papers of the C.C.S. 679 series an urgent need for 39,000 troop spaces in captured enemy shipping to supplement the trooplift available for carrying out redeployment plans.

2. Since the publication of C.C.S. 679/1,* U.S. requirements for trooplift in the Pacific have materially increased. Deficits now are serious.

3. Drastic action has been taken to augment United States resources by conversion of cargo ships, increasing air-lift, and curtailing withdrawals of U.S. troops from Europe. In spite of every possible adjustment in United States resources, the trooplift situation in the Pacific will remain serious during the last half of this year.

4. The Combined Shipping Adjustment Board (CSAB) has had the matter of distribution of captured German shipping under discussion for several weeks. Certain agreements as to manning and operation have been reached, but the United States view that the seven vessels under consideration should be allocated for the carriage of U.S. troops during the current emergency period has been opposed on the British side of the CSAB pending decision by the Combined Chiefs of Staff.

5. The United States Chiefs of Staff recommend that in order to meet emergency requirements for the movement of U.S. troops necessary for forthcoming operations, the Combined Chiefs of Staff agree to the allocation for United States purposes, so long as an emergency exists, of the following seven vessels:

Europa, Caribia, Vulcania, Patria,
Potsdam, Pretoria and Milwaukee.

---

* Not published herein.

TOP SECRET

6. Arrangements as to manning, operation, repair and conversion can be determined by the CSAB, and it is understood that the agreement proposed in paragraph 5 above in no way prejudices ultimate disposition of these vessels.

TOP SECRET

C.C.S. 679/7   19 July 1945

COMBINED CHIEFS OF STAFF

BRITISH TROOPSHIP EMPLOYMENT IN U.S. TRANS-ATLANTIC PROGRAMS, FIRST HALF OF 1946

Memorandum by the United States Chiefs of Staff

1. In C.C.S. 679/1 the following offer of trans-Atlantic lift was made:—

"For the six months following VE-Day the *Queen Mary, Queen Elizabeth* and the *Aquitania* will be retained on service in the North Atlantic, and this westbound capacity will be placed at the disposal of the United States authorities. This offer is subject to a proviso that fifty (50) berths should be reserved in each sailing if required by the British authorities."

This assistance has been estimated at equivalent to 50,000 spaces per month.

2. Subsequent to the publication of C.C.S. 679/1, the United States has taken the following steps in an attempt to expedite redeployment to meet accelerated target dates for the main operations against Japan and for repatriation:—

   a. Increased the monthly target of the Air Transport Command for trans-Atlantic lift from 15,000 to 50,000.

   b. Authorized the conversion of 100 Victory ships to carry 1,500 personnel each.

   c. Authorized the modification of 206 cargo vessels, formerly fitted for 350 personnel each, to an increased capacity of 550 personnel each.

   d. Authorized the overloading of Victory and Liberty ships by 30 percent of capacity in the Atlantic.

3. Although the measures listed in paragraph 2 above have greatly improved our ability to meet revised redeployment build-up of strategic reserve and repatriation schedules, a serious deficit in personnel shipping does exist. The United States Chiefs of Staff have recommended modification of 74 of the

TOP SECRET

100 Victory ships mentioned in paragraph 2 so that they will be suitable for trans-Pacific operation and for direct redeployment from Europe to the Pacific. It is contemplated that all captured enemy troopships, with the exception of the *Europa*, that can be placed in service, will be diverted to the Pacific. Even these expedients will not enable the United States to meet Pacific troop movement requirements and there will exist by the end of 1945 a backlog of between 250,000 and 300,000 for Pacific movements. The removal of the 74 Victorys from trans-Atlantic service will retard the withdrawal of U.S. forces from Europe and will reduce the availability of cargo shipping in the Atlantic by about 25 sailings per month.

4. At *ARGONAUT* it was considered desirable that the United States and British convert 200 cargo ships to troop carriers on a combined basis.* Up to the present time there has been no indication of British action with respect to converting a share of the cargo vessels.

5. In C.C.S. 679/1 British requirements for the movement of troops from Europe to Canada were shown to be 195,600 during the first six months after VE-day. Space was provided for 133,800, leaving a deficit of approximately 62,000 over a six-month period. The total British requirement for repatriation of Canadians is not known to the United States Chiefs of Staff; however, it is noted that five weeks' lift of the three British vessels allocated for United States trans-Atlantic troop movements would overcome the first six months' deficit.

6. The three large British passenger liners are vastly more efficient from a trooplift point of view in the North Atlantic service than in any other service. Their continued employment in this service for the repatriation of Canadian and U.S. forces will cause the greatest benefit to accrue to combined troop moving needs.

7. In order to avoid the possibility of still further invasion of United States cargo shipping resources to the detriment of combined trans-Atlantic cargo programs, it is recommended that the British trooplift represented by the two *Queens* and the *Aquitania* should be retained in the trans-Atlantic service during an additional six months for the build-up of strategic reserves in the United States and the repatriation on a combined basis of Canadian and U.S. forces.

---

* ARGONAUT Conference book, page 63.

TOP SECRET

C.C.S. 679/8   22 July 1945

COMBINED CHIEFS OF STAFF

EMPLOYMENT OF CAPTURED ENEMY OCEAN-GOING PASSENGER SHIPPING AND BRITISH TROOPSHIP EMPLOYMENT IN U.S. TRANS-ATLANTIC PROGRAMS IN THE FIRST HALF OF 1946

Memorandum by the British Chiefs of Staff

1. The British Chiefs of Staff have considered the proposals put forward by the United States Chiefs of Staff in C.C.S. 679/6 and 679/7, and consider that these proposals, the arguments in support of them and the possible effect on combined requirements for movement of personnel are so closely linked that they should be taken together.

2. The British Chiefs of Staff have taken note of the steps taken by the United States to meet revised schedules for redeployment, build-up of strategic reserve and repatriation, and of the net effect of these on Pacific movements, viz., a backlog of between 250,000 and 300,000 at the end of 1945.

3. The British Chiefs of Staff will, of course, do everything possible to assist in the movement of United States forces, particularly those destined for the Pacific, but they wish to make it clear that the personnel shipping resources allotted to them in C.C.S. 679/1 fell far short of meeting British requirements for redeployment and repatriation, which had to be severely cut.

4. Further, they wish to point out that a preliminary examination of the estimated British requirements for the first half of 1946 indicates that the total British trooplift will suffice to lift only about two men out of every three, even if the current programme is achieved without a backlog at the end of the year.

5. In view of the serious position of United States movement to the Pacific, the British Chiefs of Staff are prepared to agree that the Combined Chiefs of Staff should allocate the total lift of the seven ships listed in C.C.S. 679/6 for United States employment up to 31st December 1945. In return, they ask that the United States Chiefs of Staff allocate to them a lift of 16,000 during the rest

TOP SECRET

of 1945 for movement of the Canadians, many of whom have been absent from their homes for a very long time. The Canadian Government are pressing us very strongly in this matter.

6. The British Chiefs of Staff further suggest that a combined study on the lines of C.C.S. 679/1 of the combined requirements and combined resources (including captured enemy trooplift) for the first half of 1946 should be completed by mid-September if possible. The study would cover the recommendation in C.C.S. 679/7 and also the employment during the first half of 1946 of the seven ships to which reference is made in C.C.S. 679/6.

TOP SECRET

C.C.S. 679/9 23 July 1945

COMBINED CHIEFS OF STAFF

EMPLOYMENT OF CAPTURED ENEMY OCEAN-GOING PASSENGER SHIPPING AND BRITISH TROOPSHIP EMPLOYMENT IN U.S. TRANS-ATLANTIC PROGRAMS IN THE FIRST HALF OF 1946

Memorandum by the United States Chiefs of Staff

The United States Chiefs of Staff agree with the provisions of C.C.S. 679/8 except for the date of 31 December 1945 given in paragraph 5 as terminating the use by the United States of the six of the seven captured German ships destined for the Pacific.

After moving these ships great distances to the Pacific we shall be fortunate to obtain one trip from them before the 31 December date. By then our deployment will not have ended and the main operation will yet have to be undertaken. It would be uneconomical to remove this shipping from the Pacific after just one run. When ships may be withdrawn from the Pacific, less adaptable shipping such as the converted Victory ships should be first transferred back to the Atlantic. The lift of these ships of course will be included in the proposed review of personnel shipping to be completed by mid-September.

Accordingly, the United States Chiefs of Staff recommend that paragraphs 5 and 6 of C.C.S. 679/8 be modified as indicated in the Enclosure.

TOP SECRET

ENCLOSURE

5. In view of the serious position of United States movement to the Pacific, the British Chiefs of Staff are prepared to agree that the Combined Chiefs of Staff should allocate the total lift of the seven ships listed in C.C.S. 679/6 *for to the United States employment up to 31st December 1945* for employment as follows: the Europa until 31 December 1945; and the Caribia, Patria, Vulcania, Potsdam, Pretoria and Milwaukee until 30 June 1946. In return, they ask that the United States Chiefs of Staff allocate to them a lift of 16,000 during the rest of 1945 for movement of the Canadians, many of whom have been absent from their homes for a very long time. The Canadian Government are pressing us very strongly in this matter.

6. The British Chiefs of Staff further suggest that a combined study on the lines of C.C.S. 679/1 of the combined requirements and combined resources (including captured enemy trooplift) for the first half of 1946 should be completed by mid-September if possible. The study would cover the recommendation in C.C.S. 679/7 and also the employment *during the first half of 1946* of the seven ships to which reference is made in C.C.S. 679/6. subject to the provisions of paragraph 5 above.

Words underlined are proposed additions.
Words italicized are proposed deletions.

SECRET

C.C.S. 706/11
C.C.S. 706/14 (TERMINAL)

DISPOSAL OF ENEMY WAR MATÉRIEL IN GERMANY AND AUSTRIA

Reference:

CCS 197th Meeting, Item 3

C.C.S. 706/11 (28 June 1945) circulated a report by the Combined Administrative Committee. C.C.S. 706/14 (TERMINAL) (17 July) circulated a memorandum by the United States Chiefs of Staff proposing certain amendments to Appendices "A" and "B" to C.C.S. 706/11.

The Combined Chiefs of Staff in their 197th Meeting (20 July) approved Appendices "A" and "B" to C.C.S. 706/11, as amended in C.C.S. 706/14 (TERMINAL).

SECRET

C.C.S. 706/11   28 June 1945

COMBINED CHIEFS OF STAFF

DISPOSAL OF ENEMY WAR MATÉRIEL IN GERMANY AND AUSTRIA

Report by the Combined Administrative Committee

THE PROBLEM

1. As a matter of priority to draft a reply to SCAF 447 (Appendix "D," page 61), in which the Supreme Commander, Allied Expeditionary Force (SCAEF) requests authority to:—

   a. Fill London Munitions Assignment Board requirements from war material in Germany and Austria.

   b. Render surplus enemy warlike equipment unserviceable and dispose of it as scrap.

FACTS BEARING ON THE PROBLEM

2. See Appendix "C" (page 60).

DISCUSSION

3. Informal discussions are taking place on governmental levels as to the disposal of enemy equipment. It has been indicated informally that some nations desire the distribution of enemy war matériel among the United Nations, and are directly opposed to widespread destruction of German warlike equipment.

4. Because it appears that there will be considerable delay prior to the formulation of an intergovernmental policy on this subject, it appears necessary to make available a means by which enemy war matériel, captured or surrendered, which might be used profitably in the war against Japan, could be obtained immediately by those nations now actively engaged in the Japanese war.

SECRET

CONCLUSIONS

5. Until a policy of disposal, agreed upon by the nations represented on the European Advisory Commission, has become effective, the London Munitions Assignment Board should be empowered to assign captured or surrendered enemy matériel in the hands of forces under United States or British command in Germany and Austria to the forces of those nations employed in furtherance of the agreed strategy in the war against Japan.

6. Because of the imminent dissolution of Supreme Headquarters, Allied Expeditionary Force, instructions relative to the destruction of enemy matériel surplus to the needs of the military forces and those of the London Munitions Assignment Board are a matter for consideration by the respective United States and British Chiefs of Staff rather than the Combined Chiefs of Staff.

RECOMMENDATIONS

7. That the message in Appendix "A" be dispatched to the Supreme Commander, Allied Expeditionary Force, and the Supreme Allied Commander, Mediterranean.

8. That the message in Appendix "B" be dispatched to the London Munitions Assignment Board.

SECRET

APPENDIX "A"

DRAFT

MESSAGE TO SUPREME COMMANDER, ALLIED EXPEDITIONARY FORCE AND SUPREME ALLIED COMMANDER, MEDITERRANEAN

This is answer to SCAF 447 repeated this date to SACMED. The London Munitions Assignment Board is being empowered to assign captured or surrendered enemy matériel in the hands of forces under United States or British command in Germany and Austria to the forces of those nations employed in furtherance of the agreed strategy in the war against Japan. The treatment of enemy matériel surplus to needs of the military commanders and those required to fill London Munitions Assignment Board requirements will be the subject of instructions by the respective Chiefs of Staff to the United States and British zone commanders after the dissolution of SHAEF.

SECRET

APPENDIX "B"

DRAFT

MESSAGE TO THE LONDON MUNITIONS ASSIGNMENT BOARD

Until a policy of disposal is agreed upon by the nations represented on the European Advisory Commission and implemented, the London Munitions Assignment Board is empowered to assign captured or surrendered enemy matériel in the hands of forces under United States or British command in Germany and Austria to the forces of those nations who will employ such equipment in furtherance of the agreed strategy in the war against Japan.

SECRET

APPENDIX "C"

FACTS BEARING ON THE PROBLEM

1. FACS 159—FAN 507 authorized the destruction of captured enemy war matériel in Germany and Austria, which was surplus to the requirements of the Supreme Command and the London Munitions Assignment Board, such authority to remain in force until cessation of hostilities or until superseded by a later directive (page 4 of C.C.S. 200/5* as amended by C.C.S. 200/6*).

2. Present handling of captured and surrendered war matériel in Germany and Austria is based on FACS 149—FAN 500 (page 3 of C.C.S. 706/7*) and FACS 109—FAN 453 (page 3 of C.C.S. 706/2*) by which surplus enemy war matériel is being safeguarded, inventoried, and pooled as the property of the United Nations pending multipartite agreement as to disposal by the governments represented on the European Advisory Commission.

3. SCAEF states in SCAF 447 (Appendix "D") that long-term guarding and maintenance of warlike equipment constitutes a heavy burden on occupational forces and is considered impracticable particularly in view of the redeployment program.

4. The military advisor, European Advisory Commission, writing on behalf of the Joint Advisors, U.S. Delegation, European Advisory Commission (EAC), states that it is doubted whether EAC will be in position to consider question of disposal of enemy matériel in the near future.

5. In C.C.S. 706/7,* the Combined Chiefs of Staff agreed that if, at the time of the defeat of Germany, there was no prospect of a speedy agreement on policies for the disposal of enemy war matériel, action should be taken to seek the agreement on a governmental level of the authorities of the nations represented on the EAC for the immediate disposal of war matériel in Germany and Austria required for the war against Japan.

---

* Not published herein.

Appendix "C"

SECRET

APPENDIX "D"

From: Supreme Commander, Allied Expeditionary Force

To: Combined Chiefs of Staff

Nr: FWD 24508   SCAF 447   11 June 1945

FACS 159 authorized the destruction of enemy war material captured in Germany and Austria which was surplus to the requirements of the Supreme Command and London Munitions Assignment Board, such authority to remain in force until cessation of hostilities or until superseded by a later directive.

Present policy is accordingly based on FACS 149 and FACS 109 by which surplus enemy war material in Germany and Austria is being safeguarded, inventoried, and pooled as the property of the United Nations pending multipartite agreement as to disposal, between the governments represented in the European Advisory Commission.

Long-term guarding and maintenance of warlike equipment constitutes heavy burden on occupational forces particularly in view of redeployment program and is considered impracticable. Unless early issue of new directive is to be made request authority to:—

A. Fill London Munitions Assignment Board requirements from war material in Germany and Austria.

B. Render surplus enemy warlike equipment unserviceable and dispose as scrap.

CM-IN-10543   (11 Jun 45)

SECRET

C.C.S. 706/14 (TERMINAL) 17 July 1945

COMBINED CHIEFS OF STAFF

DISPOSAL OF ENEMY WAR MATÉRIEL IN GERMANY AND AUSTRIA

Reference:

CCS 706/11

Memorandum by the United States Chiefs of Staff

The United States Chiefs of Staff recommend that the Combined Chiefs of Staff approve Appendices "A" and "B" to C.C.S. 706/11 as amended herein.

SECRET

APPENDIX "A"

DRAFT MESSAGE

MESSAGE TO SUPREME COMMANDER, ALLIED EXPEDITIONARY FORCE

<u>FROM THE BRITISH CHIEFS OF STAFF TO THE COMMANDER IN CHIEF, BRITISH FORCES OF OCCUPATION IN GERMANY</u>

<u>FROM THE U.S. CHIEFS OF STAFF TO THE COMMANDING GENERAL, UNITED STATES FORCES, EUROPEAN THEATER</u>

<u>FROM THE COMBINED CHIEFS OF STAFF TO THE</u> *AND* <u>SUPREME ALLIED COMMANDER, MEDITERRANEAN</u>

This is answer to SCAF 447 repeated this date to SACMED. The London Munitions Assignment Board is being empowered to assign captured or surrendered enemy matériel <u>except that of non-German origin</u> in the hands of forces under U.S. or British command in Germany and Austria to the forces of those nations employed in furtherance of the agreed strategy in the war against Japan. <u>In the absence of agreement in the Control Council, the</u> *The* treatment of enemy matériel surplus to needs of the military commanders and those required to fill London Munitions Assignment Board requirements will be the subject of <u>further</u> instructions by the respective Chiefs of Staff to the United States and <u>British</u> zone commanders after the dissolution of SHAEF. <u>Meanwhile no destruction of such matériel beyond that required for public and military security should take place.</u>

Words underscored are proposed additions.
Words italicized are proposed deletions.

Appendix "A"

SECRET

APPENDIX "B"

DRAFT

MESSAGE TO THE LONDON MUNITIONS ASSIGNMENT BOARD

Until a policy of disposal is agreed upon by the nations represented on the European Advisory Commission and implemented, the London Munitions Assignment Board is empowered to assign captured or surrendered enemy matériel <u>except that of non-German origin</u> in the hands of forces under U.S. or British command in Germany and Austria to the forces of those nations who will employ such equipment in furtherance of the agreed strategy in the war against Japan.

Words underscored are proposed additions.

TOP SECRET

                    C.C.S. 842
                    C.C.S. 842/1
                    C.C.S. 842/2

FRENCH AND DUTCH PARTICIPATION IN THE WAR AGAINST JAPAN

References:

CCS 195th Meeting, Item 2
CCS 900/3, paragraph 15

In C.C.S. 842 (25 April 1945) the Representatives of the British Chiefs of Staff proposed a general over-all policy with regard to French and Dutch participation in the war against Japan and recommended that a memorandum be forwarded to the French and Netherlands Representatives to the Combined Chiefs of Staff.

In C.C.S. 842/1 (10 July) the United States Chiefs of Staff agreed in principle that the Combined Chiefs of Staff might now state a general over-all policy and recommended that the policy as set forth in C.C.S. 842/1 be accepted.

In C.C.S. 842/2 (18 July) the United States Chiefs of Staff circulated a revised memorandum for the French and Netherlands Representatives to be considered in lieu of the Enclosure to C.C.S. 842/1.

The Combined Chiefs of Staff in their 195th Meeting (18 July) approved the memorandum in the Enclosure to C.C.S. 842/2 and directed the Secretaries to forward it separately to the French and Netherlands Representatives.

TOP SECRET

C.C.S. 842   25 April 1945

COMBINED CHIEFS OF STAFF

FRENCH AND DUTCH PARTICIPATION IN THE WAR AGAINST JAPAN

References:

C.C.S. 644 Series
C.C.S. 702 Series

Memorandum by the Representatives of the British Chiefs of Staff

1. The French and Dutch Representatives to the Combined Chiefs of Staff have, on many occasions, made clear the wish of their governments to participate to the maximum extent possible in the war in the Far East. The Combined Chiefs of Staff have not, however, so far been able to meet these wishes to the full, nor in the near future will they be able to do so.

2. However, while it is obviously impossible for the French or Dutch to participate in the war in the Far East to the extent they desire, we believe it should now be recognized that these two nations, both of whom have large interests in the Far East, should participate in the war against Japan, to the extent which may be possible, and particularly in those operations aimed at the liberation of their own territories. This could be achieved by the employment in such operations of token forces, technical experts, and members of the civil administration.

3. In order to give effect to this policy we feel that the French and Dutch should be kept more generally informed of the intentions of the Combined Chiefs of Staff with regard to any operations which may affect their national interests in the Far East.

4. The British Chiefs of Staff believe therefore that the Combined Chiefs of Staff might now, with advantage, agree on a general over-all policy with regard to French and Dutch participation in the war against Japan. Specific requests from either of these nations could then be judged and answered in

the light of this agreed policy. Such a policy the British Chiefs of Staff consider might be stated as follows:—

a. Whilst it is at present impossible for the French or the Dutch to play a major part in Far Eastern operations, the French/Dutch desire to use their forces on the largest practical scale for the liberation of their own territories is recognized.

b. For the present their participation must be limited to the employment of token forces, technical experts, and members of the civil administration.

c. In implementing this policy the Combined Chiefs of Staff undertake to keep the French/Dutch generally informed of their intentions in respect of any operations that may affect French/Dutch national interests in the Far East. Discussions would thus be facilitated on French/Dutch participation in the light of available Allied resources and shipping.

5. If these principles are acceptable to the United States Chiefs of Staff we would see certain advantages in informing the French and Dutch Representatives to the Combined Chiefs of Staff accordingly. It would then be clear to them that the Combined Chiefs of Staff appreciate the very natural desire of the two governments concerned to participate to the maximum extent possible in the war against Japan. Such a communication might also assist in limiting their specific proposals with regard to their participation to those which were likely to prove possible of implementation.

6. To sum up, therefore, we recommend that the Combined Chiefs of Staff should:—

a. Accept the principles contained in paragraph 4 above.

b. Despatch the attached memorandum (Enclosure) to the French and Netherlands Representatives to the Combined Chiefs of Staff.

7. We understand that the British Foreign Secretary is addressing the United States Secretary of State on this subject in a similar vein.

TOP SECRET

ENCLOSURE

DRAFT

LETTER TO THE FRENCH AND NETHERLANDS REPRESENTATIVE
TO THE COMBINED CHIEFS OF STAFF

1. The Combined Chiefs of Staff have been giving earnest consideration to the question of French (the Netherlands) participation in the war against Japan and have instructed us to inform you that they fully recognize the French (Netherlands) desire to use their forces on the largest practical scale for the liberation of their own territories.

2. It will be appreciated however that the extent of French (the Netherlands) participation in any such operations must for the present be limited in character owing to the many and heavy other commitments on Allied shoulders and the consequent strain on Allied resources. In the view of the Combined Chiefs of Staff it will for the present only be possible to make provision for token forces, technical experts, and members of the civil administration.

3. However, the Combined Chiefs of Staff have instructed us to inform you that:—

    a. Within the limits of the Allied available resources and having regard to their other commitments, they will do all in their power to facilitate the participation of French (the Netherlands) forces in the liberation of French (the Netherlands) territories in the Far East.

    b. In order to facilitate discussion as to the best method of arranging for the above French (Netherlands) participation, they further undertake to keep you generally informed of their intentions in respect of any operations that may affect French (the Netherlands) national interests in the Far East.

TOP SECRET

C.C.S. 842/1　　　　　　　　　　　　　　　　　　　　　　　　10 July 1945

COMBINED CHIEFS OF STAFF

FRENCH AND DUTCH PARTICIPATION IN THE WAR AGAINST JAPAN

Memorandum by the United States Chiefs of Staff

1. The United States Chiefs of Staff have considered the proposals put forward by the Representatives of the British Chiefs of Staff in C.C.S. 842 and agree in principle that the Combined Chiefs of Staff might now state a general over-all policy with regard to French and Dutch participation in the war against Japan. They consider that such a policy should be stated as follows:—

   a. While it is at present impossible for French or Netherlands armed forces to play a major part in Far Eastern operations, the desire of the French/Dutch to join with us in the war against Japan and the possible provision of such assistance in the struggle in the Pacific which may be synchronized with operations already planned or under way will be taken into account by the Combined Chiefs of Staff. No French or Netherlands forces will be accepted for operations unless it has been previously agreed that complete control of such forces will be vested in the commander in chief concerned and their actual employment will be determined by him solely on military grounds. The actual use of any force must depend solely on military considerations.

   b. In implementing this policy the Combined Chiefs of Staff undertake to give the French/Netherlands representatives timely information of their intentions in respect of any operations that will directly affect French/Netherlands territories or armed forces in the Far East.

2. The United States Chiefs of Staff consider that the draft letter in the Enclosure to C.C.S. 842 should be amended accordingly.

3. It is recommended that the Combined Chiefs of Staff:—

   a. Accept the policy stated in paragraph 1 above.

   b. Dispatch the attached memorandum (Enclosure) to the French/Netherlands representatives.

TOP SECRET

ENCLOSURE

DRAFT

MEMORANDUM TO THE FRENCH AND NETHERLANDS
REPRESENTATIVES TO THE COMBINED CHIEFS OF STAFF

The Combined Chiefs of Staff have given consideration to the question of French/Netherlands participation in the war against Japan and wish to inform you of their views which are as follows:—

a. While it is at present impossible for French or Netherlands armed forces to play a major part in Far Eastern operations, the desire of the French/Dutch to join with us in the war against Japan and the possible provision of such assistance in the struggle in the Pacific which may be synchronized with operations already planned or under way will be taken into account by the Combined Chiefs of Staff. No French or Netherlands forces will be accepted for operations unless it has been previously agreed that complete control of such forces will be vested in the commander in chief concerned and their actual employment will be determined by him solely on military grounds. The actual use of any force must depend solely on military considerations.

b. In implementing this policy the Combined Chiefs of Staff undertake to give the French/Netherlands representatives timely information of their intentions in respect of any operations that will directly affect French/Netherlands territories or armed forces in the Far East.

TOP SECRET

C.C.S. 842/2　　　　　　　　　　　　　　　　　　　　18 July 1945

COMBINED CHIEFS OF STAFF

FRENCH AND DUTCH PARTICIPATION
IN THE WAR AGAINST JAPAN

Memorandum by the United States Chiefs of Staff

　　The United States Chiefs of Staff recommend that the Combined Chiefs of Staff forward the enclosed memorandum to the French and Netherlands Representatives to the Combined Chiefs of Staff in lieu of the memorandum in the Enclosure to C.C.S. 842/1.

TOP SECRET

ENCLOSURE

DRAFT

MEMORANDUM TO THE FRENCH AND NETHERLANDS REPRESENTATIVES TO THE COMBINED CHIEFS OF STAFF

The Combined Chiefs of Staff have given consideration to the question of French/Netherlands participation in the war against Japan and wish to inform you of their views which are as follows:—

a. While it is at present impracticable due chiefly to logistical difficulties for French or Netherlands armed forces to take a major part in the immediate operations in the Far East, the provision of such assistance which may be synchronized with operations will be taken into account by the Combined Chiefs of Staff. The use of such forces will depend solely on military considerations. French or Netherlands forces so accepted must operate under the complete control of the commander in chief concerned.

b. In implementing this policy the Combined Chiefs of Staff undertake to give the French/Netherlands representatives timely information of their intentions in respect of any operations that will directly affect French/Netherlands territories or armed forces in the Far East.

TOP SECRET

C.C.S. 866
C.C.S. 866/1
C.C.S. 866/2

FUTURE OF ALLIED FORCE HEADQUARTERS, MEDITERRANEAN

C.C.S. 866 (25 May 1945) circulated a memorandum by the Representatives of the British Chiefs of Staff presenting the views of the British Chiefs of Staff on the subject of the future of Allied Force Headquarters.

In C.C.S. 866/1 (7 July) the United States Chiefs of Staff stated their general agreement with the views set forth in C.C.S. 866 and recommended a message (Enclosure) for dispatch to the Supreme Allied Commander, Mediterranean.

In C.C.S. 866/2 (12 July) the Representatives of the British Chiefs of Staff stated that the British Chiefs of Staff agree to the dispatch of the message in the Enclosure to C.C.S. 866/1 subject to the amendment of paragraph 2.

By informal action on 20 July the Combined Chiefs of Staff approved the recommendation in C.C.S. 866/1 as amended by C.C.S. 866/2. The message to the Supreme Allied Commander, Mediterranean, was dispatched as FAN 601.

TOP SECRET

C.C.S. 866   25 May 1945

COMBINED CHIEFS OF STAFF

FUTURE OF ALLIED FORCE HEADQUARTERS, MEDITERRANEAN

Memorandum by the Representatives of the British Chiefs of Staff

1. The British Chiefs of Staff do not believe that the time has yet come when definite instructions on the subject of the future of Allied Force Headquarters can be given by the Combined Chiefs of Staff to the Supreme Allied Commander, Mediterranean. They would like however to acquaint the United States Chiefs of Staff of their present views on the matter.

2. The British Chiefs of Staff consider that the appointment of the Supreme Allied Commander, Mediterranean, should not be terminated until the Quadripartite Commission in Vienna has taken over control of Austria and the situation in each zone and on the lines of communication is firmly in hand. When this condition is fulfilled they believe that a small combined United States-British headquarters will be required to replace Allied Force Headquarters in Italy until:—

    a. The Allied Commission in Italy has been dissolved, and,

    b. Allied Military Government in Bolzano and the Allied commitment in Venezia Giulia have ceased.

3. The British Chiefs of Staff would be glad to know if the United States Chiefs of Staff are in general agreement with the considerations set out above.

TOP SECRET

C.C.S. 866/1   7 July 1945

COMBINED CHIEFS OF STAFF

FUTURE OF ALLIED FORCE HEADQUARTERS, MEDITERRANEAN

Memorandum by the United States Chiefs of Staff

1. The United States Chiefs of Staff are in general agreement with views set forth in C.C.S. 866, but note that since C.C.S. 866 was written, the question of combined command in Austria has been discussed in the C.C.S. 481 series.*

2. With termination of operations and redeployment of United States and British forces from the Mediterranean Theater, it should be possible to reduce progressively the size of Allied Force Headquarters (AFHQ). In this regard the United States Chiefs of Staff believe that Field Marshal Alexander should be directed to restrict AFHQ activities to essentially Allied matters and to reduce his headquarters as the number of troops in the theater and commitments diminish. It does not appear possible at this time, in view of commitments mentioned in paragraphs 2 *a.* and 2 *b.* of C.C.S. 866, to determine the future of AFHQ, but it is suggested that the situation might be reviewed about 1 September 1945.

3. In light of the foregoing it is recommended that the attached message (Enclosure) be dispatched to the Supreme Allied Commander, Mediterranean (SACMED).

---

* Not published herein.

TOP SECRET

ENCLOSURE

DRAFT

MESSAGE TO SUPREME ALLIED COMMANDER, MEDITERRANEAN

1. In view of Allied commitments in Mediterranean area, it is impossible at this time to determine when Allied Force Headquarters (AFHQ) might be dissolved as a combined command. However, Combined Chiefs of Staff desire that activities of AFHQ be restricted to essentially Allied matters and as troops are redeployed and other commitments diminish AFHQ be progressively reduced in size.

2. Request recommendations on 1 September as to future of AFHQ.

TOP SECRET

C.C.S. 866/2 12 July 1945

COMBINED CHIEFS OF STAFF

FUTURE OF ALLIED FORCE HEADQUARTERS, MEDITERRANEAN

Memorandum by the Representatives of the British Chiefs of Staff

1. The British Chiefs of Staff have informed us that they have given further consideration to the question of the dissolution of Allied Force Headquarters (AFHQ) and subsequent organization. The Supreme Allied Commander, Mediterranean, and the Commanders-in-Chief Middle East have sent the British Chiefs of Staff their comments on the original proposals, and when these have been considered the British Chiefs of Staff will put forward further draft proposals for the consideration of the United States Chiefs of Staff.

2. In the meanwhile, they agree to the dispatch of the message in the Enclosure to C.C.S. 866/1, amended as follows:—

Delete paragraph 2 and substitute:

"Direction for future of AFHQ by the Combined Chiefs of Staff will be sent you after *TERMINAL*."

TOP SECRET

>C.C.S. 877
>C.C.S. 877/1
>C.C.S. 877/2
>C.C.S. 877/4
>C.C.S. 877/5

BASIC OBJECTIVES, STRATEGY, AND POLICIES

References:

CCS 198th Meeting, Item 2
Plenary Meeting between the United States and Great Britain
CCS 900/3, sections I, II, & III

In C.C.S. 877 (14 June 1945) the United States Chiefs of Staff recommended that the Combined Chiefs of Staff approve the statement of basic objectives, strategy, and policies as set forth therein.

In C.C.S. 877/1 (30 June) the British Chiefs of Staff proposed certain amendments to C.C.S. 877.

In C.C.S. 877/2 (10 July) the United States Chiefs of Staff presented their views on the amendments proposed by the British Chiefs of Staff.

In C.C.S. 877/4 (20 July) the British Chiefs of Staff recommended that the Combined Chiefs of Staff adopt the basic objectives, strategy, and policies as amended in the Enclosure thereto.

C.C.S. 877/5 (21 July) presented further views of the United States Chiefs of Staff with regard to the amendments proposed by the British Chiefs of Staff and recommended that the Combined Chiefs of Staff approve the statement contained in the Enclosure to C.C.S. 877/4 as amended in the Enclosure to C.C.S. 877/5.

During discussion among the Combined Chiefs of Staff in their 198th Meeting (21 July) it was brought out that nothing further could be done in the matter until a decision had been reached on a higher level.

The President and Prime Minister in their Plenary Meeting with the Combined Chiefs of Staff on 24 July resolved the points of divergence. The agreed statement of basic objectives, strategy, and policies is contained in C.C.S. 900/3.

TOP SECRET

C.C.S. 877 14 June 1945

COMBINED CHIEFS OF STAFF

BASIC OBJECTIVES, STRATEGY, AND POLICIES

Memorandum by the United States Chiefs of Staff

The agreed summary of broad principles regarding the prosecution of the war, set forth in C.C.S. 776/3,* was based upon the agreed concept that Germany was the principal enemy. The unconditional surrender of Germany, and the vital importance of rapidly reorienting strength so that the maximum possible effort may now be brought to bear against Japan, make it desirable that this summary of broad principles be revised in consonance with the changed situation. Acceptance now of these principles will establish appropriate emphasis on the war against Japan, while taking cognizance of the changed situation in the European Theater. Accordingly, the United States Chiefs of Staff recommend that the Combined Chiefs of Staff approve the following statements of basic objectives, strategy, and policies.

I. *OVER-ALL OBJECTIVE*

1. In conjunction with other Allies to bring about at the earliest possible date the unconditional surrender of Japan.

II. *OVER-ALL STRATEGIC CONCEPT FOR THE PROSECUTION OF THE WAR*

2. In cooperation with other Allies to establish and maintain, as necessary, military control of Germany and Austria.

3. In cooperation with other Allies to bring about at the earliest possible date the defeat of Japan by: lowering Japanese ability and will to resist by establishing sea and air blockades, conducting intensive air bombardment, and destroying Japanese air and naval strength; invading and seizing objectives in the Japanese home islands as the main effort; conducting such operations

---

* ARGONAUT Conference book, page 157.

against objectives in other than the Japanese home islands as will contribute to the main effort; establishing absolute military control of Japan; and liberating Japanese-occupied territory if required.

III. BASIC UNDERTAKINGS AND POLICIES FOR THE PROSECUTION OF THE WAR

4. The following basic undertakings are considered fundamental to the prosecution of the war:—

   a. Maintain the security and war-making capacity of the Western Hemisphere and the British Isles.

   b. Support the war-making capacity of our forces in all areas with first priority given to those forces in combat areas.

   c. Maintain vital overseas lines of communication.

5. In order to attain the over-all objective, first priority in the provision of forces and resources of the United States and Great Britain, including re-orientation from the European Theater to the Pacific and Far East, will be given to meeting requirements of tasks necessary to the execution of the over-all strategic concept and to the basic undertakings fundamental to the prosecution of the war.

   The invasion of Japan and operations directly connected therewith are the supreme operations in the war against Japan; forces and resources will be allocated on the required scale to assure that invasion can be accomplished at the earliest practicable date. No other operations will be undertaken which hazard the success of, or delay, these main operations.

6. The following additional tasks will be undertaken in order to assist in the execution of the over-all strategic concept:—

   a. Encourage Russian entry into the war against Japan. Provide such aid to her war-making capacity as may be necessary and practicable in connection therewith.

   b. Undertake such measures as may be necessary and practicable in order to aid the war effort of China as an effective ally against Japan.

   c. Provide assistance to such of the forces of liberated areas as can fulfill an active and effective role in the present war. Within the limits of our available resources assist co-belligerents to the extent they are able to

TOP SECRET

employ this assistance in the present war. Having regard to the successful accomplishment of basic undertakings, to provide such supplies to the liberated areas as will effectively contribute to the capacity of the United Nations to prosecute the present war.

d. In cooperation with other Allies conduct operations, if required, to liberate enemy-occupied areas.

TOP SECRET

C.C.S. 877/1 30 June 1945

COMBINED CHIEFS OF STAFF

BASIC OBJECTIVES, STRATEGY, AND POLICIES

References:

CCS 877
CCS 824/5
CCS 746/10 & 746/24

Memorandum by the Representatives of the British Chiefs of Staff

1. The British Chiefs of Staff would like to propose three amendments to the memorandum put forward by the United States Chiefs of Staff (C.C.S. 877).

2. First, at the end of paragraph 4 *a.* they would like to change the words "British Isles" to read "British Commonwealth." As at present phrased, the wording would not safeguard Imperial requirements, e.g., for India and Australia.

3. Second, for the reasons already given in paragraph 5, C.C.S. 824/4,* the British Chiefs of Staff would still prefer to delete the words "or delay" in the last line of paragraph 5.

4. Third, the British Chiefs of Staff point out that since discussions regarding the formula for priorities began, the cargo shipping review has been completed and formal approval to it should be given shortly. This review will cover all present foreseen requirements, but it remains to safeguard approved military operations against additional civil requirements not now covered in the cargo shipping review. For this reason, therefore, the British Chiefs of Staff would like to suggest that a paragraph should be added to the memorandum by the United States Chiefs of Staff as follows:—

"7. The above formulae relate to cargo shipping, only in so far as additional requirements arise. Schedules of proposed military and civil

---

* Not published herein.

TOP SECRET

allocations for the period 1 July 1945 to 30 June 1946 have been agreed by the Combined Chiefs of Staff (C.C.S. 746/24*). The combined shipping authorities have given assurances (C.C.S. 746/10**) that no civil allocations additional to the above, which might prejudice approved operational requirements, will be accepted without prior consultation with the appropriate Chiefs of Staff."

5. Subject to the above remarks the British Chiefs of Staff are in full agreement with the memorandum by the United States Chiefs of Staff (C.C.S. 877), and would not propose to submit any separate formula on priorities. If the United States Chiefs of Staff feel able to accept the amendments proposed above, the British Chiefs of Staff suggest that the Combined Chiefs of Staff should adopt the formula in C.C.S. 877, as amended by this paper, at once and incorporate it in the final report of the *TERMINAL* Conference.

---

* Not published herein.
** ARGONAUT Conference book, page 54.

TOP SECRET

C.C.S. 877/2 10 July 1945

COMBINED CHIEFS OF STAFF

BASIC OBJECTIVES, STRATEGY, AND POLICIES

Memorandum by the United States Chiefs of Staff

1. With reference to the amendment proposed by the British Chiefs of Staff to paragraph 4 *a.*, "Basic Undertakings and Policies for the Prosecution of the War," of C.C.S. 877, the United States Chiefs of Staff had not proposed to change the wording of this paragraph, even though it does not fit the present situation. Now that the point has been raised, however, it is considered that the paragraph should recognize that, at this stage in the war, there is no longer any particular connection between "security" and "war-making capacity" in so far as the completion of the war against Japan is concerned. They agree to the inclusion of the term "British Commonwealth" in the statement in so far as "security" is concerned, even though the entire Commonwealth is not at war with Japan.

2. It is the view of the United States Chiefs of Staff that with the end of the war with Germany, justification does not exist for expanding the basic undertaking concerning "war-making capacity" which has been agreed during the period of a two-front war. Rather, now that our entire productive capacity is no longer being devoted to an all-out war, the wording should clearly restrict to this war the commitment in the Combined Chiefs of Staff.

3. Since the British Chiefs of Staff do not wish to continue the original wording, the United States Chiefs of Staff consider that paragraph 4 *a.* of the statement proposed in C.C.S. 877 should be deleted, the following substituted therefor, and paragraphs 4 *b.* and *c.* re-lettered accordingly:—

"4. *a.* Maintain the security of the Western Hemisphere and the British Commonwealth.

b. Maintain the war-making capacity of the U.S. and the British Isles in so far as it is connected with the prosecution of this war."

4. As to the proposal to delete the words "or delay" from the sentence, "No other operations will be undertaken which hazard the success of, <u>or delay,</u>

TOP SECRET

these main operations.", such deletion would make it meaningless in so far as establishing a priority for operations is concerned. The United States Chiefs of Staff see reasons for inclusion of the phrase and see no reason even for considering its deletion unless the British Chiefs of Staff intend to propose an operation which might delay the main operations.

5. As to the proposal that a paragraph be added relating to cargo shipping, the intent of the memorandum proposed by C.C.S. 877 was to establish broad principles for the prosecution of the war. The United States Chiefs of Staff believe that interpretation of these principles to apply to specific cases should be considered as separate matters. The statements of broad policy contained in C.C.S. 877 will serve as guides to resolve problems in allocation of forces and resources. However, after meeting requirements for the supreme operations against Japan, there may remain matters of logistical and operational priorities which will require resolution by the Combined Chiefs of Staff and will have to be considered on their merits as they arise. It is therefore suggested that priorities for cargo shipping be excluded from the statement of basic policies and remain under consideration in the C.C.S. 746 series.

TOP SECRET

C.C.S. 877/4   20 July 1945

COMBINED CHIEFS OF STAFF

BASIC OBJECTIVES, STRATEGY, AND POLICIES

Memorandum by the British Chiefs of Staff

1. We have considered the latest proposals of the United States Chiefs of Staff in C.C.S. 877/2. In the attached schedule we have set out in one column the document as proposed by the United States Chiefs of Staff, together with the amendments which we should like to see introduced. In the right-hand column we set out our comments.

2. The document, as far as paragraph 6, covers presently known military requirements. Against the possibility that additional military requirements may emerge which might conflict with presently accepted civil shipping programmes, it is considered desirable to add a further paragraph in the terms set out in paragraph 7.

3. We recommend that the Combined Chiefs of Staff adopt the basic objectives, strategy, and policies as amended in the attached, and incorporate them in the final report of the *TERMINAL* Conference.

TOP SECRET

ENCLOSURE

Memorandum by United States Chiefs of Staff with Proposed Amendments by British Chiefs of Staff

Comments by British Chiefs of Staff

I. OVER-ALL OBJECTIVE

1. In conjunction with other Allies to bring about at the earliest possible date the unconditional surrender of Japan.

II. OVER-ALL STRATEGIC CONCEPT FOR THE PROSECUTION OF THE WAR

2. In cooperation with other Allies to establish and maintain, as necessary, military control of Germany and Austria.

3. In cooperation with other Allies to bring about at the earliest possible date the defeat of Japan by: lowering Japanese ability and will to resist by establishing sea and air blockades, conducting intensive air bombardment, and destroying Japanese air and naval strength; invading and seizing objectives in the Japanese home islands as the main effort; conducting such operations against objectives in other than the Japanese home islands as will contribute to the main effort; establishing absolute military control of Japan; and liberating Japanese occupied territory if required.

We fully agree that the first priority should be given to the main operations against the Japanese Islands.

We trust, however, that other operations in the Outer Zone, which will achieve the secondary object of evicting the Japanese from all occupied territories, will receive the fullest possible consideration.

Memorandum by United States Chiefs of Staff with Proposed Amendments by British Chiefs of Staff

Comments by British Chiefs of Staff

III. BASIC UNDERTAKINGS AND POLICIES FOR THE PROSECUTION OF THE WAR

4. The following basic undertakings are considered fundamental to the prosecution of the war:—

   a. Maintain the security of the Western Hemisphere and the British Commonwealth.

   b. Maintain the war-making capacity of the United States and the British Isles in so far as it is connected with the prosecution of this war.

   <u>*a.* Maintain the security and war-making capacity of the Western Hemisphere and the British Commonwealth as necessary for the fulfillment of the strategic concept.</u>

   <u>*b.*</u> *c.* Support the war-making capacity of our forces, in all areas, with first priority given to those forces in <u>or destined for combat areas.</u>

   <u>*c.*</u> *d.* Maintain vital overseas lines of communication.

The wording of paragraph 4 *b.* as proposed by the United States Chiefs of Staff does not allow for the maintenance of the war-making capacity of such countries as Canada, India or Australia, all of which are making an important contribution towards the prosecution of the war. War-making capacity cannot be confined solely to that required for the defeat of Japan since it is also necessary to meet the requirements for military control of Germany and Austria as stated in the overall strategic concept for the prosecution of the war.

If first priority is given only to the support of the war-making capacity of forces in the combat areas, this might lead to the withholding of priority from the forces destined to relieve or support them. For example, the forces in India are required for maintaining the forces in active operations and providing reinforcements. As is known

---

Words underscored are proposed additions.
Words italicized are proposed deletions.

Memorandum by United States Chiefs of Staff with Proposed Amendments by British Chiefs of Staff

Comments by British Chiefs of Staff

many installations supporting the operations in Southeast Asia Command are outside those areas which can strictly be termed combat areas. Unless these requirements are recognised, the war-making capacity of forces in combat areas will be jeopardised.

5. In order to attain the over-all objective, first priority in the provision of forces and resources of the United States and Great Britain, including re-orientation from the European Theater to the Pacific and Far East, will be given to meeting requirements of tasks necessary to the execution of the over-all strategic concept and to the basic undertakings fundamental to the prosecution of the war.

The invasion of Japan and operations directly connected therewith are the supreme operations in the war against Japan; forces and resources will be allocated on the required scale to assure that invasion can be accomplished at the earliest practicable date. No other operations will be undertaken which hazard the success of, or delay, these main operations.

6. The following additional tasks will be undertaken in order to assist in the execution of the over-all strategic concept:

a. Encourage Russian entry into the war against Japan. Provide such

TOP SECRET

Memorandum by United States Chiefs of Staff with Proposed Amendments by British Chiefs of Staff	Comments by British Chiefs of Staff

aid to her war-making capacity as may be necessary and practicable in connection therewith.

b. Undertake such measures as may be necessary and practicable in order to aid the war effort of China as an effective ally against Japan.

c. Provide assistance to such of the forces of liberated areas as can fulfill an active and effective role in the present war. <u>or are required to maintain world order in the interests of the war effort.</u> Within the limits of our available resources assist co-belligerents to the extent they are able to employ this assistance in the present war. *Having regard to the successful accomplishment of basic undertakings, to provide such supplies to the liberated areas as will effectively contribute to the capacity of the United Nations to prosecute the present war.*

 The present wording would appear to limit this assistance strictly to those forces which can take part in the war against Japan. We feel, however, that the necessity for the maintenance of world order, particularly in Europe, must be recognised. Having brought about the liberation of Europe, it would be illogical to allow unrest to occur owing to lack of forces in the liberated areas to keep order.

d. In cooperation with other Allies conduct operations, if required, to liberate enemy-occupied areas.

 The last sentence of paragraph 6 c. is unnecessary as it is now dealt with in paragraph 7 below.

7. Cargo Shipping

<u>Present estimates of the requirements for cargo shipping indicate the position to be sufficiently manageable to provide for the maximum effort in the prosecution of the war against Japan, for the maintenance of the war-</u>

Words underscored are proposed additions.
Words italicized are proposed deletions.

TOP SECRET

| *Memorandum by United States Chiefs of Staff with Proposed Amendments by British Chiefs of Staff* | *Comments by British Chiefs of Staff* |

<u>making capacity of the British Commonwealth of Nations and the Western Hemisphere, for an additional amount for the reconstruction and rehabilitation of the United Kingdom, and for supplies to liberated areas. Should further military demands arise for maintaining the maximum war effort which would bring about a substantial conflict with British rehabilitation and reconstruction plans, and supplies to liberated areas, the shipping situation will be examined by the two Governments at time in the light of changed conditions.</u>

Words underscored are proposed additions.

TOP SECRET

C.C.S. 877/5   21 July 1945

COMBINED CHIEFS OF STAFF

BASIC OBJECTIVES, STRATEGY, AND POLICIES

Reference:

CCS 877/4

Memorandum by the United States Chiefs of Staff

1. The United States Chiefs of Staff having considered the proposals concerning the "Basic Objectives, Strategy and Policies" made by the British Chiefs of Staff in C.C.S. 877/4, wish to make their position clear. They consider that the basic undertakings should be confined to broad statements concerning the military conduct of the war. As a result of the changed circumstances arising from the defeat of Germany and the practical capability of the British Commonwealth to support its own forces in the field, they are operating on the basis that approval of the issue to allied governments of lend-lease munitions of war and military and naval equipment will be limited to that which is to be used in the war against Japan and which will not be used for any other purpose. They do not propose to subscribe to any statements which deviate from this principle. They consider that occupation forces are not a subject for combined military commitments. Matters relating to post-war armies are also not susceptible to combined military commitments. Any arrangements which the British wish to make on these subjects are beyond the purview of the United States Chiefs of Staff and should be taken up on the governmental level.

2. Considering in detail the proposed changes, the United States Chiefs of Staff have understood that throughout the entire period of the two-front war the combined commitment limited to supporting the war-making capacity of the British Isles has been satisfactory to the British Chiefs of Staff. In light of the limited information available to the United States Chiefs of Staff, it appears that the war effort of the British Commonwealth in the future is going to be less than that generated over the period when the commitment as previously worded was satisfactory; also certain portions of this war-making capacity will be devoted to other than the war effort against Japan. Since it

is realized that certain parts of the British Commonwealth will make a contribution to the war against Japan there is no objection to a statement which confines the combined military commitment to matters clearly connected with the prosecution of the war against Japan. Therefore the United States Chiefs of Staff propose to substitute in their paragraph III 4 b. the words "British Commonwealth" for "British Isles" and substitute "the war against Japan" for "this war."

3. The change proposed by the British Chiefs of Staff in paragraph 4 c. to include forces "destined for combat areas" is acceptable if rephrased to indicate clearly that it applies only to forces specifically designated for employment in combat areas against Japan. The United States Chiefs of Staff propose that the subparagraph 4 c. read in part "... those forces in or designated for employment in combat areas in the war against Japan." The proposal contained in paragraph III 6 c. that the United States make a military commitment to support forces engaged in other than the prosecution of the war against Japan is unacceptable for reasons indicated in the first paragraph of this memorandum.

4. The proposal to strike out the last sentence of paragraph III 6 c. is acceptable. However, the United States Chiefs of Staff are willing to retain it in view of the fact they do not accept the inclusion in the basic undertakings of paragraph 7 proposed by the British.

5. The proposed paragraph 7 is beyond the purview of the United States Chiefs of Staff. They are not in a position to make military commitments on the reconstruction and rehabilitation of the United Kingdom or on the matter of supplies for liberated Allies. Furthermore, the inclusion of terms concerning a specific resource such as cargo shipping in the basic undertakings is unacceptable. The purpose of the basic undertakings includes provision of a guide to the operating agencies for the allocation and the determination of priorities concerning all resources, not only cargo shipping, but forces and munitions of war. The United States Chiefs of Staff, however, will accept the inclusion in the final report to the President and Prime Minister, but not in the basic undertakings of a statement concerning cargo shipping which is limited to matters within their purview. The statement proposed by the British Chiefs of Staff changed as indicated below is acceptable to the United States Chiefs of Staff:—

CARGO SHIPPING

"Present estimates of the requirements for cargo shipping indicate the position to be sufficiently manageable to provide for the maximum effort

TOP SECRET

in the prosecution of the war against Japan, for the maintenance of the war-making capacity of the British Commonwealth of Nations and the Western Hemisphere, <u>insofar as it is connected with the prosecution of the war against Japan,</u> and for an additional amount for *the reconstruction and rehabilitation of the United Kingdom, and for supplies to liberated areas* <u>civilian requirements</u>. Should *further military demands arise for maintaining the maximum war effort which would bring about* a substantial conflict <u>arise</u> *with British rehabilitation and reconstruction plans, and supplies to liberated areas,* the shipping situation will be *examined* <u>a matter for examination</u> by the two Governments at <u>the</u> time <u>and</u> in the light of changed conditions."

6. For purposes of ready reference the statement of policy concerning strategy and basic undertakings is included in the Enclosure using the redraft of the British Chiefs of Staff in C.C.S. 877/4 and with the changes indicated above shown by italicizing and underlining.

7. It is recommended that the Combined Chiefs of Staff approve the statement in the Enclosure.

Words underscored are proposed additions.
Words italicized are proposed deletions.

TOP SECRET

ENCLOSURE

I. *OVER-ALL OBJECTIVE*

1. In conjunction with other Allies to bring about at the earliest possible date the unconditional surrender of Japan.

II. *OVER-ALL STRATEGIC CONCEPT FOR THE PROSECUTION OF THE WAR*

2. In cooperation with other Allies to establish and maintain, as necessary, military control of Germany and Austria.

3. In cooperation with other Allies to bring about at the earliest possible date the defeat of Japan by: lowering Japanese ability and will to resist by establishing sea and air blockades, conducting intensive air bombardment, and destroying Japanese air and naval strength; invading and seizing objectives in the Japanese home islands as the main effort; conducting such operations against objectives in other than the Japanese home islands as will contribute to the main effort; establishing absolute military control of Japan; and liberating Japanese-occupied territory if required.

III. *BASIC UNDERTAKINGS AND POLICIES FOR THE PROSECUTION OF THE WAR*

4. The following basic undertakings are considered fundamental to the prosecution of the war:—

    a. <u>Maintain the security of the Western Hemisphere and the British Commonwealth.</u>

    b. <u>Maintain the war-making capacity of the United States and the British Commonwealth in so far as it is connected with the prosecution of the war against Japan.</u>

    a. Maintain the security and war-making capacity of the Western Hemisphere and the British Commonwealth as necessary for the fulfillment of the strategic concept.

Words underscored are proposed additions.
Words italicized are proposed deletions.

TOP SECRET

<u>c.</u> b. Support the war-making capacity of our forces in all areas, with first priority given to those forces in or <u>designated</u> *destined* for <u>employment in</u> combat areas <u>in the war against Japan</u>.

<u>d.</u> c. Maintain vital overseas lines of communication.

5. In order to attain the over-all objective, first priority in the provision of forces and resources of the United States and Great Britain, including re-orientation from the European Theatre to the Pacific and Far East, will be given to meeting requirements of tasks necessary to the execution of the over-all strategic concept and to the basic undertakings fundamental to the prosecution of the war.

The invasion of Japan and operations directly connected therewith are the supreme operations in the war against Japan; forces and resources will be allocated on the required scale to assure that invasion can be accomplished at the earliest practicable date. No other operations will be undertaken which hazard the success of, or delay, these main operations.

6. The following additional tasks will be undertaken in order to assist in the execution of the over-all strategic concept:—

a. Encourage Russian entry into the war against Japan. Provide such aid to her war-making capacity as may be necessary and practicable in connection therewith.

b. Undertake such measures as may be necessary and practicable in order to aid the war effort of China as an effective ally against Japan.

c. Provide assistance to such of the forces of liberated areas as can fulfill an active and effective role in the present war *or are required to maintain world order in the interests of the war effort*. Within the limits of our available resources assist co-belligerents to the extent they are able to employ this assistance in the present war. <u>Having regard to the successful accomplishment of basic undertakings, to provide such supplies to the liberated areas as will effectively contribute to the capacity of the United Nations to prosecute the war against Japan.</u>

d. In cooperation with other Allies conduct operations, if required, to liberate enemy-occupied areas.

Words underscored are proposed additions.
Words italicized are proposed deletions.

TOP SECRET

7. *CARGO SHIPPING*

The proposal by the British Chiefs of Staff is not acceptable.

Words italicized are proposed deletions.

TOP SECRET

C.C.S. 880
C.C.S. 880/1
C.C.S. 880/2
C.C.S. 880/5
C.C.S. 880/7

AGENDA FOR THE NEXT
UNITED STATES - BRITISH STAFF CONFERENCE

In C.C.S. 880 (15 June 1945) the British Chiefs of Staff proposed a tentative outline agenda for the forthcoming Staff Conference.

In C.C.S. 880/1 (25 June) the British Chiefs of Staff suggested a further item for the agenda proposed in C.C.S. 880.

In C.C.S. 880/2 (27 June) the United States Chiefs of Staff agreed to the tentative outline agenda and expressed certain views regarding items (6) and (7) thereof.

In C.C.S. 880/5 (29 June) the British Chiefs of Staff replied to the views expressed by the United States Chiefs of Staff in paragraphs 2, 3, and 4 of C.C.S. 880/2.

In C.C.S. 880/7 (6 July) the United States Chiefs of Staff suggested an additional item for the tentative outline agenda (C.C.S. 880).

TOP SECRET

C.C.S. 880   15 June 1945

COMBINED CHIEFS OF STAFF

AGENDA FOR THE NEXT
UNITED STATES - BRITISH STAFF CONFERENCE

Memorandum by the Representatives of the British Chiefs of Staff

1. The British Chiefs of Staff put forward the following tentative outline agenda for the next United States - British Staff Conference:—

   (1) Progress reports on operations in the Pacific and Southeast Asia Command (SEAC).

   (2) Estimate of Japanese situation.

   (3) Development of operations in the Pacific.

   (4) British participation in the war against Japan.

   (5) Directive to the Supreme Allied Commander, Southeast Asia Command.

   (6) Control and command of the war against Japan.

   (7) Russian participation in the war against Japan.

   (8) French, Dutch, and Portuguese participation in the war against Japan.

   (9) Planning date for the end of the war against Japan.

   (10) Over-all priorities.

2. As to the preparation of papers, the British Chiefs of Staff assume that the United States Chiefs of Staff would deal with items 3, 7, 8, and 9. They themselves would be prepared to table papers on items 4, 5, and 6, and will probably wish to comment on C.C.S. 877* under item 10. They suggest that the Combined Intelligence Committee should be asked to prepare a report on item 2.

---

* Page 82.

TOP SECRET

3. The British Chiefs of Staff would be glad to have the reactions of the United States Chiefs of Staff to the above which is, of course, purely provisional at this stage.

TOP SECRET

C.C.S. 880/1   25 June 1945

COMBINED CHIEFS OF STAFF

AGENDA FOR THE NEXT
UNITED STATES - BRITISH STAFF CONFERENCE

Memorandum by the Representatives of the British Chiefs of Staff

1. The British Chiefs of Staff have now one further item to add to the tentative outline agenda proposed in C.C.S. 880. They suggest that the following item be added:

(11) Combined Chiefs of Staff Machinery after the war with Japan.

2. The British Chiefs of Staff would submit a paper on this item as a basis for discussion.

TOP SECRET

C.C.S. 880/2　　　　　　　　　　　　　　　　　　　　　　27 June 1945

COMBINED CHIEFS OF STAFF

AGENDA FOR MILITARY STAFF CONFERENCES

Memorandum by the United States Chiefs of Staff

1. The United States Chiefs of Staff agree to the tentative outline agenda for the next United States-British Staff Conference proposed by the British Chiefs of Staff in C.C.S. 880 and C.C.S. 880/1, and to the proposed scheme for the preparation of papers in connection therewith.

2. The United States Chiefs of Staff assume that the question of control and command in the war against Japan concerns the reorganization of command in the Southwest Pacific Area now under discussion by the Combined Chiefs of Staff in C.C.S. 852 Series* and in C.C.S. 878.* The United States Chiefs of Staff believe it would be desirable to resolve this matter before the forthcoming conference if at all practicable.

3. As to the matter of Russian participation in the war against Japan, there is a question as to whether discussion of this on a combined basis will be necessary, and, in any event, the United States Chiefs of Staff will not be prepared to take up the matter until after conclusion of any conversations with the Russians.

4. It is suggested that in so far as practicable the papers on each side be presented for consideration of the other prior to the conferences.

---

* Not published herein. See CCS 890 series, page 147.

TOP SECRET

C.C.S. 880/5 29 June 1945

COMBINED CHIEFS OF STAFF

AGENDA FOR MILITARY STAFF CONFERENCES

Memorandum by the Representatives of the British Chiefs of Staff

1. We communicated the views of the United States Chiefs of Staff, as set out in C.C.S. 880/2, to the British Chiefs of Staff.

2. With regard to paragraph 2 of C.C.S. 880/2, the British Chiefs of Staff say that their paper on the control and command of the war against Japan will include proposals for the reorganization of command in the Southwest Pacific.

3. With regard to paragraph 3 of C.C.S. 880/2, the British Chiefs of Staff agree that the Combined Chiefs of Staff should defer discussion of this problem until after the conclusion of any conversations with the Russians.

4. With regard to paragraph 4 of C.C.S. 880/2, the British Chiefs of Staff agree that papers should be exchanged in advance of the conference so far as practicable. They doubt, however, whether under present circumstances they will be able to present their papers on British participation in the war against Japan (item 4) and control and command of the war against Japan (item 6) more than a few days before *TERMINAL*. The directive to the Supreme Allied Commander, Southeast Asia Command (item 5) will depend upon the outcome of the Combined Chiefs of Staff discussion on British participation in the war against Japan (item 4) and cannot therefore be tabled in advance.

TOP SECRET

C.C.S. 880/7   6 July 1945

COMBINED CHIEFS OF STAFF

AGENDA FOR FORTHCOMING CONFERENCE

Memorandum by the United States Chiefs of Staff

The United States Chiefs of Staff recommend the addition to the agenda proposed in C.C.S. 880 and 880/1 of the following item, which they will prepare and present:—

(12) Report on air operations in the war against Japan.

TOP SECRET

C.C.S. 880/3
C.C.S. 880/6

SIZE OF MILITARY STAFFS FOR TERMINAL

In C.C.S. 880/3 (28 June 1945) the United States Chiefs of Staff expressed their views with regard to the size of military staffs at *TERMINAL*. The reply from the British Chiefs of Staff was circulated as C.C.S. 880/6 (30 June).

TOP SECRET

C.C.S. 880/3 28 June 1945

COMBINED CHIEFS OF STAFF

SIZE OF MILITARY STAFFS FOR TERMINAL

Memorandum by the United States Chiefs of Staff

1. With reference to the memorandum by the Representatives of the British Chiefs of Staff of 25 June,* it is the opinion of the United States Chiefs of Staff that large military staffs should not be taken to *TERMINAL* and that detailed discussions which will involve the need for a large staff on the order of *OCTAGON* and *ARGONAUT* should not be engaged in at that place. The United States Chiefs of Staff have not proposed to take with them more than very small staffs. Their understanding of the agenda proposed to date is such that they believe it should be handled quickly and easily without need for any large accompanying staff at the meeting. It is their view that in general subjects involving detailed studies and consideration should be handled within the normal mechanism of the Combined Chiefs of Staff.

2. In case the understanding the British Chiefs of Staff have of the discussions to be engaged in is such as to require a considerable staff, the United States Chiefs of Staff would like to be informed on this matter in order that they may consider it further.

---

*Not published herein.

TOP SECRET

C.C.S. 880/6   30 June 1945

COMBINED CHIEFS OF STAFF

SIZE OF MILITARY STAFFS FOR TERMINAL

Memorandum by the Representatives of the British Chiefs of Staff

We communicated the views of the United States Chiefs of Staff regarding the size of the military staffs for *TERMINAL* as set out in C.C.S. 880/3 to the British Chiefs of Staff who replied saying that they agreed that large military staffs would not be required at *TERMINAL*. The order of the staffs which they have in mind to take is approximately as follows:—

a. Each chief of staff will have with him, in addition to his personal staff, four or five staff officers.

b. In addition the secretariat will take with it enough personnel to provide for the normal administrative running of the conference.

TOP SECRET

C.C.S. 880/4

DEVELOPMENT OF OPERATIONS IN THE PACIFIC

References:

CCS 880, paragraph 1 (3)
CCS 193d Meeting, Item 4

C.C.S. 880/4, a memorandum by the United States Chiefs of Staff (29 June 1945), was noted by the Combined Chiefs of Staff in their 193d Meeting (16 July).

TOP SECRET

C.C.S. 880/4   29 June 1945

COMBINED CHIEFS OF STAFF

DEVELOPMENT OF OPERATIONS IN THE PACIFIC

Memorandum by the United States Chiefs of Staff

1. In conformity with the over-all objective to bring about the unconditional surrender of Japan at the earliest possible date, the United States Chiefs of Staff have adopted the following concept of operations for the main effort in the Pacific:—

    a. From bases in Okinawa, Iwo Jima, Marianas, and the Philippines to intensify the blockade and air bombardment of Japan in order to create a situation favorable to:

    b. An assault on Kyushu for the purpose of further reducing Japanese capabilities by containing and destroying major enemy forces and further intensifying the blockade and air bombardment in order to establish a tactical condition favorable to:

    c. The decisive invasion of the industrial heart of Japan through the Tokyo Plain.

2. We have curtailed our projected expansion in the Ryukyus by deferring indefinitely the seizure of Miyako Jima and Kikai Jima. Using the resources originally provided for Miyako and Kikai, we have accelerated the development of Okinawa. By doing this, a greater weight of effort will more promptly be brought to bear against Japan and the risk of becoming involved in operations which might delay the seizure of southern Kyushu is avoided.

3. In furtherance of the accomplishment of the over-all objectives, we have directed:—

    a. The invasion of Kyushu, target date 1 November 1945.

    b. The continuation of operations for securing and maintaining control of sea communications to and in the Western Pacific as are required for the accomplishment of the over-all objective.

    c. The defeat of the remaining Japanese in the Philippines by such operations as can be executed without prejudice to the over-all objective.

TOP SECRET

d. The seizure of Balikpapan, target date 1 July 1945.

e. The continuance of strategic air operations to support the accomplishment of the over-all objective.

4. Planning and preparation for the campaign in Japan subsequent to the invasion of Kyushu is continuing on the basis of meeting a target date of 1 March 1946 for the invasion of the Tokyo Plain. This planning is premised on the belief that defeat of the enemy's armed forces in the Japanese homeland is a prerequisite to unconditional surrender, and that such a defeat will establish the optimum prospect of capitulation by Japanese forces outside the main Japanese islands. We recognize the possibility also that our success in the main islands may not obviate the necessity of defeating Japanese forces elsewhere; decision as to steps to be taken in this eventuality must await further developments.

5. We are keeping under continuing review the possibility of capitalizing at small cost, without delaying the supreme operations, upon Japanese military deterioration and withdrawals in the China Theater.

6. We have directed the preparation of plans for the following:—

a. Keeping open a sea route to Russian Pacific ports.

b. Operations to effect an entry into Japan proper for occupational purposes in order to take immediate advantage of favorable circumstances such as a sudden enemy collapse or surrender.

TOP SECRET

C.C.S. 880/8

PLANNING DATE FOR THE END OF ORGANIZED RESISTANCE BY JAPAN

References:

CCS 880, paragraph 1 (9)
CCS 196th Meeting, Item 5
CCS 900/3, paragraph 19

    The Combined Chiefs of Staff considered C.C.S. 880/8 (7 July 1945) in their 196th Meeting (19 July) and agreed that for the purpose of planning production and the allocation of manpower, the planning date for the end of organized resistance by Japan be 15 November 1946; that this date be adjusted periodically to conform to the course of the war.

TOP SECRET

C.C.S. 880/8 7 July 1945

COMBINED CHIEFS OF STAFF

PLANNING DATE FOR THE END OF ORGANIZED RESISTANCE BY JAPAN
(For the purpose of planning production and the allocation of manpower)

Memorandum by the United States Chiefs of Staff

With reference to item (9), "Planning date for the end of the war against Japan," of the proposed agenda for United States-British military staff conferences (C.C.S. 880), the United States Chiefs of Staff recommend agreement to the following:—

a. That for the purpose of planning production and the allocation of manpower, the planning date for the end of organized resistance by Japan be 15 November 1946; that this date be adjusted periodically to conform to the course of the war.

b. The United States Chiefs of Staff desire to avoid use of the term "end of the war" in the sense proposed in the agenda, in view of the fact that certain United States laws, which should remain in effect during the period of occupation of Japan, will automatically lapse at stated periods after "the end of the war."

TOP SECRET

C.C.S. 880/9

C.C.S. 880/10

PROGRAM AND PROCEDURE FOR THE CONFERENCE

Reference:

CCS 193d Meeting, Item 1

In C.C.S. 880/9 (15 July 1945) the British Chiefs of Staff suggested a program and procedure for the conference.

In C.C.S. 880/10 (16 July) the United States Chiefs of Staff accepted the program subject to certain outlined provisions.

The Combined Chiefs of Staff in their 193d Meeting (16 July) approved C.C.S. 880/10.

TOP SECRET

C.C.S. 880/9   15 July 1945

COMBINED CHIEFS OF STAFF

PROGRAM AND PROCEDURE FOR THE CONFERENCE

Memorandum by the British Chiefs of Staff

1. We suggest that in accordance with the procedure we have adopted at previous conferences, the United States and British Chiefs of Staff should hold their domestic meetings in the morning and the Combined Chiefs of Staff should meet in the afternoon at 1430.

2. We suggest also that we should aim to work to the attached programme.

TOP SECRET

ENCLOSURE

PROGRAMME FOR TERMINAL

1st Meeting
(Monday, 16th)

1. *PROGRAMME AND PROCEDURE FOR THE CONFERENCE*
2. *ESTIMATE OF THE JAPANESE SITUATION*
3. *PROGRESS REPORTS ON OPERATIONS IN PACIFIC AND SEAC*
4. *DEVELOPMENT OF OPERATIONS IN THE PACIFIC*
5. *REPORT ON AIR OPERATIONS IN THE WAR AGAINST JAPAN*

2nd Meeting
(Tuesday, 17th)

1. *BRITISH PARTICIPATION IN THE WAR AGAINST JAPAN*
2. *CONTROL AND COMMAND IN THE WAR AGAINST JAPAN*

3rd Meeting
(Wednesday, 18th)

1. *BASIC OBJECTIVES, STRATEGY, AND POLICIES*
2. *FRENCH, DUTCH, AND PORTUGUESE PARTICIPATION IN THE WAR AGAINST JAPAN*

4th Meeting
(Thursday, 19th)

1. *DIRECTIVE TO SACSEA*
2. *RUSSIAN PARTICIPATION*
3. *RELATIONS WITH THE RUSSIANS*
4. *PLANNING DATE FOR END OF WAR AGAINST JAPAN*
5. *C.C.S. MACHINERY AFTER THE END OF WAR AGAINST JAPAN*

TOP SECRET

C.C.S. 880/10   16 July 1945

COMBINED CHIEFS OF STAFF

PROGRAM AND PROCEDURE FOR THE CONFERENCE

Memorandum by the United States Chiefs of Staff

1. The program suggested by C.C.S. 880/9 is satisfactory, subject to such rearrangement of subjects as may later appear desirable, except that:—

   a. No dates should be specified for the meetings, as such cannot be determined at this time.

   b. Whether discussion of Russian participation will prove appropriate or necessary remains to be determined. This item has been left on the agenda pending firm determination in light of later developments.

   c. It is presumed that item 3 of the 4th Meeting, as listed in the Enclosure to C.C.S. 880/9 refers to the subject matter of C.C.S. 884/2 and that the title of this item should be the same as the title of that paper, "Information for the Russians Concerning the Japanese War."

TOP SECRET

C.C.S. 884
C.C.S. 884/1
C.C.S. 884/2

INFORMATION FOR THE RUSSIANS CONCERNING
THE JAPANESE WAR

References:

CCS 196th Meeting, Item 4
CCS 900/3, paragraph 18

In C.C.S. 884 (22 June 1945) the British Chiefs of Staff suggested that their policy for imparting information to the Russians be coordinated with the policy of the United States Chiefs of Staff.

In C.C.S. 884/1 (8 July) the United States Chiefs of Staff stated that they did not consider the matter an appropriate one for combined agreement.

In C.C.S. 884/2 (15 July) the British Chiefs of Staff suggested that the matter be discussed further at *TERMINAL*.

The Combined Chiefs of Staff considered the C.C.S. 884 series in their 196th Meeting (19 July) and agreed to the conclusions recorded in item 4 of that meeting.

TOP SECRET

C.C.S. 884 22 June 1945

COMBINED CHIEFS OF STAFF

INFORMATION FOR THE RUSSIANS CONCERNING THE JAPANESE WAR

Memorandum by the Representatives of the British Chiefs of Staff

1. The Head of the British Military Mission in Moscow, General Gammell, has asked the British Chiefs of Staff to inform him, in the event of Russia declaring war on Japan, what information he should pass to the Russians on Japanese dispositions and estimated intentions, and on British dispositions and operational plans.

2. The British Chiefs of Staff feel that it is desirable for the policy adopted by them in imparting information to the Russians on these subjects to be coordinated with the policy of the United States Chiefs of Staff.

3. The British Chiefs of Staff suggest that General Gammell and General Deane should be empowered to hand over information on Japanese dispositions and intentions, and also on Allied dispositions only if it is asked for, and then only on a basis of reciprocity. The British Chiefs of Staff as agents of the Combined Chiefs of Staff would provide General Gammell with the necessary information on Southeast Asia Command, and they assume that the United States Chiefs of Staff would provide General Deane with information about the Pacific, Southwest Pacific, and China Theatres. Coordination between General Gammell and General Deane would however be necessary in order to ensure that information is passed on American forces in a theatre under the operational control of the British Chiefs of Staff, and vice versa.

4. So far as Allied intentions in all theatres are concerned, the British Chiefs of Staff consider that information should be passed to the Russians only on the authority of the Combined Chiefs of Staff on each occasion.

5. We should be glad to have the views of the United States Chiefs of Staff on this matter.

TOP SECRET

C.C.S. 884/1   8 July 1945

COMBINED CHIEFS OF STAFF

INFORMATION FOR THE RUSSIANS CONCERNING THE JAPANESE WAR

Memorandum by the United States Chiefs of Staff

1. The United States Chiefs of Staff have considered the proposals of the British Chiefs of Staff in C.C.S. 884 concerning the information which should be given to the Russians on intelligence, dispositions, and plans in the war against Japan.

2. The United States Chiefs of Staff consider this matter is not an appropriate one for combined agreement. However, they will not, without prior agreement of the appropriate British authorities, pass to the Russians any information on dispositions or operational plans of Allied forces in areas of British strategic responsibility or any information that has been obtained from a British source.

TOP SECRET

C.C.S. 884/2　　　　　　　　　　　　　　　　　　　　　　　15 July 1945

COMBINED CHIEFS OF STAFF

INFORMATION FOR THE RUSSIANS CONCERNING THE JAPANESE WAR

Memorandum by the British Chiefs of Staff

1. The British Chiefs of Staff have considered the reply by the United States Chiefs of Staff (C.C.S. 884/1) to their memorandum (C.C.S. 884) concerning the information which should be given to the Russians if they enter the war against Japan.

2. The British Chiefs of Staff cannot agree that this is an inappropriate matter for combined agreement.

3. Hitherto throughout the war against Germany, it has been customary, although not obligatory, for the United States and British Chiefs of Staff to consult together as to the measure and means of our dealings with the Russians. The British Chiefs of Staff consider that on the whole this policy has been wise and profitable, and they see no reason, now that Germany has been defeated and Russia is not yet at war with Japan, to depart from it. They are not aware that it has aroused resentment on the part of the Russians, who nevertheless must have been aware of our joint collaboration.

4. If the British and American staffs now take an independent and quite possibly divergent line as regards passing information to the Russians, it seems possible that the Russians will be tempted to play one of us off against the other.

5. For the above reasons the British Chiefs of Staff would be grateful for an opportunity of discussing this matter further with the United States Chiefs of Staff at *TERMINAL*.

TOP SECRET

C.C.S. 889
C.C.S. 889/1
C.C.S. 889/2
C.C.S. 889/3

BRITISH PARTICIPATION IN THE WAR AGAINST JAPAN

References:

CCS 194th Meeting, Item 2
CCS 900/3, paragraph 10

C.C.S. 889 (6 July 1945) circulated the proposal by the British Chiefs of Staff for the British contribution to the final phase of the war against Japan.

The reply of the United States Chiefs of Staff was circulated as C.C.S. 889/1 (17 July).

The Combined Chiefs of Staff considered C.C.S. 889 and C.C.S. 889/1 in their 194th Meeting (17 July). Their conclusions are recorded in item 2 of that meeting.

In C.C.S. 889/2 (18 July) the United States Chiefs of Staff circulated for the information of the Combined Chiefs of Staff extracts of a message from General MacArthur concerning British participation in the war against Japan.

In C.C.S. 889/3 (21 July) the United States Chiefs of Staff circulated information for the Combined Chiefs of Staff in connection with item 2 *b.* of the conclusions reached on this subject in their 194th Meeting.

TOP SECRET

C.C.S. 889   6 July 1945

COMBINED CHIEFS OF STAFF

BRITISH CONTRIBUTION TO THE FINAL PHASE OF THE WAR AGAINST JAPAN

References:

CCS 452 Series
CCS 619 Series
CCS 691 Series

Memorandum by the Representatives of the British Chiefs of Staff

1. We have been instructed to present the attached memorandum on the British contribution to the final phase of the war against Japan, which the British Chiefs of Staff have prepared for discussion at the next conference.

2. The views of the Australian and New Zealand Governments on the proposals formulated have been requested but have not yet been received.

TOP SECRET

ENCLOSURE

BRITISH CONTRIBUTION TO THE FINAL PHASE
OF THE WAR AGAINST JAPAN

Memorandum by the British Chiefs of Staff

1. It has been agreed that the over-all objective for the war against Japan is to force the unconditional surrender of the Japanese by:—

a. Lowering Japanese ability and will to resist by establishing sea and air blockades, conducting intensive air bombardment, and destroying Japanese naval and air strength.

b. Invading and seizing objectives in the industrial heart of Japan.

2. It is agreed that the invasion of Japan is the supreme operation of the war. The prospect of the recapture of Singapore in November 1945, together with the opening of the Malacca Straits, enables us to offer, in addition to the British Pacific Fleet and the very long range (VLR) bomber force, a British, Dominion, and Indian land force to take part in this invasion. Owing to limitations of shipping, however, such a project will only absorb a part of the forces at present deployed in Southeast Asia Command. We have therefore planned that British forces should continue operations in the Outer Zone as far as limitations of other resources allow.

3. We propose, therefore, that British participation in the final phase of the war against Japan should take the following form:—

a. The British Pacific Fleet as at present planned.

b. A VLR bomber force of 10 squadrons increasing to 20 squadrons at a later date when more airfields become available.

c. A British Commonwealth force to participate in *CORONET* under American command, of three to five divisions, all to be carried in British shipping and provided with the necessary assault lift. This force would be supported by the East Indies Fleet, augmented by the British Pacific Fleet as necessary, and by a tactical air component of some 15 squadrons. The exact size, composition, and role of this force can only be determined by consultation between British and United States staffs in the light of United States operational plans, the target date of *CORONET*, and its relation to

TOP SECRET

the date of the capture of Singapore. Our preliminary investigations show that it might take one of the following forms:—

(i) A force of one or possibly two divisions in the assault together with two or three divisions in the build-up, administratively largely self-supporting.

(ii) A force of three divisions in the assault and immediate follow-up and one or possibly two divisions in the build-up, relying, to a considerable degree, on American administrative assistance.

(iii) A force of up to five divisions in the build-up administratively largely self-supporting. We should naturally prefer a course which allowed us to take part in the assault.

d. Operations in the Outer Zone to maintain pressure against the Japanese across the Burma-Siam frontier. In addition, plans for operations against Siam, for the establishment of bridgeheads in Java or Sumatra, and for the recapture of Hong Kong will be studied. A decision will be made at a later date as to whether, and if so when, any of these operations will be undertaken.

4. We therefore propose that the Combined Chiefs of Staff should approve the British contribution to the final phase of the war against Japan, as set out in this memorandum.

TOP SECRET

C.C.S. 889/1   17 July 1945

COMBINED CHIEFS OF STAFF

BRITISH PARTICIPATION IN THE WAR AGAINST JAPAN

Memorandum by the United States Chiefs of Staff

1. The United States Chiefs of Staff reaffirm their previous agreement to the proposals in subparagraphs 3 *a.* and *b.* of C.C.S. 889. In connection with the latter proposal it should be noted that there is little prospect that airfield space for more than ten squadrons of a British very long range (VLR) bomber force will become available at least before 1 December 1945.

2. As to paragraph 3 *c.*, the United States Chiefs of Staff agree in principle to the participation in the final phase of the war against Japan of a British Commonwealth land force, subject to satisfactory resolution of operational problems by Commander in Chief, U.S. Army Forces, Pacific, and Commander in Chief, U.S. Pacific Fleet, and to the clarification of certain factors which the United States Chiefs of Staff believe will be controlling. Their views on some of these factors follow:—

    a. It is essential that a firm commitment be received as to dates of availability and composition of forces in order to plan for their participation in the final effort and to effect adjustments of the United States redeployment program. It is not practicable to plan on using forces whose availability is contingent upon their release following the conclusion of a separate major operation. Hence it appears these forces cannot at present be planned for use earlier than the build-up phase of *CORONET*.

    b. The difficulties incident to the employment of Indian troops (language complications and the necessity for prior acclimatization) make it doubtful that the Indian division can be effectively employed.

    c. Arrangements have already been made with the Canadian Government to organize and equip along United States lines one Canadian division, to operate as a part of a United States corps.

    d. It is noted that agreement of the Dominions concerned has not yet been obtained.

    e. A solution must be found to the complicated logistical problems involved.

f. The forces should be concentrated in the Pacific or in the United States well in advance of the date scheduled for their participation in the campaign.

g. The question of the provision of assault lift requires clarification.

h. It is considered impracticable to superimpose upon the already adequate U.S. tactical air forces a small British tactical air force, since this would overload prospective airfields and introduce complications resulting from additional aircraft types.

i. The effect of the proposals upon continued operations in the Southeast Asia Command requires further examination.

TOP SECRET

C.C.S. 889/2   18 July 1945

COMBINED CHIEFS OF STAFF

BRITISH PARTICIPATION IN THE WAR AGAINST JAPAN

Memorandum by the United States Chiefs of Staff

The following extracts of a message from General MacArthur to the War Department under date of 9 July 1945 concerning British participation in the war against Japan are furnished for the information of the British Chiefs of Staff:—

The scope of the British proposal for participation in *CORONET* presents problems not heretofore encountered when the Canadian and French contingents were considered.

These problems must be viewed in their proper perspective as they relate to the specific operation in contemplation unless complexity, particularly as applies to logistics, and lack of homogeneity of forces destroy combat effectiveness or require a delay in target date.

This operation, as at present visualized, is confined to narrow limits. There will be no opportunity to assign separate sectors of responsibility along national lines.

The assault is to be made into heavily defended areas and calls for the closest coordination of air, naval, and ground forces, and within the ground forces themselves. Acceptance of the British in the assault with the differences in organization, composition, equipment, training procedures, and doctrines will complicate command, operations, and logistic support. Redeployment geared to the support of homogeneous forces and now well advanced, would have to undergo a large-scale readjustment, particularly taking into consideration a parallel line of British logistic channels, including separate bases, storage, issuance and maintenance facilities, and personnel therefor.

British forces participating in operations against Singapore in November could not be prepared for the assault phase in *CORONET*. It is

TOP SECRET

considered doubtful that these forces could participate even in the follow-up. Certainly, to utilize considerable numbers of troops without adequate opportunity on the part of higher commanders of this area to exercise command functions prior to their use would be a most dangerous expedient.

Moreover, it would be entirely unsatisfactory to have the availability of troops scheduled for *CORONET* dependent in any way upon their release from another campaign. Availability of these troops as well as all others committed must be certain for a fixed date.

The following general plan is suggested as being one which will obviate the full impact of the objectionable features indicated above.

This plan takes into consideration previous communications relating to the use of Australian forces as well as Canadian forces.

A. Limit British Empire participation to one corps of three divisions; one British, one Canadian, and one Australian.

B. Re-equip British division and corps troops and Australian division with American equipment, logistic support to be provided by the United States on the same scale as provided for our troops.

C. The Australian division to be either the 7th or 9th Division, now concentrated in the Borneo-Morotai area.

D. British division and corps troops to be concentrated by 1st December in the Borneo-Morotai area or, as an alternate, in the United States, if these units can be equipped there.

E. Amphibiously train one British division and one Canadian division prior to arrival in concentration area. The Australian division is already amphibiously trained.

F. Lift this corps on assault shipping to be provided by the British to arrive in the objective area about Y plus 10. It will there be used as the AFPAC assault reserve afloat. Canadian division to be lifted directly from the United States, Australian division from the Borneo-Morotai area, and British division and corps troops from either area depending on where it is concentrated.

G. Fight this corps as an integral corps within a United States Army. Utilize divisions separately within American corps if the exigencies of the situation so demand.

TOP SECRET

I doubt the advisability of employing troops of native origin in this complex operation where homogeneity of language within the corps is required.

Likewise, there is a question of the advisability of utilizing troops of tropical origin in a temperate zone without an extended period of acclimatization. Hence, the acceptance of Indian troops is not concurred in. The British division should be Anglo-Saxon.

The foregoing comments are equally applicable to Allied air components, aggravated by the difficulties of integrating relatively small air forces in tactical operations under the restrictions imposed by a comparatively limited air deployment potential. There are ample American air forces in or projected for this area to support all troops in *CORONET* operation.

TOP SECRET

C.C.S. 889/3   21 July 1945

COMBINED CHIEFS OF STAFF

BRITISH PARTICIPATION IN THE WAR AGAINST JAPAN

Memorandum by the United States Chiefs of Staff

    General MacArthur and Admiral Nimitz welcome the visit of a British corps commander and accompanying officers. General MacArthur suggests that they should arrive at an early date, and if practicable by 1 August.

    It is suggested that further matters connected with this visit be handled on an operational basis between the British Joint Staff Mission and the operating agencies concerned of the War and Navy Departments.

TOP SECRET

C.C.S. 890
C.C.S. 890/1
C.C.S. 890/2

CONTROL AND COMMAND IN THE WAR AGAINST JAPAN

References:

CCS 195th Meeting, Items 4 & 5
CCS 199th Meeting, Item 6
CCS 900/3, paragraph 8

In C.C.S. 890 (9 July 1945) the British Chiefs of Staff presented their views on command and control in the war against Japan.

In C.C.S. 890/1 (17 July) the United States Chiefs of Staff replied to C.C.S. 890.

In C.C.S. 890/2 (18 July) the British Chiefs of Staff commented on C.C.S. 890/1.

The Combined Chiefs of Staff in their 195th Meeting (18 July) considered C.C.S. 890/2. Their conclusions with regard to paragraphs 2, 3, and 4 of C.C.S. 890/2 are recorded in item 4 of that meeting, and their conclusions with regard to paragraphs 5 and 6 are recorded in item 5.

TOP SECRET

C.C.S. 890   9 July 1945

COMBINED CHIEFS OF STAFF

CONTROL AND COMMAND IN THE WAR AGAINST JAPAN

Memorandum by the Representatives of the British Chiefs of Staff

1. We have been instructed to present the attached memorandum on command and control in the war against Japan which the British Chiefs of Staff have prepared for discussion at the next conference.

2. The views of the Australian and New Zealand Governments on the proposals formulated have been requested but have not yet been received.

TOP SECRET

ENCLOSURE

CONTROL AND COMMAND IN THE WAR AGAINST JAPAN

Memorandum by the British Chiefs of Staff

1. In considering the proposals made by the United States Chiefs of Staff on the transfer of command in the Southwest Pacific Area, we have reviewed the whole question of command and control in the war against Japan under the following headings:—

    I. Southeast Asia Command (SEAC) and Southwest Pacific Area (SWPA)

        (a) Boundaries of command

        (b) Chain of command

        (c) Date of transfer

    II. Higher Strategic Control of the War against Japan

I. SOUTHEAST ASIA COMMAND AND SOUTHWEST PACIFIC AREA

2. We agree with the United States Chiefs of Staff that there should shortly be some alteration in the responsibility for SWPA. In our view, the transfer of this responsibility will involve alterations in the boundaries of the Supreme Allied Commander, Southeast Asia's (SACSEA) command. We make the following proposals:—

BOUNDARIES OF COMMAND

3. SACSEA's boundaries should be extended as follows:—

Beginning at the junction of the Sino-Burmese frontier and the Sino-Indo-China frontier, along the frontier between Indo-China and China to the coast; thence down the coast of Indo-China to a point 15 degrees N; thence through the Balabac Strait along the 1939 boundary line between the Philippines and Borneo to latitude 05 degrees N; thence eastward to 05 degrees N, 128 degrees E; thence southwestward to 02 degrees S, 123 degrees E; thence southeastward to 08 degrees S, 125 degrees E; thence southwestward to 18 degrees S, 110 degrees E.

TOP SECRET

The main difference from the proposal so far made to us by the United States Chiefs of Staff is the inclusion of Indo-China, as well as Siam, in SEAC. This we consider important so that there may be unity of control of the major operations in this area when they develop and of previous subversive and paramilitary operations.

This line of demarcation would add Borneo, Java, and the Celebes to SEAC.

4. Boundaries of Australian command should now be defined as follows:—

05 degrees N, 128 degrees E; thence to 05 degrees N, 130 degrees E; thence south to the Equator; thence to the International Date Line.

The main difference between this line of demarcation and that proposed by the United States Chiefs of Staff is that all Australian mandated territories are now included in the area. This is naturally the desire of the Australian Government, with which we are in sympathy. It would, of course, be possible for United States forces to make use of the facilities in Manus and Guadalcanal.

CHAIN OF COMMAND

5. We propose that the chain of command and responsibility should then be as follows:—

a. SEAC — no change.

b. Australian command — in this area there should be an Australian commander under the Australian Chiefs of Staff. The British Chiefs of Staff should be the link between the Australian and Combined Chiefs of Staff.

DATE OF TRANSFER

6. In our view SACSEA may not be ready to assume his additional responsibilities until after the recapture of Singapore. We, therefore, propose that, subject to further examination with the United States Chiefs of Staff, the transfer of command should take place shortly after that time. This need not preclude the gradual turnover in the meantime of bases, ports, or airfields by agreement between the Australians and General MacArthur.

TOP SECRET

II. *HIGHER STRATEGIC CONTROL IN THE WAR AGAINST JAPAN*

7. The present arrangements for the higher strategic control in the war against Japan are:—

a. SEAC (C.C.S. 319/5*):

Under the Combined Chiefs of Staff with the British Chiefs of Staff acting as their agents.

b. Pacific and Southwest Pacific Areas:

In these areas the Combined Chiefs of Staff exercise jurisdiction over grand strategic policy and over the allocation of forces and war materials but the United States Chiefs of Staff are responsible for all matters appertaining to operational strategy.

8. We feel that the time has now come when we should take upon ourselves a greater share of the burden of strategic decisions which will be required before Japan is defeated. Although our contribution in the Pacific must always remain small in comparison with that of the United States, it is natural that our interest and concern should grow as more of our forces begin to be deployed in the Pacific area. Moreover, when the Straits of Malacca have been opened, there will no longer be the same natural geographical division between SEAC and the Pacific. All operations in the war against the Japanese would then form one strategic concept.

9. We therefore propose for consideration that the control of the different theatres in the war against Japan should now be organised as follows:—

a. The Combined Chiefs of Staff will exercise general jurisdiction over strategic policy and the proper coordination of the Allied efforts in all theatres engaged against the Japanese.

b. The United States Chiefs of Staff acting as agents of the Combined Chiefs of Staff will exercise jurisdiction over all matters pertaining to operations in the Pacific Ocean area and China.

c. The British Chiefs of Staff acting as agents of the Combined Chiefs of Staff will exercise jurisdiction over all matters pertaining to operations in SEAC and SWPA.

d. The Combined Chiefs of Staff will exercise jurisdiction over allocation of forces and war materials as between all theatres engaged against the Japanese.

---

*QUADRANT Conference book, page 260.

TOP SECRET

C.C.S. 890/1   17 July 1945

COMBINED CHIEFS OF STAFF

CONTROL AND COMMAND IN THE WAR AGAINST JAPAN

Memorandum by the United States Chiefs of Staff

With reference to the proposed boundaries for the extension of command of the Supreme Allied Commander, Southeast Asia, suggested by the British Chiefs of Staff, the United States Chiefs of Staff have no objection from the military viewpoint to the inclusion of Indo-China south of latitude 15 degrees N. in the new area. This, however, is a matter primarily for decision by the Generalissimo and a shift does not appear practicable until such time as his agreement is obtained. Until that time it appears operations can go forward on the present basis.

As to the boundaries of the Australian command, this is a matter on which the solution worked out between the British and Australian Chiefs of Staff should be acceptable to the United States Chiefs of Staff.

On the matter of the northern boundary of the area, the United States Chiefs of Staff reaffirm the necessity for retaining control by the United States of the Admiralty Islands for the reasons set forth in paragraph 3 of C.C.S. 852/1.*

The proposal to extend the British sphere of responsibility east of the present boundary of the Southwest Pacific Area does not appear necessary or desirable until United States activities are cleared from the area, at which time the transfer should be effected. Aside from United States military resources in the area which must continue to be rolled up under United States military control, there are no military objectives or problems in the area except Ocean and Nauru Islands. At such time as British forces are prepared to recapture these islands, the United States will offer no objection.

The objective of the United States Chiefs of Staff in proposing the transfer has been to release United States resources and commanders from the

---
*Not published herein.

TOP SECRET

responsibility for containing and mopping up the Japanese forces in the area in order that they might concentrate on the main effort. Hence they have proposed 15 August as the date of turnover. Their objective would not be achieved by delaying the turnover until such time as Admiral Mountbatten is in position to advance through the Malacca Straits. Furthermore, it does not appear that retention of the area under United States responsibility until the end of the year will result in any activity additional to that which would occur if the area passed to Admiral Mountbatten on 15 August. The forces employed in the area are already primarily Australian. It is possible that if the British Chiefs of Staff do not desire to take over the area shortly, the Australian Chiefs of Staff might be able to do so with subsequent adjustment with Admiral Mountbatten within the British Empire.

In summary, with regard to the matter of the Southeast Asia Command and the Southwest Pacific Area, the United States Chiefs of Staff consider that the immediate action should be to pass to the British Chiefs of Staff as of 15 August or very shortly thereafter the area with boundaries as outlined in C.C.S. 852/1.

Concerning the matter of higher strategic control in the war against Japan, the thought of the United States Chiefs of Staff is that the role of the Combined Chiefs of Staff in the European war cannot appropriately be applied to the Pacific war. In the Pacific war there exist two clearly delineated areas that, commanded by Admiral Mountbatten with the extensions proposed in the foregoing paragraphs, constitute an area of British Empire responsibility associated with the Portuguese, the Dutch, and perhaps eventually the French. The initial operational interest of the United States in this area has now greatly decreased. The Pacific area is devoted to the main effort, is organized under a command and control set-up peculiar to the United States, and has forces and resources overwhelmingly United States unless the Chinese, and possibly Russian, contribution is considered. Any change in the present control system which would involve added complications and more cumbersome procedures is unacceptable.

It appears that the interest of the United States in Admiral Mountbatten's expanded theater now includes little more than sufficient review of operations to determine their impact on Allied operations and from the standpoint of lend-lease requirements, that they are adjusted to the main effort, and that they do not have an unduly adverse effect on the supply line to China through India and Burma. In line with this thought the British Chiefs of Staff may wish to consider some readjustment of the status of the Southeast Asia

TOP SECRET

Command under the Combined Chiefs of Staff, perhaps along the line of the present status of the Pacific Theater.

In summary, the United States Chiefs of Staff believe that increased participation of the Combined Chiefs of Staff in the Pacific Theater is impracticable.

TOP SECRET

C.C.S. 890/2   18 July 1945

COMBINED CHIEFS OF STAFF

CONTROL AND COMMAND IN THE WAR AGAINST JAPAN

Memorandum by the British Chiefs of Staff

1. The British Chiefs of Staff have considered the memorandum by the United States Chiefs of Staff (C.C.S. 890/1) on Control and Command in the War against Japan. They have the following comments to make.

2. They fully understand that it will ultimately be necessary to obtain the agreement of the Generalissimo to the inclusion of Indo-China in Southeast Asia Command. They are anxious, however, that the United States Chiefs of Staff should support them in recommending to the President and the Prime Minister that they should press the Generalissimo to agree to this transfer. They suggest, therefore, that a recommendation to this effect should be included in the final report of the *TERMINAL* Conference.

3. The British Chiefs of Staff note that the United States Chiefs of Staff consider it necessary to retain control of the Admiralty Islands. They, therefore, withdraw their proposal for the inclusion of these islands in the Australian command. They also agree not to press for the eastward extension of the present boundary of the Southwest Pacific Area until United States activities are cleared from the area. They note that the United States Chiefs of Staff would offer no objection to British operations against Ocean and Nauru Islands.

4. The British Chiefs of Staff realize the advantages of an early transfer of the Southwest Pacific Area but are up against two difficulties. The first is the fact that Admiral Mountbatten is now fully engaged on planning further operations. The assumption of further responsibilities at this particular stage must inevitably embarrass him. Secondly, we have no idea what degree of assistance the United States Chiefs of Staff are at present providing to the Borneo operations nor when those operations are due to be completed. On present information, therefore, we cannot assess the commitment we should be undertaking if we agree to the transfer on any particular date. We should like, therefore, to discuss this further with the United States Chiefs of Staff.

TOP SECRET

5. On the question of the higher strategic control of the war against Japan, the British Chiefs of Staff wish to reiterate and amplify their view that they should now be given a larger share of control of strategy on the lines suggested in C.C.S. 890. They desire to bring to the notice of the United States Chiefs of Staff the following particular considerations:—

a. The United States and Great Britain are the two major powers allied against Japan, and thus jointly responsible for the prosecution of the war. It is most desirable that they should consult freely on all matters of major strategic importance relating to the conduct of the war.

b. The British Chiefs of Staff have an inescapable responsibility to advise His Majesty's Government on the use to which British forces are put in all theatres of war.

c. Although the United States are of course providing the major share, the war against Japan, like that against Germany, is being fought with pooled United States and British resources, particularly shipping. It is right, therefore, that the British should have full understanding and knowledge of the proposed methods of applying these resources.

6. The British Chiefs of Staff wish to make it clear that the full extent of what they are asking is that they should be consulted on major strategic policy. They have no intention of suggesting interference with the operational control now accorded to General MacArthur and Admiral Nimitz in whom they have the utmost confidence.

The British Chiefs of Staff ask, therefore, that the United States Chiefs of Staff should reconsider their attitude on this question.

TOP SECRET

C.C.S. 890/3

COMMAND IN INDO-CHINA

References:

CCS 195th Meeting, Item 4
CCS 199th Meeting, Item 4
CCS 900/3, paragraph 14

In C.C.S. 890/3 (22 July 1945) the British Chiefs of Staff presented their views on the reorganization of command in Indo-China.

The Combined Chiefs of Staff in their 199th Meeting (23 July) approved the recommendation in paragraph 3 of C.C.S. 890/3 subject to the amendment of the statement therein as indicated in paragraph 14, C.C.S. 900/3.

TOP SECRET

C.C.S. 890/3   22 July 1945

COMBINED CHIEFS OF STAFF

COMMAND IN INDO-CHINA

Memorandum by the British Chiefs of Staff

1. We agree that as a first step in reorganising command in Indo-China, there is advantage in dividing the country into two, leaving the northern portion in China Theatre and allotting the southern portion to Southeast Asia Command. This organisation of command should be subject to review in the light of the development of operations in that area.

2. We have examined the run of communications in Indo-China and suggest that the most satisfactory dividing line would be latitude 16°N.

3. We, therefore, recommend that the Combined Chiefs of Staff should include in their final report to the Prime Minister and President, a statement on the following lines:—

"We consider it important that there shall be unity of control of major operations in the Indo-China-Siam area when they develop and of previous subversive and para-military operations. As the first step in securing this unity of control, we are agreed that the best arrangement would be to include that portion of Indo-China lying south of latitude 16° North in Southeast Asia Command. This arrangement would continue General Wedemeyer's control of that part of Indo-China which covers the flank of projected Chinese operations in China, and would enable Admiral Mountbatten to prepare the ground in the southern half of Indo-China where any initial operations by him would develop.

"We recommend that the President and the Prime Minister should approach the Generalissimo to secure his agreement to this arrangement."

TOP SECRET

C.C.S. 891

C.C.S. 891/1

COMBINED CHIEFS OF STAFF MACHINERY
AFTER THE WAR WITH JAPAN

Reference:

CCS 196th Meeting, Item 3

C.C.S. 891 (15 July 1945) and C.C.S. 891/1 (19 July) circulated memoranda by the British Chiefs of Staff and the United States Chiefs of Staff respectively.

The Combined Chiefs of Staff took note of C.C.S. 891 and C.C.S. 891/1 in their 196th Meeting (19 July).

TOP SECRET

C.C.S. 891 15 July 1945

COMBINED CHIEFS OF STAFF

COMBINED CHIEFS OF STAFF MACHINERY
AFTER THE WAR WITH JAPAN

Memorandum by the British Chiefs of Staff

1. We should like at *TERMINAL* to discuss with our United States colleagues the question of the continuation of machinery for combined United States/British collaboration in the military sphere after the defeat of Japan.

2. Since 1941 the machinery of the Combined Chiefs of Staff and its associated committees has worked smoothly and effectively. For the reasons which follow, we consider that it would be a retrograde step to allow this machinery to fall into disuse merely because Germany and Japan have been defeated and there are no supreme allied commanders to receive the instructions of the Combined Chiefs of Staff.

3. As we see it, the world, all too unfortunately, is likely to remain in a troubled state for many years to come. Major problems will constantly arise affecting both American and British interests. In many cases these interests may well be closely identified, and in many cases also they will have important military implications.

4. For these reasons we consider that some machinery for the continuation of joint and combined United States/British collaboration is desirable. For example, it may be to the great advantage both of the United States and ourselves that some machinery should exist for the mutual exchange of information. Some measure of uniformity in the design of weapons and in training may also be mutually beneficial.

5. It is not our intention in this paper to attempt to fashion the form or the structure of the machinery which may be found necessary for the above purpose after hostilities have ended. All that we suggest at this stage is that we should now recommend to our respective governments that they should approve the maintenance of the framework of the Combined Chiefs of Staff

TOP SECRET

organization after the war with Japan, and the principle of consultation on matters of mutual interest.

6. We do not think that the maintenance of the Combined Chiefs of Staff machinery after the end of hostilities need in any way cut across or impinge upon the Military Staff Committee of the World Security Organization. There is plenty of room and work for both.

TOP SECRET

C.C.S. 891/1   19 July 1945

COMBINED CHIEFS OF STAFF

COMBINED CHIEFS OF STAFF MACHINERY
AFTER THE WAR WITH JAPAN

Memorandum by the United States Chiefs of Staff

With reference to C.C.S. 891, the political relationship of the United States with other nations in the period following this war is not yet sufficiently defined to permit the United States Chiefs of Staff to discuss at this date the post-war relationships between the respective military staffs.

The United States Chiefs of Staff will bring up for consideration the problem of the most effective military machinery to be used from now forward and prior to the end of the Japanese war.

TOP SECRET

C.C.S. 892

PROGRESS REPORT
ON OPERATIONS IN THE SOUTHEAST ASIA COMMAND

References:

CCS 880, paragraph 1 (1)
CCS 193d Meeting, Item 3

The Combined Chiefs of Staff took note of C.C.S. 892 (15 July 1945) in their 193d Meeting (16 July).

TOP SECRET

CCS 892　　　　　　　　　　　　　　　　　　　15 July 1945

COMBINED CHIEFS OF STAFF

PROGRESS REPORT
ON OPERATIONS IN THE SOUTHEAST ASIA COMMAND

Note by the Secretaries

The enclosed report by the Supreme Allied Commander, Southeast Asia, is circulated for information.

　　　　　　　　　　　　　　　　　　　A. J. McFARLAND,
　　　　　　　　　　　　　　　　　　　A. T. CORNWALL-JONES,
　　　　　　　　　　　　　　　　　　　Combined Secretariat.

TOP SECRET

ENCLOSURE

PROGRESS REPORT
ON OPERATIONS IN THE SOUTHEAST ASIA COMMAND

PART I

CURRENT OPERATIONS

1. *NAVAL*

   a. Enemy. Two damaged cruisers and one destroyer constitute the only major Japanese forces. Few motor torpedo boats and submarines may be available to them. It is believed Japanese naval forces have no major offensive capabilities though there is a possibility of suicide attacks by small boats and one-man submarines.

   b. Own Forces. Japanese cruiser of Nachi class was sunk in recent action by destroyers and recent naval air operations in southern Malaya were successful in obtaining good photo cover of *ZIPPER* areas. Sweeps and operations are being carried out continuously in the Andaman Sea. Submarine patrols have been maintained in the Malacca Straits and have inflicted steady losses on Japanese coastal shipping. Between 1 January 1945 and 15 June 1945 at least 176 merchant vessels totalling 11,400 tons have been destroyed by naval forces, in addition to 15 landing craft and 17 minor war vessels.

2. *GROUND FORCES*

   a. Enemy. Japanese troops remaining in Burma west of the Sittang River are in two main groups excepting a few small bodies of disorganised stragglers. One group of 4/5000 in the central Pegu Yomas and foothills northwest of Pegu is slowly moving to cross the road and railway between Yaunglebin and Pyu while a second group of approximately 1/2000 in the hills east of Prome is splitting into small groups to cross the road and railway between Myohla and Toungoo and between Toungoo and Pyu. East of the Sittang River the 56th Division has withdrawn from the Kalaw area to Kemapyu and southeast of Toungoo apparently to relieve the 15th Division on the Mawchi road while the latter pulls back to Papun. Total enemy troops in the Mawchi road—Kemapyu area are approximately 4,000. The Sittang line in the Mokpalin area is held by the 18th and 53d Divisions

TOP SECRET

and a number of non-divisional units with an estimated total strength of 10,500. There are estimated to be 10,000 enemy troops in the immediate Moulmein area but without offensive capabilities while there are a further 13,000 troops east of the Sittang between Papun and Moulmein who are also without offensive capabilities and who are in the process of regrouping and reorganisation.

b. *Own Troops.*

(i) All operations in Burma are now under control in Twelfth Army with headquarters in Rangoon whose task is to destroy all enemy west of the Sittang River. The Twelfth Army assumed operational responsibility for the North Combat Area Command on 1 July and it is expected that Chinese forces will complete withdrawal from this area by 15 July.

(ii) The 82d Division is responsible for the Arakan in the Taungup area.

(iii) On the Irrawaddy River axis operating into the Pegu Yomas are 268th Indian Infantry Brigade responsible for area Allanmyo Schwedaung exclusive and 20th Indian Division with 22d East African Brigade under command responsible for area Schwedaung Yandoon-Taukkyan inclusive.

(iv) The 6th Brigade of 2d Division is responsible for the defence of the Rangoon area.

(v) On the Mandalay-Rangoon road and railway axis 19th Indian Division under IV Corps is responsible for area from north of Pyjnmana to Pyu exclusive patrolling north of Toungoo and pushing east on the Toungoo-Mawchi road where it is now at MS (milestone) 25* with little opposition. It will maintain pressure on this axis throughout the monsoon. The 17th Indian Division under IV Corps is responsible for Pyu-Daik-U area inclusive. It has one brigade in Walew area which will establish base at Taunggyi and patrol north, south and east. Patrols will not go further east than Loilem nor south than Loikaw. Patrols have entered Heho in which area there is now slight opposition. Many broken bridges on this road hinder operations. The 7th Division under IV Corps responsible for the Pegu area has just relieved 5th Division which is concentrating in Mingaladon area for rest and reorganisation before ZIPPER. It will be necessary to relieve further divisions to prepare for ZIPPER during the monsoon.

---

* See Map facing page 174.

TOP SECRET

(vi) There has been considerable rain in south Burma which greatly hinders operations by rendering Chaungs unfordable, carrying away bridges and flooding level ground. Operations have been undertaken waist deep in mud and water and areas have been reported under ten feet of water in the Sittang area. Movement off roads is virtually impossible for wheels in these conditions thus sometimes necessitating infantry attacking prepared positions without artillery support. In flooded areas even movement on tracks has sometimes been restricted to a rate of 1,000 yards per hour.

3. *AIR*

a. Enemy. Enemy air activity has been negligible since July 1944. Present estimated enemy strength of operational aircraft including reconnaissance type planes in Thailand, French Indo-China, Sumatra, and Malaya is 275.

b. Own Forces.

(i) Support of ground troops is being provided by a composite tactical group consisting of two light bomber squadrons, six single-engine fighter/ground attack (short range) squadrons, five single-engine fighter/general reconnaissance (long range) squadrons, one air jungle rescue and one single-engine fighter/fighter-reconnaissance (short range) squadron.

(ii) Strategic operations are being carried out by four heavy bomber squadrons based in the Calcutta area.

(iii) Special duty operations by one special duty squadron, one misemployed heavy bomber squadron and two misemployed general reconnaissance squadrons are being carried out in Siam and Malaya.

(iv) Eight transport squadrons are engaged in air supply operating mainly from all-weather airfields in Chittagong, Akyab and Kyaukpyu areas.

(v) Seven all-weather fields including one to heavy bomber standard are being constructed in the Rangoon area to support future operations with target date of 15 August.

(vi) In the Cocos Islands one heavy-bomber squadron is expected to be operational by 15 July and one more by 31 July. It is intended to phase in two more heavy-bomber squadrons by 10 September and 1 October respectively. A flight of Mosquitoes photo-reconnaissance 34 is now based on Cocos.

PART II

4. *a. Enemy.* Jap troops in Burma are believed to have no offensive capabilities. Estimated that troops in Mokpalin and in Moulmein will hold present positions until forced out by our offensive action. Retreat from Moulmein will probably be toward Bangkok. Jap reinforcements coming into Malaya are expected to be spread evenly throughout the country although there are indications that they are paying particular attention to the defences of southern Malaya. Jap combatant strength in Malaya and the Kra Isthmus will probably rise to the equivalent of two and one-half divisions by September in addition to approximately 40,000 non-divisional troops.

b. Own Forces.

(i) *Navy.* Naval strikes will continue during the period before ZIPPER and shipping sweeps will be maintained.

(ii) *Army.* No operations are contemplated east of the Sittang River until after the monsoon except along the Toungoo-Mawchi and Thazi-Taunggyi roads. Activities will be confined to destroying Japs remaining west of the Sittang River. Preparations are in hand for ZIPPER. Part of the forces will be mounted from Burma.

(iii) *Air.* Strategic bombing policy has following priorities: enemy shipping, Banpong-Singapore railway, Bangkok-Pegu railway. Arrangements are in hand for the co-ordination of strategic bombing, mining and anti-shipping operations with the Southwest Pacific Area and China Theatre.

PART III

ADMINISTRATIVE

5. *Current Tasks.* Chief among the current administrative tasks other than the mounting of further operations are the reconstruction of the lines of communication within Burma, the preparation of an advanced base in the Rangoon area, and the rehabilitation of the irrigation system of the country. Subsidiary tasks are the preparation of Trincomalee to support naval operations and of the Cocos Islands as a staging base for aircraft in transit to the Pacific and as a heavy bomber base to support coming operations.

TOP SECRET

6. *Burma Lines of Communication.* After 1 October 1945 apart from 100 tons/day of civil affairs stores being flown from Imphal into the remote districts of North Burma and 300 tons/day of bulk petrol, oil and lubricants (POL) being moved by pipeline and inland water transportation (IWT) from Manipur road to Myingyan in central Burma all stores required in Burma will be imported through Rangoon. The development of lines of communication northwards from Rangoon is therefore a primary task.

7. *Rail and Inland Water Transport Line of Communication.* There are two rail routes north from Rangoon, one to Prome and the other via Toungoo to Mandalay. In view of the extensive demolitions on the latter route the former has been given first priority for reconstruction. Stores will be transshipped at Prome, the remainder of the journey being made by IWT up the Irrawaddy River to Myingyan and Mandalay. There are still several breaks in the Rangoon-Prome line and until these are repaired the best combination of rail and road is being used. The present capacity of the Rangoon-Prome route is 250 tons/day. It is planned to reach the target of 600 tons/day by 15 August. Thereafter this figure will be increased monthly. The rail line of communication to Mandalay via Toungoo is planned to be opened by the end of 1945. In addition to the Prome-Myingyan service IWT is already in operation between Rangoon and Pegu and is the main artery of supply for troops based on the Pegu area. Present capacity of this route is 100 tons/day.

8. *Road Line of Communication.* Of the two main roads leading northwards priority is being given to development of the Rangoon to Mandalay route via Pegu, Toungoo, and Thazi. However, in view of the fact that the road north of Pegu is likely to be breached for short periods during the monsoon, it is not planned to use this road for regular maintenance convoys until after the monsoon.

9. *Burma Oil Fields.* A complete reconnaissance of the Burma oil fields has been carried out. A production of up to 4,000 barrels daily of crude oil could be achieved within three months but due to the demolition of refining facilities the production of this crude oil involves the waste of valuable residues and is only being employed to the extent dictated by difficulties of supply from other sources. This situation will persist until adequate refining facilities can be provided. This would take too long for it to be of value to military operations against Japan and will not, therefore, be undertaken as a military responsibility. The oil companies concerned are in agreement with this policy in so far as it affects their interests.

10. *Rangoon Base.* Limited facilities are being provided for light naval forces. Base installations, hospitals, and reserves are being provided to maintain a

force of five equivalent divisions together with corps army base and line of communication troops and air forces. Stocks are to be 30 days reserves plus 15 days working stock. These should be in place by 1 November 1945. An airbase is being constructed to provide the following:—

a. North of line Pegu-Henzada two all-weather fighter-bomber, three all-weather transport fields.

b. South of line Pegu-Henzada by 15 August three all-weather fighter, three all-weather medium bomber, one all-weather heavy bomber fields with subsequent addition by 31 December of two fine-weather medium bomber, two fine-weather heavy bomber fields and the conversion of the previous three all-weather fighter fields to medium bomber standard.

The development of Rangoon port is proceeding satisfactorily. The target capacity of 6000 tons/day of dry stores and 1500 tons/day of bulk POL should be achieved in August. At present 4500 tons/day of dry stores are being cleared through the port. Four million gallons of bulk POL tankage will be in operation by mid-July.

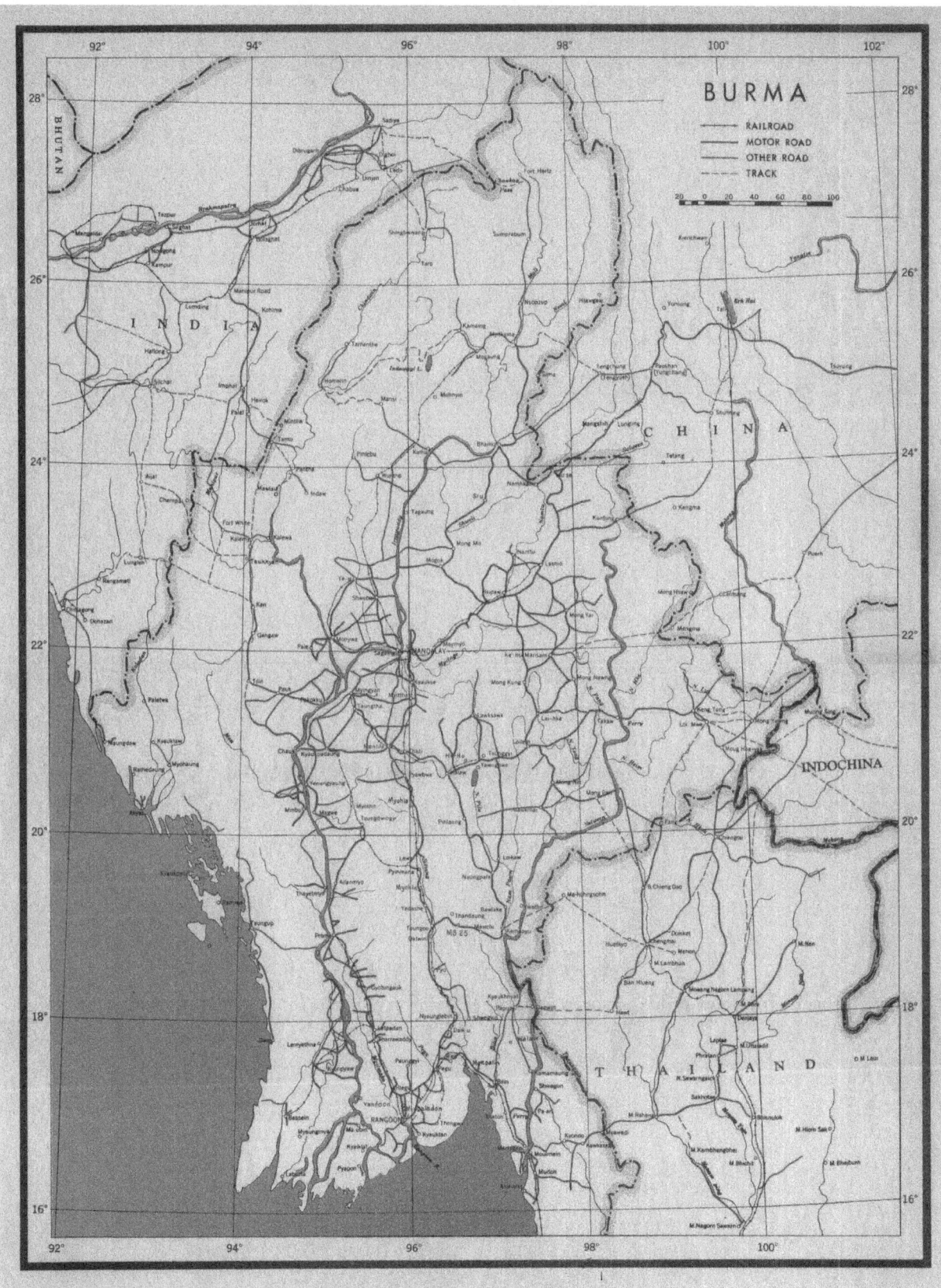

TOP SECRET

C.C.S. 892/2

DIRECTIVE TO THE SUPREME ALLIED COMMANDER, SOUTHEAST ASIA

References:

CCS 197th Meeting, Item 2
CCS 200th Meeting
CCS 900/3, paragraph 13

In C.C.S. 892/1 (20 July 1945) the British Chiefs of Staff presented a proposed directive to the Supreme Allied Commander, Southeast Asia.

The Combined Chiefs of Staff in their 197th Meeting (20 July) approved C.C.S. 892/1 as amended during discussion. The agreed directive was subsequently circulated as C.C.S. 892/2.

TOP SECRET

C.C.S. 892/2   20 July 1945

COMBINED CHIEFS OF STAFF

DIRECTIVE TO THE SUPREME ALLIED COMMANDER, SOUTHEAST ASIA

Note by the Secretaries

The Combined Chiefs of Staff approved the attached directive to the Supreme Allied Commander, Southeast Asia* at their 197th Meeting, 20 July 1945, with the understanding that the British Chiefs of Staff would take steps to obtain the agreement of the Australian, New Zealand, and Dutch governments to the proposed command set-up in Southwest Pacific and Southeast Asia.

A. J. McFARLAND,

A. T. CORNWALL-JONES,

Combined Secretariat.

---

* The Appendix as published herein is revised to conform with the boundary description as finally approved by the Combined Chiefs of Staff and included in their report to the President and Prime Minister.

TOP SECRET

ENCLOSURE

DRAFT

DIRECTIVE TO THE SUPREME ALLIED COMMANDER, SOUTHEAST ASIA

1. Your primary task is the opening of the Straits of Malacca at the earliest possible moment. It is also intended that British Commonwealth land forces should take part in the main operations against Japan which have been agreed as the supreme operations in the war; and that operations should continue in the Outer Zone to the extent that forces and resources permit.

BOUNDARIES OF COMMAND

2. The Eastern boundary of your command will be extended to include Borneo, Java, and the Celebes.

Full details of this extension are contained in the Appendix (page 179).

3. Further information will be sent to you regarding Indo-China.

4. It is desirable that you assume command of the additional areas as soon as practicable after the 15th August, 1945. You will report to the Combined Chiefs of Staff the date on which you expect to be in a position to undertake this additional responsibility.

5. From that date, such Dominion and Dutch forces as may be operating in your new area will come under your command. They will, however, continue to be based on Australia.

6. The area to the east of your new boundary will be an Australian command under the British Chiefs of Staff.

BRITISH PARTICIPATION IN MAIN OPERATIONS AGAINST JAPAN

7. It has been agreed in principle that a British Commonwealth land force of from three to five divisions and, if possible, a small tactical air force should

TOP SECRET

take part in the main operations against Japan in the spring of 1946. Units of the East Indies Fleet may also take part. Certain important factors relating to this are still under examination.

8. You will be required to provide a proportion of this force together with the assault lift for two divisions. The exact composition of this force and its role and the mounting and supporting arrangements will be discussed between Admiral Nimitz, General MacArthur and the British force commanders, and will receive final approval by the Combined Chiefs of Staff.

9. The requirements for the force taking part in the main operations against Japan must have priority over all the other tasks indicated below.

OPERATIONS IN THE OUTER ZONE

10. Subject to the fulfillment of the higher priority commitments given above, you will, within the limits of available resources, carry out operations designed to:—

   a. Complete the liberation of Malaya.

   b. Maintain pressure on the Japanese across the Burma-Siam frontier.

   c. Capture the key areas of Siam.

   d. Establish bridgeheads in Java and/or Sumatra to enable the subsequent clearance of these areas to be undertaken in due course.

11. You will submit a programme of operations to the Combined Chiefs of Staff as soon as you are in a position to do so.

DEVELOPMENT OF BASES

12. You will develop Singapore and such other bases as you may require to the extent necessary for operations against the Japanese.

TOP SECRET

APPENDIX

EASTERN BOUNDARY OF SOUTHEAST ASIA COMMAND

Beginning on the coast of Indo-China at 16° north; thence to intersect at 7°40′ north latitude 116° east longitude, the boundary between the Commonwealth of the Philippine Islands and British North Borneo; thence along the 1939 boundary line of the Philippines to latitude 05° north longitude 127° east; thence southwestward to 02° south 123° east; thence southeastward to 08° south 125° east; thence southwestward to 18° south 110° east.

SECRET

C.C.S. 893

GENERAL PROGRESS REPORT ON RECENT OPERATIONS
IN THE PACIFIC

References:

CCS 880, paragraph 1 (1)
CCS 193d Meeting, Item 3

The Combined Chiefs of Staff took note of C.C.S. 893 (15 July 1945) in their 193d Meeting (16 July).

SECRET

C.C.S. 893   16 July 1945

COMBINED CHIEFS OF STAFF

GENERAL PROGRESS REPORT ON RECENT OPERATIONS IN THE PACIFIC

References:

C.C.S. 880
C.C.S. 880/2

Memorandum by the United States Chiefs of Staff

The enclosed general progress report on recent operations in the Pacific is presented for consideration by the Combined Chiefs of Staff.

SECRET

ENCLOSURE

GENERAL PROGRESS REPORT ON RECENT OPERATIONS
IN THE PACIFIC

*PROGRESS OF TWENTIETH AIR FORCE; CENTRAL PACIFIC,
AND SOUTHWEST PACIFIC OPERATIONS
1 FEBRUARY 1945—1 JULY 1945*

1. Appendices "A" and "B" (pages 187 and 189) contain a graphic presentation of the Pacific situation on 1 July 1945 as compared with the situation on 1 February 1945.

TWENTIETH AIR FORCE

2. The Commanding General, Army Air Forces, will submit a separate report on this subject (C.C.S. 894).

CENTRAL PACIFIC

3. Operations in the Central Pacific have consisted principally of the capture, occupation, and development of Iwo Jima in the Bonins and of Okinawa and adjacent islands in the Ryukyus, and in preparing bases throughout the area for the support of further operations.

4. The seizure of Iwo Jima was preceded by carrier strikes on the Tokyo-Yokohama area, the first against the Japanese mainland. On 19 February, after extensive surface and air bombardment, Marine amphibious troops landed on Iwo Jima. Enemy opposition was bitter and the island was not completely secured until 16 March. Strong naval surface and air forces provided support throughout the operation.

5. Between 26 and 29 March United States troops occupied islands of the Kerama Group, southwest of Okinawa. After nine days of intensive surface and air bombardment, troops of the Tenth Army, including Marine amphibious troops, landed on Okinawa on 1 April. The northern tip of the island was reached by the 24th, but in the south enemy opposition was extremely stubborn. Organized enemy resistance did not cease until 21 June. Naval forces

SECRET

gave support throughout the protracted operation, fighting off almost daily enemy bombing and suicide attacks, from which we suffered considerable losses. On the morning of 7 April a Japanese force, en route to attack our surface forces off Okinawa, was intercepted by our carrier aircraft about 50 miles southwest of Kyushu, and the battleship *Yamato*, a light cruiser of the *Agano* class, and another light cruiser or destroyer-leader, and several destroyers were sunk. Our carrier forces, assisted by a carrier force of the British Pacific Fleet, provided air support for our troops and struck at targets ranging from the Sakishima Islands in the south to Tokyo in the north. During the operation several islands of the Okinawa group were occupied. Capture of other islands of the group continued through June.

6. Almost continuous air patrols from Okinawa and Iwo Jima bases are now maintained over southern Kyushu, the Yellow Sea, and southern Honshu. The Central Pacific air forces, Army, Navy, and Marine continued to attack enemy installations and shipping in the Bonins and Carolines and are inflicting heavy losses on enemy installations, aircraft, and shipping.

7. The submarine campaign in the Western Pacific has been prosecuted with vigor and extended into the Sea of Japan. The results have been most gratifying as considerable toll continues to be taken of the greatly reduced Japanese shipping and naval vessels.

NORTH PACIFIC

8. Operations in the North Pacific have consisted of periodic air attacks on the northern Kuriles, of surface ship raids into the Sea of Okhotsk, and bombardments of Paramushiro and Matsuwa Islands. A task group of cruisers and destroyers of the North Pacific Force recently intercepted and destroyed a Japanese convoy in a sweep through the Okhotsk Sea.

SOUTHWEST PACIFIC

9. The Philippine Islands campaign has reached a climax with the successful execution of the following:—

a. The bitterly fought Luzon campaign which began 9 January 1945 is approaching completion. Amphibious landings on southern Bataan and coordinated amphibious-parachute operations on Corregidor in mid-February gave us control of Manila Bay. Continued pressure in all directions up to the present eliminated most of the resistance on Luzon.

b. The Visayan group is under our control as a result of numerous operations beginning with the landing on the south coast of Panay on 18 March, followed by successive landings on Cebu, Negros, et cetera.

c. The successful landing at Zamboanga, Mindanao on 10 March followed by landings in the southern part of the island on 17 April and the north coast on 10 May in conjunction with subsequent operations on Mindanao has cut the enemy into three groups. These isolated Japanese groups are being rapidly reduced. Simultaneous with this operation islands in the Sulu Archipelago were secured in April.

d. Port and air facilities were secured on Palawan in February.

10. Allied forces, mostly Australian, made amphibious landings on Borneo as follows:—

a. Tarakan Island was assaulted 1 May, initial objectives being secured by 19 May and the remaining enemy forced to the hills in the northeastern part of the island. Organized resistance ceased on 23 May 1945.

b. Initial landings were made at Brunei Bay on 10 June; the air strips at Brunei town and Labuan Island were secured two days later; Labuan Island was completely cleared by 15 June and a greater part of the Brunei Bay objective has been secured.

c. A third force landed on 1 July at Balikpapan against initial light opposition. Enemy resistance stiffened somewhat as the beachhead was expanded but the Australians in this area apparently are making rapid progress toward their objective in the Balikpapan-Manggar area.

11. Allied forces continue to reduce and contain by-passed enemy garrisons in New Guinea, the Bismarcks, and the Solomons.

12. Army, Navy, and Marine air units in conjunction with naval surface units have conducted intensive preparatory and participating bombardment in cooperation with the amphibious operations described above.

SECRET

APPENDIX "A"

REVIEW OF PACIFIC SITUATION

1 JULY 1945

Appendix "A"

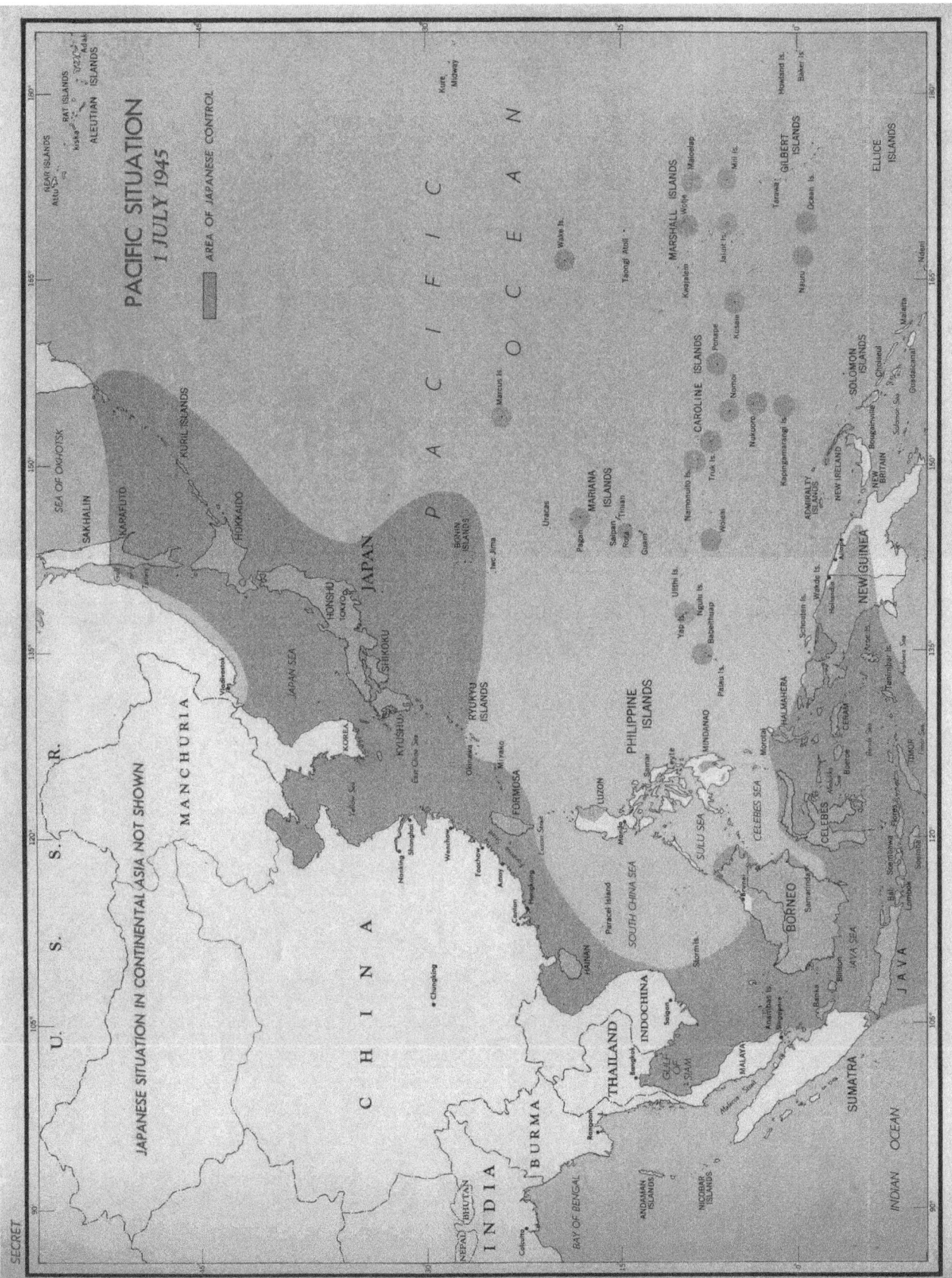

SECRET

APPENDIX "B"

REVIEW OF PACIFIC SITUATION

1 FEBRUARY 1945

TOP SECRET

C.C.S. 893/1

PROGRESS REPORT ON OPERATIONS IN CHINA,
APRIL 1944 THROUGH JUNE 1945

Reference:

CCS 193d Meeting, Item 3

C.C.S. 893/1 (19 July 1945) circulated for the information of the Combined Chiefs of Staff a report by the United States Chiefs of Staff containing General Wedemeyer's estimate of the situation in China.

TOP SECRET

C.C.S. 893/1
19 July 1945

COMBINED CHIEFS OF STAFF

PROGRESS REPORT ON OPERATIONS IN CHINA,
APRIL 1944 THROUGH JUNE 1945

Memorandum by the United States Chiefs of Staff

In April and May of 1944 the Japanese completed their control of the Pinhan Railroad, thus connecting their forces in the Yellow River and Tungting Lake areas. At the same time they launched a drive south from Tungting Lake, overrunning the principal Fourteenth Air Force bases in southeast China. In November this force was joined by forces advancing along the West River from Canton and shortly afterwards Nanning was captured and a junction made with the Japanese in French Indo-China. China was cut from every angle and the Japanese controlled all of the main lines of communication except in southwest China.

During this period the Fourteenth Air Force, in spite of its loss of important bases, continued to support the Chinese. Air superiority was maintained in China and Japanese lines of communication, supply dumps, and troop concentrations were constantly harassed. Japanese shipping off the China Coast was watched closely and all profitable targets attacked. During 1944, 631,000 tons of Japanese shipping were sunk.

During the period of 15 June 1944 to 17 January 1945 the XX Bomber Command flew twenty-three missions against strategic targets from bases in the China Theater. Efforts were directed primarily against harbor and dock areas, steel works, aircraft factories, railroad installations, and supply storage areas. Nine missions were flown against targets in Japan proper, five against Manchuria, three against China, and six against Formosa.

Operations in the China Theater are uniquely dependent upon supply by air. During the month of November 1944, 39,000 tons were air transported into the theater but by January 1945 air deliveries had increased to 47,000 tons as a result of increased numbers of aircraft in use and the acquisition of facilities in North Burma and in June 57,750 tons were air delivered. With the future aircraft augmentation of the Air Transport Command to a total of some 825

TOP SECRET

transport aircraft as now planned, it is estimated that approximately 106,000 tons per month will be flown into China by next May.

To utilize most effectively the meager United States supplies that reach China, it was decided to concentrate United States training and equipment on a relatively small group of selected Chinese units. This program, referred to as the Chinese Army Program, is now well underway, and some 550,000 Chinese troops are presently being equipped with United States weapons and trained in United States techniques.

This program includes 39 divisions organized into 13 armies and four field armies which are being trained and equipped by the United States. Included in this total are the five Chinese divisions which were formerly in the Chinese Army in India (CAI). Additionally United States instructional personnel is being attached to other armies but no U.S. supply or equipment is at present planned for them.

The China Theater has two bomber, four fighter, and four miscellaneous groups in the United States Fourteenth Air Force; one bomber and two fighter groups in the Chinese American Composite Wing; and two bomber and two fighter groups in the Chinese Air Force. It is intended to transfer the Tenth Air Force from India to China before the end of the year, placing both the Tenth and the Fourteenth Air Forces under the present Headquarters, U.S. Army Air Forces, India-Burma Theater, which will also be transferred.

General Wedemeyer's estimate of the situation in China is attached (Appendix "A").

TOP SECRET

APPENDIX "A"

ESTIMATE OF THE SITUATION

By the Commanding General, U.S. Forces, China Theater

1. Mission: From the United States point of view the mission of the China Theater is to divert, contain, and destroy maximum Jap forces and to increase the military effectiveness of the Chinese Army.

2. Situation and possible lines of action:—

   a. Enemy. The enemy is strengthening his forces and position in Manchuria and North China against the Russian threat, and in Shanghai and the coastal area north of Shanghai against the United States Pacific threat. On the central and south China fronts he continues his deliberate withdrawal northward from the Liuchow (109°16' - 24°18'), Kweilin (110° 08' - 25°20'), Hengyang (112°35' - 26°56') corridor, but will fight strong delaying actions. In the Canton, Hong Kong, Kukong area he has approximately 100,000 troops, with indications of northward movement from the area, especially down the Kan River. The withdrawal from the Luichow Peninsula continues by land and sea. Although it is not clear that he intends to completely evacuate the peninsula, he has greatly weakened his forces there. All Jap forces south of the French Indo-China border are now considered isolated from the north with the exception of minor evacuations by boat and/or plane.

   b. Supply. Line of communications supply situation governs the maximum Jap forces that the Chinese can contain and destroy. It is the determining factor in the speed of operations to follow the Jap withdrawal in Central and South China and to take advantage of the opportunities thus afforded. Present operations by Chinese units are ahead of schedule and have required an earlier forward displacement of supplies than was originally anticipated. The resulting drain on supplies, particularly petrol, oil, and lubricants (POL), which is a major item in Hump tonnage, must be compensated. This, plus the requirement for the air force in China, makes the seizure of a port and additional air routes into China a major requirement. The securing of a major port in the Canton-Hong Kong area and an intermediate port at Fort Bayard on the Luichow Peninsula fulfills this requirement. Additional tonnage may be realized by opening an Air Transport Command (ATC) route from the Philippines to air terminals in the

Appendix "A"

TOP SECRET

Nanning-Liuchow-Tanchuk (110°33' - 23°24') area, or in the Luichow Peninsula area, when it is secured. Present estimates predict from the air route a small gain of about 3,000 tons per month after the first month of operation with Luichow Town as base, and from 5,000 tons in mid-September to 16,000 tons in November from Fort Bayard port. Thus, commencing with November, tonnage from these sources will be sufficient to commit approximately five more divisions than was originally planned. The Fort Bayard area should be captured and exploited immediately and the possibilities of the air route thoroughly explored.

c. *Relative Strength.* Enemy troops are superior to the Chinese in training, equipment, organization for battle, and experience. Consequently, the Chinese ground troops must be committed only where they can enjoy local superiority. Only the five Chinese Army in India (CAI) divisions are rated as excellent and ready for combat. Commencing with mid-July the Alpha divisions begin to complete their 13 weeks training program. By 1 September 18 divisions, including the five CAI divisions, will be ready for combat. Two more will be ready by 1 November. Not until the presently estimated requirement of a total of 34 divisions are equipped, supplied, and trained can the Chinese afford to attack northeastwards against the Yangtze River corridor into the main strength of the Jap forces. To create such a Chinese capability and support such an effort requires the backing of a major port. The port area with the necessary capacity is the Canton-Hong Kong area. It is estimated these ports can be captured by the forces allotted to operation *CARBONADO* with the support of the China Theater air forces. The first Chinese main effort should be to capture the Canton-Hong Kong area.

d. *Time and Space.* The only forces immediately available to interfere with the Jap withdrawal from the Liuchow-Kweilin-Hengyang corridor are the air, clandestine, and non-Alpha divisions in the area. If Fort Bayard is secured by 15 August, it will be possible to augment the flow of supplies to *CARBONADO* forces, and permit a diversion of Hump supplies to the Paoching area to permit the ground forces there to operate against the Hengyang and the Kan River corridors without waiting for the capture of the Canton-Hong Kong port. This will permit a major interdiction of Jap lines of communication to the Jap Canton-Hong Kong garrison, or will disrupt their withdrawal in event Japanese decide earlier to evacuate in preference to isolation.

e. *Enemy Capabilities.*

(1) Against the first part of the China Theater mission, the Japanese can:

(a) Withdraw forces from the Shanghai area to the Jap homeland and Ryukyu Islands.

Appendix "A"

TOP SECRET

(b) Withdrawal north of the Yangtze River some of or all of their Canton-Hong Kong area forces for further withdrawal from China.

(2) Against the second part of the mission the enemy can by stubborn defense of ports delay the program of training and equipping the Chinese forces.

f. Own Lines of Action.

(1) To capture the ports of Canton-Hong Kong at the earliest date possible with a view to subsequent large-scale operations against the Japanese main body behind the Yangtze River. In the meantime, to utilize air and clandestine forces and such ground forces as supplies and the training program permit in operations to harass, divert, and maintain pressure of Jap forces throughout China.

(2) To contain the Canton-Hong Kong Japs, and strike northeastward against the main body of Japanese in China along and north of the Yangtze River.

3. *Analysis of Possible Lines of Action.* Should course (1) be adopted, the enemy might move some of his Shanghai area troops from China. China Theater would be unable to prevent this. However, there are at present no indications that he will do this and each week he waits will make it more difficult due to the paucity of his shipping and its increasing vulnerability to the air and sea operations of United States Pacific forces. If the enemy embarks on a withdrawal northward of some of his Canton-Hong Kong forces, they will become subject to air and clandestine attacks initially and to ground force attacks commencing about November. Canton-Hong Kong area would be easier to capture. A complete evacuation of the Canton-Hong Kong area would subject all the moving troops to air and guerrilla attacks and expedite our entry into the ports. It would, however, permit a large number of Japs to escape north of the Yangtze River. This would not be a serious loss if by then the Jap could not evacuate his forces from China to Japan. Should the enemy decide to defend the China ports to the last in the German manner, his forces will automatically be contained in China, and it becomes imperative that we capture Canton-Hong Kong ports and proceed according to plan.

Should we adopt course (2) and move northwards prior to the capture of a major port, it is unlikely that our move would hold in China any Shanghai area forces the Japs decided to move. Our strength would be insufficient. The training program and preparation for major Chinese offensives would be delayed due to lack of a major port.

Appendix "A"

TOP SECRET

4. *Comparison of Own Lines of Action.* The degree to which China Theater can divert, contain, and destroy Jap forces in China is dependent on the speed with which the capabilities of the Chinese forces can be developed to the required strength. Similarly the speed of the development of Chinese troops is dependent on the expeditious augmentation of supplies and of facilities. This requires ports.

Therefore, course (1) appears the best one to adopt as it best accomplishes the first part of our mission and concurrently achieves the greatest degree of progress on the second part of the mission.

5. *Decision.* To capture and develop the port area of Canton-Hong Kong at earliest date possible with a view to subsequent operations against the Jap forces in the Yangtze River-Shanghai area. The plan is:—

   a. To maintain pressure on the enemy.

   b. To capture Fort Bayard.

   c. To secure the Nanning-Liuchow-Kweilin-Tanchuk area, develop the airfields and prepare the area as a base for future operations against the Canton-Hong Kong port area.

   d. To capture the Canton-Hong Kong area.

Appendix "A"

TOP SECRET

APPENDIX "B"

GROUND SITUATION CHINA THEATER 1 APRIL 1944
SHOWING U.S. AIRFIELDS
THAT WERE SUBSEQUENTLY OVERRUN BY JAPANESE DRIVES

Appendix "B"

TOP SECRET

APPENDIX "C"

LINE SHOWING MAXIMUM TERRITORY OCCUPIED BY JAPANESE IN SOUTH CHINA DURING 1944-1945 INCLUDING MAJOR U.S. AIRFIELDS LOST TO THE JAPANESE

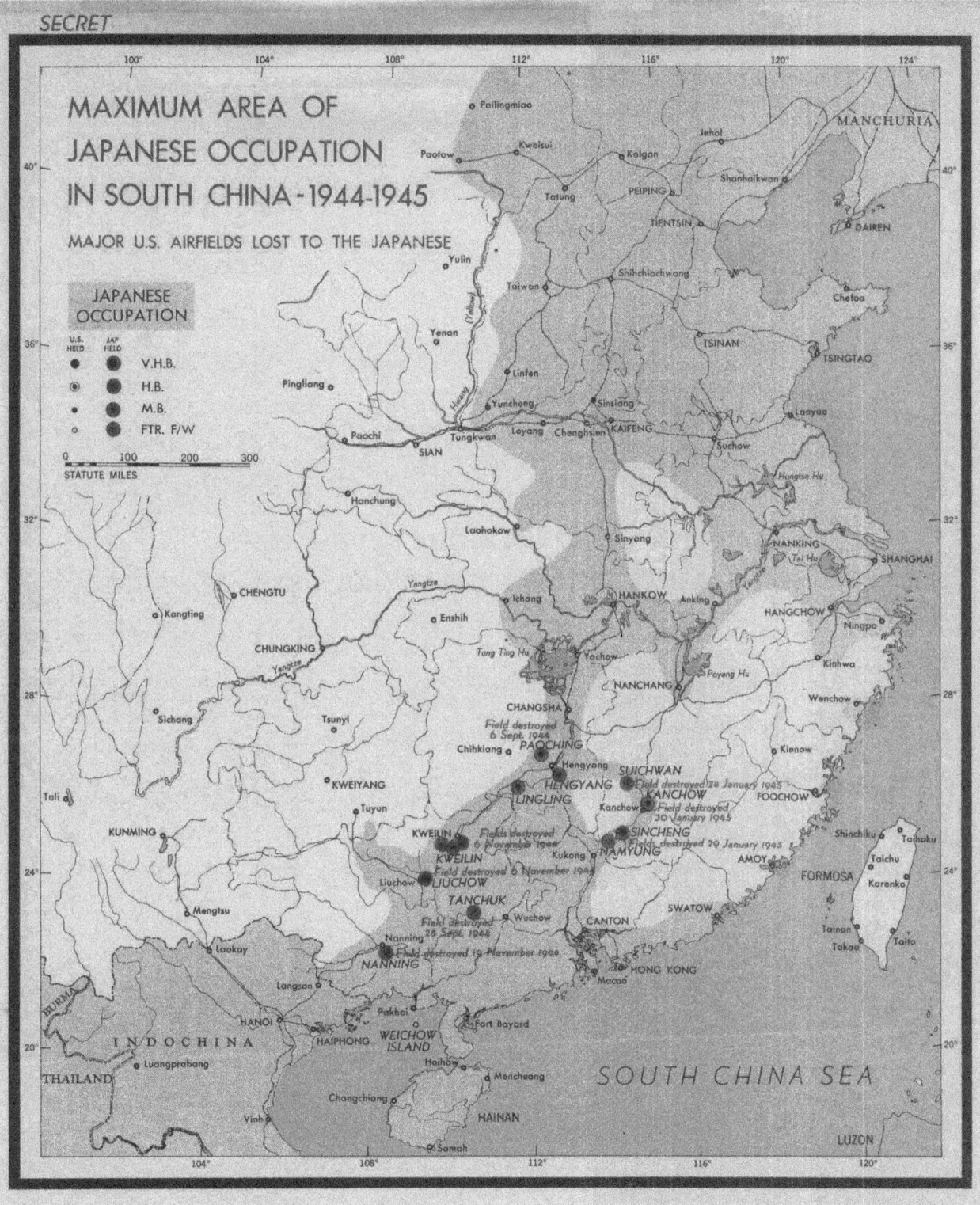

TOP SECRET

APPENDIX "D"

GROUND SITUATION CHINA 6 JUNE 1945
SHOWING MAJOR U.S. AIRFIELDS HELD BY JAPANESE AND CHINESE

Appendix "D"

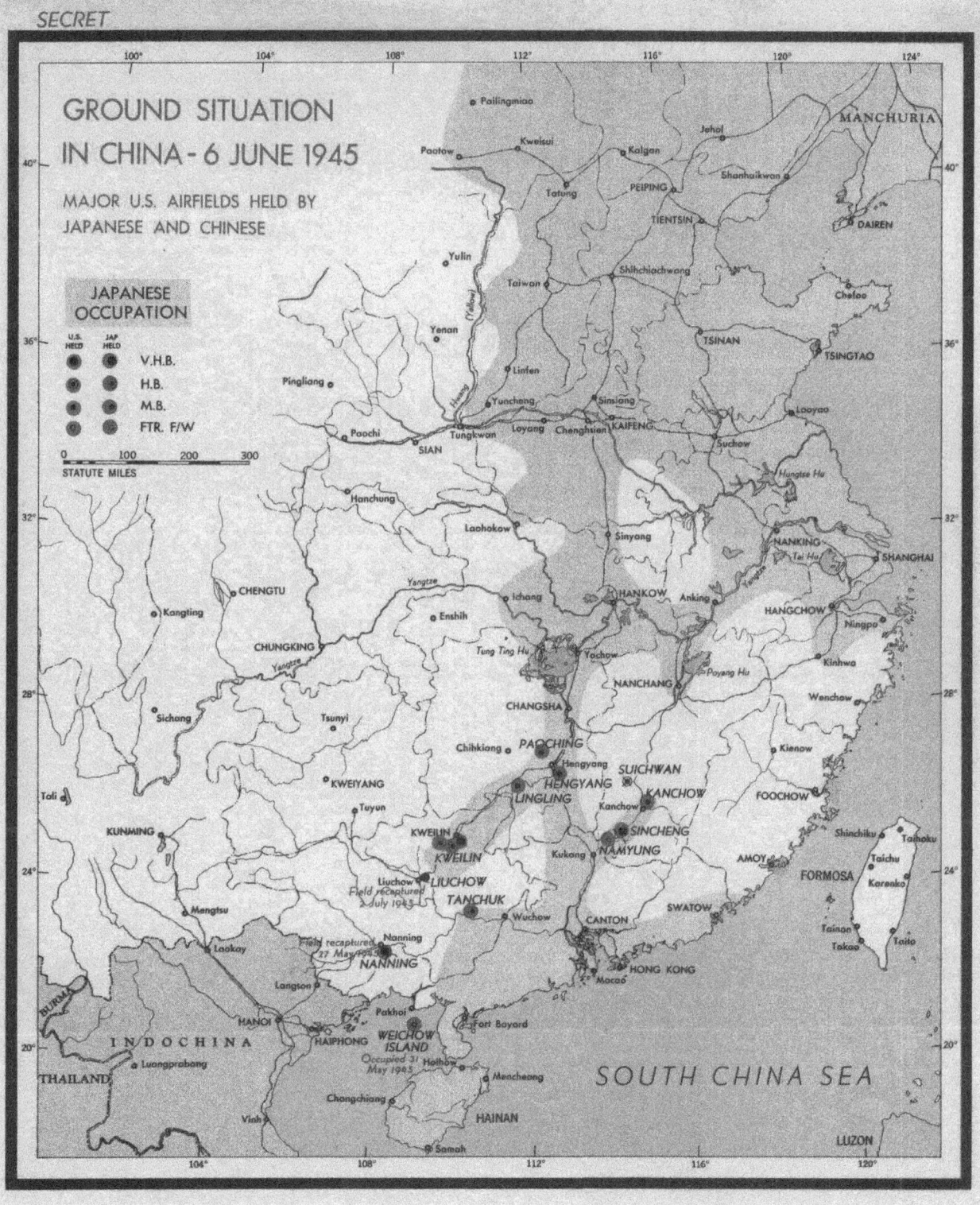

TOP SECRET

C.C.S. 894

REPORT ON ARMY AIR OPERATIONS IN THE WAR AGAINST JAPAN

References:

CCS 880/7
CCS 193d Meeting, Item 5

The Combined Chiefs of Staff took note of C.C.S. 894 (16 July 1945) in their 193d Meeting (16 July).

TOP SECRET

C.C.S. 894   16 July 1945

COMBINED CHIEFS OF STAFF

REPORT ON ARMY AIR OPERATIONS IN THE WAR AGAINST JAPAN

Reference:

C.C.S. 880/7

Memorandum by the United States Chiefs of Staff

The enclosed report by the United States Chiefs of Staff on Army air operations in the war against Japan is presented for consideration by the Combined Chiefs of Staff.

TOP SECRET

ENCLOSURE

PART I

STRATEGIC BOMBING OPERATIONS

The mission of strategic bombardment against Japan is substantially the same as was the objective of our Allied air forces operating against Germany. This mission is to achieve the earliest possible progressive destruction and dislocation of the Japanese military, industrial, and economic systems, and to undermine the morale of the Japanese people to the point where their capacity for war is decisively weakened. It is our conviction that a relatively speedy and economical accomplishment of this mission is well within our capabilities.

There are peculiar and complex problems involved. Perhaps the most troublesome of these, at the outset, was the problem of distances. Distances were great and range limitations dominated much of our early thinking about Pacific operations. For example, the distance from the Hawaiian Islands to Guam is 3,815 statute miles, from Guam to Tokyo, 1,500 statute miles, and from Manila to Tokyo, 2,150 statute miles. Fortunately for us, the Japanese counted much too heavily on our inability to cope with this situation. Whether they banked on our conducting a prolonged island-to-island offensive or felt secure in the possession of their air defense, is not relevant here. The fact is, we caught them unprepared.

We had other problems—the problem of perfecting our B-29; the problem of weather. We knew that bombing weather over Japan was worse than over Europe; we did not know how much worse. We found out quickly enough and adapted our techniques accordingly. The North Pacific monsoon area is bad—not bad enough to stop us. As for the B-29—it has turned out to be a superior airplane.

On the credit side of the ledger we had a number of basic factors to consider. The compactness of Japan's industry had been one of her initial advantages. Where Germany's industry had been spread over the greater part of her territory in 25 or 30 complexes, Japan's is concentrated in three great centers and two smaller ones. Where much of Germany's industry had been buried far in the interior, Japan has, so to speak, no interior. She has not,

TOP SECRET

to any appreciable extent, had a chance to go underground. And it is too late now to move lock, stock, and barrel over to the Asiatic mainland.

We know, of course, that Japan has built up considerable stock piles of raw materials. She has hoarded petroleum from the Indies, rubber and tin from the Indies and Malaya, lead, tungsten, and zinc from Burma, nickel from the Celebes, bauxite from the Indies and Malaya. But this torrent of supplies has been cut to a trickle by our Navy and our Far Eastern Air Forces who now dominate the shipping lanes of the China seas. The attrition we have forced on the Japanese merchant fleet has also seriously cut into the flow of iron ore, copper, aluminous shale, magnesium and other vital materials from the Manchuria-North China area. Increasingly, from now on, Japan will have to fight this war with resources on hand. And we know from our intelligence that as a result of strategic bombardment, these resources are dwindling by the day.

Japan's industry is far more vulnerable to air attack than Germany's had been. Approximately 47 percent of her priority war industries are concentrated in her six major cities—Tokyo, Kawasaki, Osaka, Kobe, Nagoya, and Yokohama. An equivalent percentage had been spread over 25 cities of the Reich. Naturally, distribution of industrial labor force runs along the same lines. Berlin had 6 percent of Germany's industrial workers; Tokyo had 14 percent. In Hamburg there had been under 6,000 people to the square mile; in Osaka over 45,000. In Tokyo's unbelievably supersaturated Asakusa ward, there had been—and we use the past tense advisedly—over 130,000 people to the square mile. Today there is hardly a building left in Asakusa. To sum up, 20 Japanese cities contain 22 percent of the total population, 53 percent of all numbered targets, 69 percent of all key targets, and 74 percent of all priority targets.

Further, it should be borne in mind that much of Japan's industry is extremely backward—almost feudal—in character. A formidable proportion of it is conducted on a contracting and subcontracting basis. Statistics of the immediate post-war years show that plants employing five or more persons totaled 15,000 apiece in Tokyo and Osaka, 5,000 in Nagoya, and that the great bulk of these employed less than thirty workers. These feeder plants are scattered throughout all but the most restricted of residential sections and housed, for the most part, in highly inflammable structures.

Early in March, therefore, we decided to launch a series of low level incendiary night attacks against Japanese urban areas. We knew this meant an increased bomb load, greater bombing accuracy, less intense winds at bombing altitude, better radar returns, less strain on the airplane and

208

TOP SECRET

equipment. What we had not expected was the comparative ineffectiveness of Japanese anti-aircraft at altitudes ranging from 10,000 to as low as 5,000 feet.

Results have been immensely gratifying. By the end of June we had completely burned out—leveled to ashes—more than 115 square miles of highly industrialized urban areas, all of them containing high priority targets. In a single mission against Tokyo, the following strategic damage was accomplished. Two petroleum plants destroyed, one damaged. One shipbuilding yard destroyed, two damaged. Eleven civilian production factories destroyed, five damaged. Eight storage plants damaged. Two freight yards destroyed, six other transportation facilities damaged. Two public utilities destroyed, seven damaged. More than 50 percent of the built-up area of Tokyo, 26 percent of Osaka, 22 percent of Nagoya, 51 percent of Kobe, 44 percent of Yokohama, no longer exist. What this means in terms of economic dislocation need hardly be enlarged on. We intend to keep on hitting specific priority targets in these cities, but we no longer regard them as functioning industrial units. Millions of skilled workers have not only been rendered homeless and temporarily useless, but are today forced to subsist in conditions approaching chaos. With these major cities well on the road to extinction, we have been able to continue the strategic effort by directing missions to smaller, but nevertheless important industrial communities. Of these, Nagasaki, Kagoshima, Yokkaichi, Toyohashi, Fukuoka, and Shizuoka have been respectively 11, 41, 50, 52, 20, and 66 percent destroyed.

Our successes on night incendiary missions have not prevented us from varying our tactics and techniques. We have repeatedly thrown Japanese defenses off balance by dispersing elements of our striking force, by alternating day and night attacks, coming in at different altitudes, attacking in a variety of formations, with or without fighter escort. And we have carried on our sustained campaign of precision bombing against high priority targets, notably the Japanese aircraft industry.

Nineteen of the thirty-odd aircraft frame and engine plants in the Japanese home islands have been attacked by B-29's to date. At least six of these have been so severely damaged that production has ceased. We shall not enter into assessments of damage to individual factories. But taking the most conservative intelligence estimates, we may safely conclude that strategic bombardment has cut Japan's potential aircraft production for the first six months of this year by 6,400 airplanes. Add to this the attrition losses that our Army and Navy squadrons have inflicted on the Japanese air force, and the handwriting on the wall becomes legible indeed. Japan lost some 40 percent of her air strength in the Philippine campaign alone. Her monthly production of aircraft, which was an estimated 2,350 last December, declined to

TOP SECRET

approximately 1,100 in May. The results of our June attacks have not yet been finally appraised.

The Japanese air force remains a threat to our surface forces, largely by the employment of suicide aircraft, but unless there is some unusual development and production, our air offensive will not be subject to serious interference. Their anti-aircraft defense has improved, but it is most unlikely that they will ever be able to attain the concentration or accuracy of German flak.

In consequence, our loss rate has been relatively light. During the first quarter of 1945, 35 aircraft were lost out of every 1,000 that were airborne. During the second quarter, this figure dropped to 15 aircraft out of every 1,000 airborne. Decreases in rates have occurred in losses due both to enemy action and operational factors. Some of these decreases are due, of course, to our acquisition of emergency landing fields on Iwo Jima.

The performance of the B-29 has been a source of deep satisfaction to us. Its bomb load has been about four times as great as that of the United States heavy bombers in Europe. During their first operational year—through June, that is—our B-29's have dropped more than 100,000 tons of bombs of all types. By the end of this year, we expect to deliver that figure every month. By April of next year, our plans call for 177,000 tons monthly, which will be the greater part of the 243,000 tons per month that will be dropped on Japan by the entire Army Air Forces. At this moment we have 854 B-29's deployed in the Marianas. These include the 150 that had previously been operating out of China and India. By March of next year, we expect our B-29 force to be at full strength—nearly 2,000 aircraft divided equally between the Marianas and the Ryukyus. The problem of deploying this number of B-29's in the Ryukyus is not simple. In fact, it will be one of the outstanding feats of this war in the development of air bases and the unloading of supplies which will have to be done mostly over the beaches. Airdromes are being built on Okinawa, within 350 miles of the Japanese homeland, which means that construction and unloading will be subject to enemy air attack. In addition to the B-29's in the Ryukyus, the tactical air force will be there, in turn involving a logistical problem of major proportions. For airdrome and base construction in the Ryukyus, it will require more engineers than were employed for that purpose in England. The development of Okinawa where most of these forces must be based due to the landmass required is an island approximately 68 miles long and varying from around ten miles to three miles in width. This island had practically no development. Docks are being constructed to get the required tonnage unloaded. Before an airfield can be started roads must be built to the sites. Our

TOP SECRET

forces will require approximately 23 airfields; the difficulties are obvious. We are pushing our resources to the limit to accomplish this development, even so it will be near the end of the year before our forces are deployed. The build-up will be gradual; as a field is contructed it will be occupied by our fighters and bombers which only then may join in the fight against the Japanese homeland. This is not an easy job but it will be done.

In the employment of these forces in the Ryukyus supplementing the present forces in the Marianas, we expect to achieve the disruption of the Japanese military, industrial, and economic systems. We are already well advanced in the destruction of the aircraft industry and will continue to destroy aircraft factories and will maintain Japanese aircraft production below the attrition to assure the impotence of the Japanese air force. We will also continue the over-all attack on Japanese industry through incendiary attacks on her urban industrial areas. The weather, as stated before, is one of the major factors affecting future operations. On days when visual bombing is possible we will attack specific targets in the Japanese industrial system. These attacks will be directed against the aircraft industry, arsenals, storage, oil. In connection with the arsenals, we intend to knock out, first, Japan's principal producer of anti-aircraft weapons, upon which she will have to place steadily increasing reliance for defense as the Japanese air force becomes more impotent. In order to take full advantage of the incendiary attacks on urban industrial areas and visual attacks on precision targets, we expect to completely disrupt the Japanese transportation system. We estimate that this can be done with our forces available in the month prior to the invasion of Japan. Japan, in fact, will become a nation without cities, with her transportation disrupted and will have tremendous difficulty in holding her people together for continued resistance to our terms of unconditional surrender.

PART II

TACTICAL AIR OPERATIONS

In our progress westward toward Japan, we moved by "island hopping"—primary objective of this strategy was to advance our network of airbases deeper and deeper into the Japanese perimeter. We did this also to secure our own communications by isolating and neutralizing Japanese strongpoints, and to provide ourselves with forward bases where we could accumulate supplies and assemble forces for our next move. From the standpoint of tactical air operations, our ordinary procedure was the same as in the land campaigns in Europe.

Circumstances, of course, varied as the size of the island battlefields, and their location, varied. At Leyte, we went ashore for the first time beyond the effective cover of our land-based air power. Thanks to the valiant work of the Navy's carrier-based planes, we made the landing good, and were able to establish our airfields. This was not done cheaply. Naval vessels cannot operate within range of still effective land-based air power without taking losses. In this case, strategic considerations outweighed this tactical consideration; and we took the calculated risk.

A similar situation confronted us at Okinawa, and we were obliged to take shipping losses. Considerations of strategy here again outweighed tactical considerations. However, the success of this difficult campaign, which has brought the Japanese home islands within operational range of our light and medium air components, is of such importance as to far more than repay its cost to us.

Of the many Pacific tactical air operations, we think the most striking example of the effective use of tactical air power, in cooperation with ground troops and the Navy, to achieve decisive results at a minimum cost in lives and matériel was the work of the Far Eastern Air Forces in the Lingayen-Central Luzon campaign.

The job assigned to the Fifth and Thirteenth Air Forces involved the destruction of enemy air, sea, and land forces. It can be summarized as follows:—

1. Destruction of enemy air strength by:

    a. Destruction of aircraft.

    b. Neutralization of enemy installations throughout the Southwest Pacific Area.

2. Protection of amphibious forces.

3. Denial of movement of hostile reserves and reinforcements by sea.

4. Support of ground troops by:

    a. Destruction of lines of communication.

    b. Destruction of enemy installations and concentrations.

During the latter part of December the Japanese had built up their air strength in Luzon to an estimated peak of about 532 operational aircraft on 4

TOP SECRET

January. Between 5 January and 15 January the bulk of that air strength was broken, and by 24 January it had been reduced to practically nothing—an estimated 34 planes.

At the same time we had been directing heavy air attacks at targets in Formosa, in the Netherlands East Indies, and points in the Philippines other than on Luzon. These attacks were made to destroy enemy bases and concentrations, thus preventing the reinforcement of the dwindling Japanese air force in Luzon, and to protect our own operations. Attacks against these targets were particularly heavy during the first six days of January and were continued steadily except for a period of bad weather around the 13th. The widespread effectiveness of these attacks was shown by a marked reduction of enemy air strength throughout the Southwest Pacific Area. Counting the enemy's heavy Luzon losses, his over-all air strength in the whole area was cut to less than half—from a peak of about 1,243 aircraft to about 500 by the end of the month. Most of the 500 were based on Formosa where they could offer no effective opposition to our Philippine ground operations. In the course of the month we had dropped 6,825 tons of bombs and expended more than five and a half million rounds of ammunition.

Throughout this period we had been prepared to deal with Japanese attempts to bring reinforcements to Luzon. Probably because the Japanese recognized that such attempts could not succeed, they made none of any consequence.

The task of protecting the amphibious forces was assigned jointly to the Navy and to the Far East Air Forces. Our losses were 46 vessels damaged or sunk. The principal tactics used by the enemy was suicide bombing. All but four of the successful attacks were of this type. While ineffective, in the sense of never seriously jeopardizing the success of any of our amphibious operations, the suicide tactic was a constant and destructive nuisance. Neither fighter cover nor anti-aircraft fire was able to prevent attacks. The only technique so far found successful is the destruction of the enemy's airbases. We directed heavy strikes against the Luzon airfields on 6, 7, and 8 January, with the result that there was only one day (the 12th) following 8 January when more than one suicide attack was successful. The total Japanese effort was 42 such attacks, the last on the 18th. This reflects the progress made in knocking out the enemy's airfields and destroying his air force.

The landings at Lingayen Gulf took place on 9 January 1945. The Far Eastern Air Force cooperated with the ground forces by the tactical bombing and strafing of lines of communication and vehicles, and of military installations and concentrations. The effectiveness of the attacks is indicated by the following quotation from an Intelligence Summary: "The Fifth Air Force announced on 16 January that, since 25 December, its units had destroyed 79 locomotives (50 percent of pre-war total), 466 railroad cars (25 percent of pre-war total), 486 motor trucks, and 67 staff cars."

The damage done to the enemy was so great that, on 19 January, the Commanding General, Sixth Army, recommended to the Commanding General, Fifth Air Force, that, in the future, attacks against the bridges be limited to those specifically requested, and that attacks on rolling stock be limited to trains in motion. The destruction of lines of communication had, in fact, gone so far that it was no longer a question of crippling the Japanese defense effort, but of impeding our own advance. We had flown a total of 3,713 sorties and dropped 2,634 tons of bombs on these targets. Specific pinpoint targets—the Calumpit, Plaridel, Baliuag, and Calaug bridges and the closing of the highway through Belete Pass—had been hit promptly with precision. The work of the attack and medium bombers and bomb-carrying fighters responsible for the destruction of the bridges was particularly good.

While this was going on behind the possible Japanese defensive positions, the job of direct cooperation with our fast moving ground columns was under way. Heavies, medium and fighter bombers were blasting out the road blocks and Jap strong points directly ahead of our spearheads driving south. Almost two thousand sorties were flown and 1,530 tons of bombs dropped on military installations and concentrations.

A comparison of losses with results achieved indicates the outstanding success of the operation. A total of 447 aircraft of all types were lost from all causes. Four hundred eighty-six Army Air Force officers and enlisted men were killed or missing during the month of January. By that time the enemy air force had been totally destroyed, all major resistance had been overcome. Except for the difficult but strategically unimportant mopping-up operations, the Philippines were again ours as the result of the cooperation between our three services—naval, ground, and air.

Our greatest problem of tactical air operations is, however, yet to come. Now that we are established in the Ryukyus, we have the herculean task before us of developing ports, roads, and airdromes sufficient to accommodate 50 groups of aircraft by 1 November. This amounts to approximately 3,000 aircraft operating off of 23 airfields. The distance from our bases in the Ryukyus to the target area in Kyushu further complicates the problem of effective coordination with the assault forces. It is approximately 400 miles to the target areas in the southern portion of Kyushu and some 550 miles to the northern part of Kyushu over which distance it will be necessary to conduct tactical air operations on an unprecedented scale.

Once we have attained a foothold on the Japanese homeland, we will be faced again with the necessity of securing airfield sites as early as possible to establish the necessary air support of our ground forces ashore. In the objective area, there are estimated to be some nine airfield sites on which it is planned to eventually deploy up to 40 groups of approximately 2,400 aircraft. To achieve this planned build-up of air, it will be essential to move the full force of our engineering effort to the objective area as early as possible and operate under the similar difficult conditions which are being experienced now in the Ryukyus. Once firmly established in Kyushu our tactical air operations will assume the familiar pattern of destroying the remnants of the Japanese air force, isolation of the battlefield areas and direct coordination with the ground forces in overcoming enemy resistance.

The Kyushu operation will have for its objective the rapid seizure of an area in southern Kyushu sufficient for establishment of overpowering land-based air forces to cover the final decisive thrust into the industrial heart of Japan. When the operation is completed we will face a situation similar to that experienced in Europe after the Rhine break-through. There will be an overlapping of operating spheres of strategical and tactical air forces. By that time, profitable targets in the Japanese mainland will have become scarce and strategic functions will necessarily merge with the tactical. Our aircraft heretofore operating over great distances will then be operating against targets considerably closer to their bases which will permit optimum employment of all aircraft. With the merging of the strategical and tactical functions, the coordination of operations will become increasingly necessary as never before. With a tactical air force of some 2,400 aircraft operating "wheels down, bucket brigade" backed up by 1,300 B-29's of the Strategic Air Force located in the Marianas 1,600 miles away and from the Ryukyus 1,000 miles away, the full destructive power of the air force will be brought against the remaining elements of the Japanese war machine.

TOP SECRET

C.C.S. 895
C.C.S. 895/1
C.C.S. 895/2

PARTICIPATION OF TWO FRENCH COLONIAL INFANTRY DIVISIONS IN FAR EASTERN OPERATIONS

References:

CCS 194th Meeting
CCS 196th Meeting, Item 2
CCS 900/3, paragraph 16

In C.C.S. 895 (16 July 1945) the United States Chiefs of Staff requested the comments of the British Chiefs of Staff regarding the employment of two French colonial infantry divisions in Far Eastern operations.

C.C.S. 895/1 (18 July) circulated comments by the British Chiefs of Staff.

In C.C.S. 895/2 (19 July) the United States Chiefs of Staff proposed a revised memorandum to be forwarded by the Combined Chiefs of Staff to the Chief of the French Military Mission to the United States in lieu of Enclosure "B" to C.C.S. 895.

The Combined Chiefs of Staff in their 196th Meeting (19 July) approved the memorandum in the Enclosure to C.C.S. 895/2.

TOP SECRET

C.C.S. 895   16 July 1945

COMBINED CHIEFS OF STAFF

PARTICIPATION OF TWO FRENCH COLONIAL INFANTRY DIVISIONS IN FAR EASTERN OPERATIONS

Memorandum by the United States Chiefs of Staff

There are attached (Enclosure "A") a memorandum in which the French propose to place a French corps of two infantry divisions under American command in the Pacific war and (Enclosure "B") a reply proposed by the United States Chiefs of Staff. Since the British Chiefs of Staff may have views as to the areas in which these French troops should be employed, though perhaps not under United States command, their comment or concurrence is requested. General MacArthur proposes, if the French corps is assigned to him, to use it in the main effort against Japan in late spring of 1946.

TOP SECRET

ENCLOSURE "A"

République Française
MISSION MILITAIRE FRANÇAISE
AUX ÉTATS-UNIS

Washington 9, D. C.

No. 432/EM   May 29, 1945

MEMORANDUM FOR: General George C. Marshall
                                            Chief of Staff, U.S. Army

SUBJECT: French participation in Far Eastern operations

During conversations between President Truman and Mr. Bidault, Minister of Foreign Affairs of the French Provisional Government, on the one hand, and President Truman, General Marshall and General Juin on the other, the principle of a French participation in the war against Japan was viewed favorably.

Following these conversations, the French Government puts at the entire disposal of the American command, for operations in the Far East, an army corps comprising two divisions, besides corps-supporting and service units.

This army corps should include:—

1) The 9th Colonial Infantry Division, already well trained, having taken a brilliant part in the French and German campaigns.

In order to be able to operate in the Pacific war zone, this division would only require certain transfers of personnel (replacement by volunteers of men unfit for overseas duty).

The above will be ready to be shipped by the end of June.

It seems advisable that the 9th Division receive its equipment in the theater of operations.

2) The 1st Colonial Infantry Division of the Far East, planned several months ago. This division, whose colored troops will be replaced by trained

Enclosure "A"

TOP SECRET

European volunteers, from the French 1st Army, will be ready by the end of July, provided it receives its equipment on time.

It is to be expected that the latter unit, in view of the previous training of its personnel, will be ready for combat duty a month after receipt of its equipment.

To save time, immediate delivery of its equipment is therefore suggested.

In case the above is delivered only in the theater of operations, a corresponding delay would be needed by the 1st Division, from the time of receipt of its equipment, to participate in actual combat.

3) Supporting units and services of the army corps would also be ready by the end of July. Details of its equipping will have to be worked out in accord with the American command.

This army corps being put at the entire disposal of the American command, it seems logical to the French General Staff to give its units an organization similar to that of corresponding American units in the Far East.

It is therefore requested, in regard to divisions as well as to supporting army corps units and services, that the types of units to be organized, be exactly defined.

It is finally suggested, in order to facilitate further negotiations, that Supreme Headquarters, Allied Expeditionary Force, be authorized to deal directly with the French command in what concerns details of the matters herewith referred to.

/s/ A. M. Brosin de Saint Didier

Enclosure "A"

TOP SECRET

ENCLOSURE "B"

DRAFT

Memorandum for the Chief of the French Military Mission to the United States

1. With reference to your memorandum of 29 May 1945 addressed to the Chief of Staff, U.S. Army, the United States Chiefs of Staff accept in principle that portion of your proposal whereby the French Government puts at the entire disposal of the American command a French army corps of two infantry divisions, with corps-supporting and service units on the U.S. scale, for operations in the war against Japan. This acceptance in principle is with the understanding that the agreement on this matter with the French Government will include the following provisions:—

   a. This French corps will be, both during the period of hostilities and in the post-hostilities readjustment period until released by the United States, subject to the complete command and control of the United States command in the same manner as a U.S. army corps.

   b. Movement of the corps from France will be contingent upon the French corps having, in the opinion of the United States command, a combat efficiency based on United States standards.

   c. Assurance that adequate trained replacements will be provided by the French Government as necessary.

   d. Maximum use will be made of equipment provided under the North African and Metropolitan Rearmament Programs.

   e. The implementation of this agreement including matters such as accompanying supporting and service units, provisions for equipment, and the planning and timing for the movement and employment of the corps will be in accordance with plans and arrangements to be determined by the United States military authorities who will deal directly with the French military authorities.

2. Pressing requirements for operations in the Pacific during the coming months make certain that it will not be possible to move this corps from France for at least several months after the dates you suggest, and it appears unlikely that this corps will be committed to operations prior to the spring of 1946.

Enclosure "B"

TOP SECRET

3. The United States Chiefs of Staff will advise you further in this matter subsequent to the conclusion of a governmental agreement.

Enclosure "B"

TOP SECRET

C.C.S. 895/1   18 July 1945

COMBINED CHIEFS OF STAFF

PARTICIPATION OF TWO FRENCH COLONIAL INFANTRY DIVISIONS IN FAR EASTERN OPERATIONS

Memorandum by the British Chiefs of Staff

1. We have examined the proposals by the United States Chiefs of Staff for the employment of two French colonial infantry divisions in Far Eastern operations, as set out in C.C.S. 895.

2. In the light of the discussion at C.C.S. 194th Meeting held on 17 July 1945, we suggest it would be preferable for the two French divisions to be employed in due course in French Indo-China.

3. The question of under whose command this force would operate would, we suggest, be decided in the light of the situation at the time.

TOP SECRET

C.C.S. 895/2 19 July 1945

COMBINED CHIEFS OF STAFF

PARTICIPATION OF TWO FRENCH COLONIAL INFANTRY DIVISIONS IN FAR EASTERN OPERATIONS

Memorandum by the United States Chiefs of Staff

The United States Chiefs of Staff have considered the comments of the British Chiefs of Staff in C.C.S. 895/1 as to the employment of the two French divisions and recommend that the enclosed memorandum be forwarded by the Combined Chiefs of Staff to the Chief of the French Military Mission to the United States in lieu of Enclosure "B" to C.C.S. 895.

TOP SECRET

ENCLOSURE

DRAFT

MEMORANDUM FOR THE CHIEF OF THE FRENCH
MILITARY MISSION IN THE UNITED STATES

The Combined Chiefs of Staff accept in principle your offer of a French corps of two infantry divisions to serve in the Pacific war on the understanding that:—

a. Whether the corps will serve under U.S. or British command and the area in which it will operate will be determined later.

b. Final acceptance of the corps will involve an agreement with the government concerned on basic matters including command, combat efficiency, replacements, and logistical support.

c. Maximum use will be made of equipment provided under the North African and Metropolitan Rearmament Program.

d. The time of movement will be in accordance with the priority of the operations in which it is to be used. Pressing shipping and other requirements for operations in the Pacific make certain that the corps cannot be moved from France for at least several months. Whether used in the main effort or in the South China Sea area, it will not be possible to commit it to operations prior to the spring of 1946.

SECRET

C.C.S. 896

C.C.S. 896/1

INTERNATIONALIZATION OF THE DANUBE RIVER

By informal action on 24 July 1945 the Combined Chiefs of Staff approved the dispatch of the letter in Enclosure "A" to C.C.S. 896 to the Department of State and the Foreign Office.

SECRET

C.C.S. 896 21 July 1945

COMBINED CHIEFS OF STAFF

INTERNATIONALIZATION OF THE DANUBE RIVER

Memorandum by the United States Chiefs of Staff

1. The free efficient use of such rivers as the Rhine, the Weser, the Elbe, and the Danube in the supply of the armies of occupation and in maintaining the bare needs of the civilian populations under their control is essential in view of the limited means of transportation available to fulfill their task.

2. Adequate machinery in the formation of the Rhine Navigation Agency under the Allied Control Council in Germany, and the active measures presently under way to clear the river of obstruction, scheduled for completion in the United States and British zones by 1 September and in the French zone by 15 October, promise to meet the basic needs served by the Rhine. Russia has now no representative on that agency because it has no supply interest. However, politically, it might be expedient to consider favorably a request from Russia for such membership.

3. The Weser and the Elbe while important in the restoration of the German economy are not so vital to the fulfillment of immediate supply needs of the occupying armies.

4. The Danube, however, though largely clear of obstructions and open to use, cannot fulfill its proper role as a transportation artery in the supply of the armies of occupation and of the populations under their control, unless a Danube Navigation Agency similar to that set up for the Rhine is organized promptly. The need for action is stated in SCAF 471, 3 July 1945, (Enclosure "B").

5. There are certain embarrassments to the formation of such an agency. Local Russian commanders have no authority to act. The river lies both in Germany and Austria and its regulation therefore involves the Allied Control Councils of both countries. The request does not include French membership although politically they are necessarily eligible and no vital disadvantage should result from their inclusion. A Russian protest to representation of the

SECRET

British and the French on the ground that they have no frontage on the river may lead to their request for membership on the Rhine Navigation Agency.

6. The opportunity for the creation of a Danube Navigation Agency will probably never be more favorable than at this conference attended by the heads of state and their foreign ministers to whom the Chiefs of Staff may now so effectively appeal for assistance.

The United States Chiefs of Staff recommend that the Combined Chiefs of Staff forward the enclosed letter (Enclosure "A") to the Department of State and to the Foreign Office.

SECRET

ENCLOSURE "A"

DRAFT

LETTER TO DEPARTMENT OF STATE AND THE FOREIGN OFFICE

The Supreme Commander, Allied Expeditionary Force, on 3 July 1945, urged the consideration at *TERMINAL* of internationalization of the Danube. While recognizing the necessity to re-establish at the earliest practicable date the international character of the Danube waterway to meet the over-all question of navigation of the Danube and the rights of all states having interest, he emphasizes the immediate need of an interim Danube Navigation Agency composed of U.S., U.K., and U.S.S.R. representatives, set up in a manner similar to that followed in the creation of the present Rhine Navigation Agency to meet the current problems of supplying the armies of occupation in Austria and the populations dependent upon them.

There are certain difficulties to the creation of such an interim agency. Local Russian commanders lack authority to discuss questions involving navigation of the river within the Russian zone. The river flows through both Germany and Austria thus involving the two Allied Control Councils of Germany and Austria. These councils include the French. The Rhine Agency has no Russian membership. The SCAEF proposal does not include a French representative for the Danube Agency. It is evident that politically all four nations must be eligible to membership on such an agency. It is equally apparent that in the creation of a Danube Navigation Agency there should be but one national representative for each of the four allied nations mutually acceptable to the Allied Control Councils of both Germany and Austria.

It is believed that the opportunity presented by this conference to come to an agreement with the Russian Government creating an interim Danube Navigation Agency should be seized in order to meet the immediate military needs and responsibilities of our armies of occupation in their own supply and that of the civilian population under their control. It is accordingly recommended that the necessary action be taken to consummate this purpose at *TERMINAL*.

Enclosure "A"

SECRET

ENCLOSURE "B"

From: Supreme Commander, Allied Expeditionary Forces

To: Combined Chiefs of Staff

SCAF 471

3 July 1945

Prior to the official date of surrender of the German Armed Forces the officer in command of the Combined German-Hungarian Navies moved all craft on the Danube into the U.S. area. Affidavits have been secured to the effect that all craft were within our area prior to this time.

The Russians have contended that certain ships did not arrive until after the official date and have placed demands through the U.S. Third Army that certain of this shipping be returned to the Russian zone.

They have been advised that restitution of such property is a matter now under consideration by the governments.

However, we have offered to enter into local agreements for the use of this shipping to our mutual benefit. Russian commanders contacted had no authority to discuss questions which involved large-scale navigation of the river within the Russian zone.

The situation is further complicated in that much of the shipping now under our control formerly belonged to Yugoslavia, Czechoslovakia, and other nations. The over-all questions of navigation of the Danube and the rights of these various allied nations therefore requires clarification.

It is recommended that policy in this connection should be directed toward the re-establishment of the international character of the Danube waterway and that as an initial step there should be set up at the earliest possible date an interim Danube Navigation Agency similar to the Rhine Navigation Agency.

The initial membership would consist of U.S., U.K., and U.S.S.R. representation and to be expanded to include as soon as expedient representation from all other nations interested in Danube navigation with a view to the eventual re-establishment of a permanent International Danube Authority.

Enclosure "B"

SECRET

Immediate questions requiring early decision are the policy for return of Yugoslav and Czechoslovakian as well as Soviet shipping and establishment of agreements for mutual use of available equipment in order to restore navigation on the river as well as relative priorities.

The urgency of this international problem would suggest, if appropriate, its inclusion in the agenda for the forthcoming Big Three Conference.

CM-IN-2876   (4 Jul 45)

Enclosure "B"

SECRET

C.C.S. 896/1 24 July 1945

COMBINED CHIEFS OF STAFF

INTERNATIONALIZATION OF THE DANUBE RIVER

Memorandum by the British Chiefs of Staff

1. The British Chiefs of Staff have considered the memorandum by the United States Chiefs of Staff in which they recommend that the Combined Chiefs of Staff should forward a letter (Enclosure "A" to C.C.S. 896) to the Department of State and the Foreign Office.

2. The British Chiefs of Staff concur in the despatch of this letter as proposed.

CONFIDENTIAL

C.C.S. 897
C.C.S. 897/1

PROVISION OF PERSONNEL SHIPPING FOR THE REQUIREMENTS
OF ALLIED GOVERNMENTS

References:

CCS 199th Meeting, Item 3
CCS 900/3, paragraph 22

The Combined Chiefs of Staff in their 199th Meeting (23 July) approved the memorandum in Enclosure "A" to C.C.S. 897, subject to amendments agreed in discussion. The amended memorandum as approved and forwarded to the Combined Shipping Adjustment Board was subsequently circulated as C.C.S. 897/1.

CONFIDENTIAL

C.C.S. 897   21 July 1945

COMBINED CHIEFS OF STAFF

PROVISION OF PERSONNEL SHIPPING FOR THE REQUIREMENTS OF ALLIED GOVERNMENTS

Report by the Combined Military Transportation Committee
(On its own initiative, in consultation with
the Combined Shipping Adjustment Board)

THE PROBLEM

1. To ensure the efficient coordination of the demands for personnel shipping submitted by Allied governments, other than British and American military movements, and to provide a machinery for dealing with essential personnel movements other than those already approved.

FACTS BEARING ON THE PROBLEM

2. See Enclosure "B."

DISCUSSION

3. See Enclosure "C."

CONCLUSIONS

4. It is concluded that:

The following procedure will ensure the efficient coordination of all those Allied demands:—

    a. The current procedure for handling the United States and United Kingdom personnel shipping for military requirements will be continued. This procedure will permit on an operational basis the opportune use of such shipping on return voyages, or legs of such voyages, to move passengers of any of the Allied governments.

b. All requirements of the Allied governments for the movement of passengers, whether military or civilian, involving definite additional commitments of shipping, whether on a short- or long-term basis, should be submitted to the United Maritime Authority (UMA) in terms of the shipping space required. The Combined Shipping Adjustment Board should confer with the Combined Chiefs of Staff as to practicability of meeting such requirements. On military requests of the other Allied governments the decision will rest with the Combined Chiefs of Staff.

c. As regards the movement of civilians for which provision is not made under *a.* and *b.* above, the matter may be referred to the appropriate agencies of the United Kingdom and United States to decide whether passenger vessels should be withdrawn at the expense of the military effort. Ships, if so allocated, would operate under the control of the United Maritime Authority on the basis of the "Agreement on Principles" but would be retained in the common pool and assigned for particular voyage employment as might be decided from time to time.

RECOMMENDATIONS

5. *a.* That the foregoing conclusions be approved by the Combined Chiefs of Staff.

b. That the letter in Enclosure "A" be forwarded to the Combined Shipping Adjustment Board.

CONFIDENTIAL

ENCLOSURE "A"

DRAFT

MEMORANDUM FOR THE COMBINED SHIPPING ADJUSTMENT BOARD

1. The Combined Chiefs of Staff have been studying the problem of providing passenger carrying shipping to meet the urgent demands for the essential military operations in the prosecution of the war against Japan, and for the provision of such shipping of this type to meet other requirements as can be made available without adversely affecting military operations.

2. The available passenger space is insufficient to meet all the urgent requirements of the United Nations, and coordination of demands is, therefore, essential in order to determine priority and to secure shipping efficiency as well as to ensure the fullest consideration being given to all claimants.

3. The Combined Chiefs of Staff have, therefore, agreed that in accordance with the "Agreement on Principles," dated 5 August 1944, contained in the UMA report, October, 1944, the following procedure in respect of the submission of demands should be adopted by all the Allied nations:—

   a. The current procedure for handling the United States and United Kingdom personnel shipping for military requirements will be continued. This procedure will permit on an operational basis the opportune use of such shipping on return voyages, or legs of such voyages, to move passengers of any of the Allied governments.

   b. All requirements of the Allied governments for the movement of passengers, whether military or civilian, involving definite additional commitments of shipping, whether on a short- or long-term basis, should be submitted to the United Maritime Authority in terms of the shipping space required. The Combined Shipping Adjustment Board should confer with the Combined Chiefs of Staff as to practicability of meeting such requirements. On military requests of the other Allied governments the decision will rest with the Combined Chiefs of Staff.

   c. As regards the movement of civilians for which provision is not made under *a.* and *b.* above, the matter may be referred to the appropriate agencies of the United Kingdom and United States to decide whether passenger vessels should be withdrawn at the expense of the military effort. Ships,

Enclosure "A"

CONFIDENTIAL

if so allocated, would operate under the control of the United Maritime Authority on the basis of the "Agreement on Principles" but would be retained in the common pool and assigned for particular voyage employment as might be decided from time to time.

4. Vital demands for shipping should therefore be submitted to the United Maritime Authority for consideration.

5. The Combined Shipping Adjustment Board is requested to transmit the foregoing statement of policy to the United Maritime Executive Board in Washington and London.

Enclosure "A"

CONFIDENTIAL

ENCLOSURE "B"

FACTS BEARING ON THE PROBLEM

1. The tonnage of the Allied Nations under the control of the United Maritime Authority (UMA) is administered in accordance with the "Agreement of Principles," dated 5 August 1944. As regards cargo, this agreement and the procedures of the UMA provide fully for the requirements of the contracting governments to be taken into account in the disposition of available tonnage. This report deals only with the sea transport of personnel.

2. The "Agreement on Principles" contains the following provision in Article 7 (c):—

"... In order to meet the special case of military requirements those ships which have been taken up under agreements made by United States Government and/or United Kingdom Government with the other governments having authority for those ships for use as troopships, hospital ships, and for other purposes in the service of the armed forces, shall remain on charter as at present to the War Shipping Administration (WSA) and/or the Ministry of War Transport (MWT), as the case may be, under arrangements to be agreed between the governments severally concerned. (Any further ships required for such purposes shall be dealt with in a like manner.)

"The fact that these ships are assigned to military requirements shall not prejudice the right of the governments concerned to discuss with the central authority the measures to be taken to provide ... shipping for their essential requirements within the scope of paragraph 1 of the Agreement."

3. As regards personnel ships suitable for long sea voyage employment, estimates of military needs indicate the necessity for every suitable vessel being under the direct control (by time charter) of the WSA or the MWT. The estimates of available trooplift as submitted to the Combined Chiefs of Staff are based on the assumption that all the Allied passenger ships at present in service, or recovered as a result of liberation or capture, will be under the direct control of the Combined (Anglo-American) shipping authorities. On the other hand, it has always been recognized that there might be requests for the movement of military and civilian personnel sponsored by other Allied governments. The last paragraph of Article 7 (c) as above, expressly reserves "the right of the governments concerned to discuss with the central authority the measures to be taken to provide shipping for their essential requirements," and was

Enclosure "B"

CONFIDENTIAL

inserted at the request of the other Allies to provide for this expectation. These requirements might include:—

a. Movement of military personnel of the forces under the control of these governments, or repatriation of prisoners of war, or

b. Movement of civilian passengers of high priority (including essential civilian personnel in colonial territories), displaced persons, etc.

CONFIDENTIAL

ENCLOSURE "C"

DISCUSSION

1. The procedure of the UMA for the allocation of shipping to contracting governments depends upon the assumption that there are appropriate authorities to approve and sponsor the requirements of those governments for shipping space. As regards cargo, this is provided for by arrangements already in force. As regards other Allied personnel movements, however, there is at present no authority responsible for guiding the UMA on questions of priority, and in this class of shipping, owing to the acute shortage, it is clear that some guidance will be necessary.

2. The available personnel lift is not adequate to meet all the urgent requirements of the United Nations. Coordination of demands is, therefore, indispensable in order to determine priority and to secure shipping efficiency. In any case, it is presumed that the appropriate chiefs of staff or theater commander would be concerned with any substantial movement of personnel. Once it is determined that a particular government has personnel movements of an approved character to carry out, it would be in accordance with the procedure of the UMA to allocate ships or space to that government for the approved movements. It should be noted that under existing conditions the combined shipping authorities are bound to advise that such arrangements can not be made on any substantial scale at present without affecting existing plans for military moves.

CONFIDENTIAL

C.C.S. 897/1   24 July 1945

COMBINED CHIEFS OF STAFF

PROVISION OF PERSONNEL SHIPPING FOR THE REQUIREMENTS OF ALLIED GOVERNMENTS

Note by the Secretaries

The Combined Chiefs of Staff in their 199th Meeting amended and approved the memorandum in Enclosure "A" to C.C.S. 897. The memorandum as forwarded to the Combined Shipping Adjustment Board is enclosed for information.

                                                A. J. McFARLAND,
                                                A. T. CORNWALL-JONES,
                                                Combined Secretariat.

CONFIDENTIAL

ENCLOSURE

MEMORANDUM FOR THE COMBINED SHIPPING ADJUSTMENT BOARD

1. The Combined Chiefs of Staff have been studying the problem of providing passenger carrying shipping to meet the urgent demands for the essential military operations in the prosecution of the war against Japan, and for the provision of such shipping of this type to meet other requirements as can be made available without adversely affecting military operations.

2. The available passenger space is insufficient to meet all the urgent requirements of the United Nations, and coordination of demands is, therefore, essential in order to determine priority and to secure shipping efficiency as well as to ensure the fullest consideration being given to all claimants.

3. The Combined Chiefs of Staff have, therefore, agreed that in accordance with the "Agreement on Principles," dated 5 August 1944, contained in the UMA report, October, 1944, the following procedure in respect of the submission of demands should be adopted by all the Allied nations:—

a. The current procedure for handling the United States and United Kingdom personnel shipping for military requirements will be continued. This procedure will permit on an operational basis the opportune use of such shipping on return voyages, or legs of such voyages, to move passengers of any of the Allied governments.

b. All requirements of the Allied governments for the movement of passengers, whether military or civilian, involving definite additional commitments of shipping, whether on a short- or long-term basis, should be submitted to the United Maritime Authority in terms of the shipping space required. The Combined Shipping Adjustment Board should confer with the Combined Chiefs of Staff as to practicability of meeting such requirements. On military requests of the other Allied governments the decision will rest with the Combined Chiefs of Staff.

c. When a satisfactory arrangement in regard to the movement of civilians cannot be made under *a.* and *b.* above, the matter may be referred to the appropriate authorities of the United Kingdom and United States to decide whether passenger vessels should be withdrawn at the expense of the military effort. Ships, if so allocated, would operate under the control of the United Maritime Authority on the basis of the "Agreement on

CONFIDENTIAL

Principles" but would be retained in the common pool and assigned for particular voyage employment as might be decided from time to time.

4. Vital demands for shipping should, therefore, be submitted to the United Maritime Authority for consideration.

5. The Combined Shipping Adjustment Board is requested to transmit the foregoing policy to the United Maritime Executive Board in Washington and London.

TOP SECRET

C.C.S. 900/3

REPORT TO THE PRESIDENT AND PRIME MINISTER

References:

CCS 199th Meeting, Item 5
Plenary Meeting between the U. S. and Great Britain

C.C.S. 900 (21 July 1945) circulated a draft of the final report to the President and Prime Minister embodying only the conclusions of the Combined Chiefs of Staff so far agreed to.

The Combined Chiefs of Staff in their 199th Meeting (23 July) approved the draft report in C.C.S. 900 as amended in discussion.

In C.C.S. 900/1 (23 July) the United States Chiefs of Staff recommended a revised Appendix "C" for substitution in lieu of Appendix "C" to C.C.S. 900.

C.C.S. 900/2 (23 July) circulated for consideration of the President and Prime Minister a draft of the final report of the Combined Chiefs of Staff, which included the agreed conclusions in C.C.S. 900 and the revised Appendix "C" in C.C.S. 900/1. Appendix "A" thereto presented the views of the United States Chiefs of Staff and the British Chiefs of Staff respectively on matters on which agreement had not yet been reached.*

In their Plenary Meeting with the Combined Chiefs of Staff on 24 July the President and Prime Minister approved the final report as agreed during the discussion.

The final report, as approved by the President and Prime Minister, was subsequently circulated as C.C.S. 900/3.

---

* For convenience of reference, Appendix "A" to C.C.S. 900/2 is reproduced on page 266.

TOP SECRET

C.C.S. 900/3 24 July 1945

COMBINED CHIEFS OF STAFF

REPORT TO THE PRESIDENT AND PRIME MINISTER

Note by the Secretaries

The enclosed final report of the Combined Chiefs of Staff as approved by the President and Prime Minister is circulated for information.

A. J. McFARLAND,
A. T. CORNWALL-JONES,
Combined Secretariat.

TOP SECRET

ENCLOSURE

REPORT TO THE PRESIDENT AND PRIME MINISTER OF
THE AGREED SUMMARY OF CONCLUSIONS REACHED BY THE
COMBINED CHIEFS OF STAFF AT THE "TERMINAL" CONFERENCE

1. The agreed summary of conclusions reached at the *TERMINAL* Conference is submitted herewith.

I. *OVER-ALL OBJECTIVE*

2. In conjunction with other Allies to bring about at the earliest possible date the unconditional surrender of Japan.

II. *OVER-ALL STRATEGIC CONCEPT FOR THE PROSECUTION OF THE WAR*

3. In cooperation with other Allies to bring about at the earliest possible date the defeat of Japan by: lowering Japanese ability and will to resist by establishing sea and air blockades, conducting intensive air bombardment, and destroying Japanese air and naval strength; invading and seizing objectives in the Japanese home islands as the main effort; conducting such operations against objectives in other than the Japanese home islands as will contribute to the main effort; establishing absolute military control of Japan; and liberating Japanese-occupied territory if required.

4. In cooperation with other Allies to establish and maintain, as necessary, military control of Germany and Austria.

III. *BASIC UNDERTAKINGS AND POLICIES FOR THE PROSECUTION OF THE WAR*

5. The following basic undertakings are considered fundamental to the prosecution of the war:—

a. Maintain the security and war-making capacity of the Western Hemisphere and the British Commonwealth as necessary for the fulfillment of the strategic concept.

b. Support the war-making capacity of our forces in all areas, with first priority given to those forces in or designated for employment in combat areas in the war against Japan.

TOP SECRET

    c. Maintain vital overseas lines of communication.

  6. In order to attain the over-all objective, first priority in the provision of forces and resources of the United States and Great Britain, including re-orientation from the European Theater to the Pacific and Far East, will be given to meeting requirements of tasks necessary to the execution of the over-all strategic concept and to the basic undertakings fundamental to the prosecution of the war.

  The invasion of Japan and operations directly connected therewith are the supreme operations in the war against Japan; forces and resources will be allocated on the required scale to assure that invasion can be accomplished at the earliest practicable date. No other operations will be undertaken which hazard the success of, or delay, these main operations.

  7. The following additional tasks will be undertaken in order to assist in the execution of the over-all strategic concept:—

    a. Encourage Russian entry into the war against Japan. Provide such aid to her war-making capacity as may be necessary and practicable in connection therewith.

    b. Undertake such measures as may be necessary and practicable in order to aid the war effort of China as an effective ally against Japan.

    c. Provide assistance to such of the forces of liberated areas as can fulfill an active and effective role in the present war in accordance with the over-all strategic concept. Within the limits of our available resources assist co-belligerents to the extent they are able to employ this assistance in the present war. Having regard to the successful accomplishment of basic undertakings, to provide such supplies to the liberated areas as will effectively contribute to the capacity of the United Nations to prosecute the war against Japan.

    d. In cooperation with other Allies conduct operations, if required, to liberate enemy-occupied areas.

IV. *THE WAR AGAINST JAPAN*

Strategic Direction of the War

  8. We have discussed the strategic direction of the war against Japan and have agreed as follows:—

TOP SECRET

 a. The control of operational strategy in the Pacific Theater will remain in the hands of the United States Chiefs of Staff.

 b. The United States Chiefs of Staff will provide the British Chiefs of Staff with full and timely information as to their future plans and intentions.

 c. The United States Chiefs of Staff will consult the British Chiefs of Staff on matters of general strategy on the understanding that in the event of disagreement the final decision on the action to be taken will lie with the United States Chiefs of Staff.

 d. In the event the British Chiefs of Staff should decide that they cannot commit British troops in support of a decision made by the United States Chiefs of Staff as indicated in *c.* above, the British Chiefs of Staff will give to the United States Chiefs of Staff such advance notice of their decision as will permit them to make timely rearrangements.

 e. In the event the U.S.S.R. enters the war against Japan, the strategy to be pursued should be discussed between the parties concerned.

Operations in the Pacific

9. We have taken note of the plans and operations proposed by the United States Chiefs of Staff in Appendix "A."

10. We have considered the scope and nature of British participation in operations in the Pacific area. Our conclusions are as follows:—

 a. The British Pacific Fleet will participate as at present planned.

 b. A British very long range bomber force of 10 squadrons, increasing to 20 squadrons when more airfields become available, will participate. There is little prospect that airfield space for more than 10 squadrons of this force will become available before 1 December 1945 at the earliest.

 c. We have agreed in principle that a Commonwealth land force and, if possible, a small tactical air force, should take part in the final phase of the war against Japan, subject to the satisfactory resolution of operational and other problems. In addition, some units of the British East Indies Fleet may also take part.

11. In connection with paragraph 10 *c.* above, we have agreed that the appropriate British commanders and staff should visit Admiral Nimitz and General MacArthur and draw up with them a plan for submission to the Combined Chiefs of Staff.

TOP SECRET

Operations in Southeast Asia Command

12. We have discussed the instructions that should be issued to the Supreme Allied Commander, Southeast Asia, and have agreed upon the terms of the directive in Appendix "B."

Reallocation of Areas and Command in the Southwest Pacific and Southeast Asia Areas

13. We have agreed in principle that that part of the Southwest Pacific Area lying south of the boundary described in Appendix "C" should pass from United States to British command as soon as possible. The British Chiefs of Staff have undertaken to obtain the agreement of the Australian, New Zealand, and Dutch Governments to these proposals and to investigate and report the earliest practicable date on which the transfer can be effected.

14. We consider it desirable that initially Admiral Mountbatten control operations undertaken in southern Indo-China since these are more closely related to those of Southeast Asia Command than to those of the China Theater. We are agreed that the best arrangement would be to include that portion of Indo-China lying south of latitude 16° north in Southeast Asia Command. This arrangement would continue General Wedemeyer's control of that part of Indo-China which covers the flank of projected Chinese operations in China, and would enable Admiral Mountbatten to prepare the ground in the southern half of Indo-China where any initial operations by him would develop.

We recommend that an approach to Generalissimo Chiang Kai-shek be made by our two governments to secure his agreement to this arrangement.

At a later date it may prove to be desirable to place all or part of the remainder of Indo-China within the sphere of operations of the Southeast Asia Command.

French and Dutch Participation in the War

15. We have considered the arrangements which can be made for French and Dutch participation in the war against Japan and our conclusions are as follows:—

a. While it is at present impracticable due chiefly to logistical difficulties for French or Netherlands armed forces to take a major part in the immediate operations in the Far East, the provision of such assistance which may be synchronized with operations will be taken into account. The use of such forces will depend solely on military considerations. French or Netherlands forces so accepted must operate under the complete control of the commander in chief concerned.

b. The French/Netherlands representatives will be given timely information of our intentions in respect of any operations that will directly affect French/Netherlands territories or armed forces in the Far East.

16. We have considered an offer by the French of a French corps of two infantry divisions to serve in the Pacific war and have agreed on the following reply:—

"*a.* Whether the corps will serve under U.S. or British command and the area in which it will operate will be determined later.

"*b.* Final acceptance of the corps will involve an agreement with the government concerned on basic matters including command, combat efficiency, replacements, and logistical support.

"*c.* Maximum use will be made of equipment provided under the North African and Metropolitan Rearmament Programs.

"*d.* The time of movement will be in accordance with the priority of the operations in which it is to be used. Pressing shipping and other requirements for operations in the Pacific make certain that the corps cannot be moved from France for at least several months. Whether used in the main effort or in the South China Sea area, it will not be possible to commit it to operations prior to the spring of 1946."

Portuguese Participation in the War

17. We have examined a report by an Anglo-American Military Mission which discussed with the Portuguese military authorities Portuguese proposals for participation in such operations as may eventually be conducted to expel the Japanese from Portuguese Timor. We have informed the State Department and the Foreign Office of our views, which are set out in Appendix "D."

Information for the Russians Concerning the Japanese War

18. We have discussed the policy to be followed by the British and the United States Chiefs of Staff in passing to the Russians information and intelligence concerning the Japanese war and have agreed as follows:—

a. The United States and British Chiefs of Staff will pass to the Russians such operational information and intelligence regarding the theaters in which they are respectively responsible as either may wish and without bargaining.

b. The United States and British Chiefs of Staff will consult together before passing to the Russians any information and intelligence other than operational. Neither party will pass to the Russians information or intelligence derived wholly or in part from the other party's sources without their consent.

Planning Date for the End of Organized Resistance by Japan

19. We recommend that for the purpose of planning production and the allocation of manpower, the planning date for the end of organized resistance by Japan be 15 November 1946 and that this date be adjusted periodically to conform to the course of the war.

V. MISCELLANEOUS

Personnel Shipping

20. We have considered the employment of certain captured enemy ocean-going passenger shipping and have agreed that the total lift of the *EUROPA, CARIBIA, VULCANIA, PATRIA, POTSDAM, PRETORIA,* and *MILWAUKEE* should be allocated for United States employment up to 31 December 1945. We have taken note that the United States Chiefs of Staff will allocate to the United Kingdom a lift of 16,000 during the remainder of 1945 for the movement of Canadians.

21. We have directed the completion by 15 September 1945 of a study of the combined requirements and combined resources, including captured enemy trooplift, for the first half of 1946.

Personnel Shipping for the Requirements of Allied Governments

22. We have considered the best means of insuring the efficient coordination of the demands for personnel shipping submitted by Allied governments, other than British and American military movements, and of providing a machinery for dealing with essential personnel movements other than those already

TOP SECRET

approved. We have forwarded to the Combined Shipping Adjustment Board the memorandum contained in Appendix "E."

Cargo Shipping

23. Present estimates of the requirements for cargo shipping indicate the position to be sufficiently manageable to provide for the maximum effort in the prosecution of the war against Japan, for the maintenance of the war-making capacity of the British Commonwealth of Nations and the Western Hemisphere in so far as it is connected with the prosecution of the war against Japan, for an additional amount for the reconstruction and rehabilitation of the United Kingdom, for supplies to liberated areas, and for essential programs of the Western Hemisphere.

Should substantial conflict arise, the shipping situation will be a matter for examination by the two governments at the time and in the light of changed conditions.

APPENDIX "A"

PLANS AND OPERATIONS IN THE PACIFIC
(See paragraph 9 of the Report)

1. In conformity with the over-all objective to bring about the unconditional surrender of Japan at the earliest possible date, the United States Chiefs of Staff have adopted the following concept of operations for the main effort in the Pacific:—

   a. From bases in Okinawa, Iwo Jima, Marianas, and the Philippines to intensify the blockade and air bombardment of Japan in order to create a situation favorable to:

   b. An assault on Kyushu for the purpose of further reducing Japanese capabilities by containing and destroying major enemy forces and further intensifying the blockade and air bombardment in order to establish a tactical condition favorable to:

   c. The decisive invasion of Honshu.

2. We have curtailed our projected expansion in the Ryukyus by deferring indefinitely the seizure of Miyako Jima and Kikai Jima. Using the resources originally provided for Miyako and Kikai, we have accelerated the development of Okinawa. By doing this, a greater weight of effort will more promptly be brought to bear against Japan and the risk of becoming involved in operations which might delay the seizure of Kyushu is avoided.

3. In furtherance of the accomplishment of the over-all objectives, we have directed:—

   a. The invasion of Kyushu.

   b. The continuation of operations for securing and maintaining control of sea communications to and in the western Pacific as are required for the accomplishment of the over-all objective.

   c. The defeat of the remaining Japanese in the Philippines by such operations as can be executed without prejudice to the over-all objective.

   d. The seizure of Balikpapan. (This operation is now approaching successful completion.)

   e. The continuance of strategic air operations to support the accomplishment of the over-all objective.

TOP SECRET

4. Planning and preparation for the campaign in Japan subsequent to the invasion of Kyushu are continuing on the basis of meeting the target date for the invasion of Honshu. This planning is premised on the belief that defeat of the enemy's armed forces in the Japanese homeland is a prerequisite to unconditional surrender, and that such a defeat will establish the optimum prospect of capitulation by Japanese forces outside the main Japanese islands. We recognize the possibility also that our success in the main islands may not obviate the necessity of defeating Japanese forces elsewhere; decision as to steps to be taken in this eventuality must await further developments.

5. We are keeping under continuing review the possibility of capitalizing at small cost upon Japanese military deterioration and withdrawals in the China Theater, without delaying the supreme operations.

6. We have directed the preparation of plans for the following:—

a. Keeping open a sea route to Russian Pacific ports.

b. Operations to effect an entry into Japan proper for occupational purposes in order to take immediate advantage of favorable circumstances such as a sudden enemy collapse or surrender.

Appendix "A"

TOP SECRET

APPENDIX "B"

DIRECTIVE TO THE SUPREME ALLIED COMMANDER, SOUTHEAST ASIA
(See paragraph 12 of the Report)

The following directive has been approved by the Combined Chiefs of Staff on the understanding that the British Chiefs of Staff will obtain the agreement of the Australian, New Zealand, and Dutch Governments to the proposed reallocation of areas and command set-up in Southwest Pacific and Southeast Asia.

1. Your primary task is the opening of the Straits of Malacca at the earliest possible moment. It is also intended that British Commonwealth land forces should take part in the main operations against Japan which have been agreed as the supreme operations in the war; and that operations should continue in the Outer Zone to the extent that forces and resources permit.

2. The eastern boundary of your command will be extended to include Borneo, Java, and the Celebes.

Full details of this extension are contained in the Annex hereto.

3. Further information will be sent to you regarding Indo-China.

4. It is desirable that you assume command of the additional areas as soon as practicable after 15 August 1945. You will report to the Combined Chiefs of Staff the date on which you expect to be in a position to undertake this additional responsibility.

5. From that date, such Dominion and Dutch forces as may be operating in your new area will come under your command. They will, however, continue to be based on Australia.

6. The area to the east of your new boundary will be an Australian command under the British Chiefs of Staff.

7. It has been agreed in principle that a British Commonwealth land force of from three to five divisions, and, if possible, a small tactical air force, should take part in the main operations against Japan in the spring of 1946. Units

TOP SECRET

of the British East Indies Fleet may also take part. Certain important factors relating to this are still under examination.

8. You will be required to provide a proportion of this force together with the assault lift for two divisions. The exact composition of this force and its role and the mounting and supporting arrangements will be discussed between Admiral Nimitz, General MacArthur, and the British force commanders, and will receive final approval by the Combined Chiefs of Staff.

9. The requirements for the force taking part in the main operations against Japan must have priority over all the other tasks indicated below.

10. Subject to the fulfillment of the higher priority commitments given above, you will, within the limits of available resources, carry out operations designed to:—

    a. Complete the liberation of Malaya.

    b. Maintain pressure on the Japanese across the Burma-Siam frontier.

    c. Capture the key areas of Siam.

    d. Establish bridgeheads in Java and/or Sumatra to enable the subsequent clearance of these areas to be undertaken in due course.

11. You will submit a program of operations to the British Chiefs of Staff as soon as you are in a position to do so.

12. You will develop Singapore and such other bases as you may require to the extent necessary for operations against the Japanese.

Appendix "B"

TOP SECRET

ANNEX TO APPENDIX "B"

EASTERN BOUNDARY OF SOUTHEAST ASIA COMMAND
(See paragraph 2 of Appendix "B")

Beginning on the coast of Indo-China at 16° north; thence to intersect at 7°40′ north latitude 116° east longitude, the boundary between the Commonwealth of the Philippine Islands and British North Borneo; thence along the 1939 boundary line of the Philippines to latitude 05° north longitude 127° east; thence southwestward to 02° south 123° east; thence southeastward to 08° south 125° east; thence southwestward to 18° south 110° east.

Annex to Appendix "B"

TOP SECRET

APPENDIX "C"

BOUNDARY BETWEEN THE BRITISH AND U.S. AREAS OF COMMAND
IN THE SOUTHWEST PACIFIC
(See paragraph 13 of the Report)

Beginning on the coast of Indo-China at 16° north; thence to intersect at 7°40′ north latitude 116° east longitude, the boundary between the Commonwealth of the Philippine Islands and British North Borneo; thence along the 1939 boundary line of the Philippines to latitude 05° north longitude 127° east; thence east to 05° north 130° east; thence south to the equator; thence east to 140° east; thence generally southeast to 02°20′ south 146° east; thence east to 02°20′ south 159° east; thence south.

Appendix "C"

TOP SECRET

APPENDIX "D"
(See paragraph 17 of the Report)

The Combined Chiefs of Staff have communicated to the Department of State and the Foreign Office the following views on Portuguese participation in the war against Japan:—

a. The Combined Chiefs of Staff are agreed on the acceptance of Portuguese assistance in such operations as may be conducted eventually to expel the Japanese from Portuguese Timor. While they have made no agreement with the Portuguese military authorities as to the direct use of Portuguese forces, they have recognized the possibility of such use and agreed that plans will be worked out as a result of the studies conducted in staff conversations in Lisbon.

b. As between the two military forces offered by Portugal (a regimental combat team of 4,000 or a battalion combat team of 2,200, both including 400 native troops), the larger force is likely to be the more acceptable. Steps are being taken to allocate a suitable training area.

c. The air component offered by Portugal should under no circumstances be included in the acceptance of the Portuguese offer in view of the small number of planes available and the state of the training of the pilots, mechanics, and radio specialists.

d. There is no objection from the military viewpoint to Portugal receiving munitions when they can be spared but negotiation as to the basis for transfer is an action to be taken on a governmental level.

e. The Combined Chiefs of Staff in accepting Portuguese participation do not intend to enter into a commitment for the retaking of Portuguese Timor. Neither is acceptance to be construed as a commitment to use Portuguese troops in any other area.

f. Military operations against Portuguese Timor must for the present await the completion of operations against higher priority Japanese-held objectives. The Combined Chiefs of Staff will notify the Portuguese military authorities of impending operations against Portuguese Timor in time for them to prepare their troops for participation therein. Details as to the assembly, shipment, training, and equipping of the Portuguese force will be decided by the Combined Chiefs of Staff at the appropriate time.

They have informed the State Department and the Foreign Office that they have no objection to the disclosure of any of the above information to the

Appendix "D"

TOP SECRET

Portuguese if the Department of State or Foreign Office deem it necessary in diplomatic conversations. The participation of Portuguese forces in the liberation of Portuguese Timor is considered of little military importance in the war against Japan.

Appendix "D"

APPENDIX "E"

MEMORANDUM FOR THE COMBINED SHIPPING ADJUSTMENT BOARD
(See paragraph 22 of the Report)

1. The Combined Chiefs of Staff have been studying the problem of providing passenger carrying shipping to meet the urgent demands for the essential military operations in the prosecution of the war against Japan, and for the provision of such shipping of this type to meet other requirements as can be made available without adversely affecting military operations.

2. The available passenger space is insufficient to meet all the urgent requirements of the United Nations, and coordination of demands is, therefore, essential in order to determine priority and to secure shipping efficiency as well as to ensure the fullest consideration being given to all claimants.

3. The Combined Chiefs of Staff have, therefore, agreed that in accordance with the "Agreement on Principles," dated 5 August 1944, contained in the United Maritime Authority's report, October, 1944, the following procedure in respect of the submission of demands should be adopted by all the Allied nations:—

a. The current procedure for handling the United States and United Kingdom personnel shipping for military requirements will be continued. This procedure will permit on an operational basis the opportune use of such shipping on return voyages, or legs of such voyages, to move passengers of any of the Allied governments.

b. All requirements of the Allied governments for the movement of passengers, whether military of civilian, involving definite additional commitments of shipping, whether on a short- or long-term basis, should be submitted to the United Maritime Authority in terms of the shipping space required. The Combined Shipping Adjustment Board should confer with the Combined Chiefs of Staff as to practicability of meeting such requirements. On military requests of the other Allied governments the decision will rest with the Combined Chiefs of Staff.

c. When a satisfactory arrangement in regard to the movement of civilians cannot be made under *a.* and *b.* above, the matter may be referred to the appropriate authorities of the United Kingdom and United States, to decide whether passenger vessels should be withdrawn at the expense of the military effort. Ships, if so allocated, would operate under the control

CONFIDENTIAL

of the United Maritime Authority on the basis of the "Agreement on Principles" but would be retained in the common pool and assigned for particular voyage employment as might be decided from time to time.

4. Vital demands for shipping should, therefore, be submitted to the United Maritime Authority for consideration.

5. The Combined Shipping Adjustment Board is requested to transmit the foregoing policy to the United Maritime Executive Board in Washington and London.

Appendix "E"

TOP SECRET

APPENDIX "A" TO C.C.S. 900/2

III. BASIC UNDERTAKINGS AND POLICIES FOR THE PROSECUTION OF THE WAR

U.S. Proposals	British Proposals
4. The following basic undertakings are considered fundamental to the prosecution of the war:—	
a. Maintain the security of the Western Hemisphere and the British Commonwealth.	Delete a. and b. and substitute:—
b. Maintain the war-making capacity of the United States and the British Commonwealth in so far as it is connected with the prosecution of the war against Japan.	a. Maintain the security and war-making capacity of the Western Hemisphere and the British Commonwealth as necessary for the fulfillment of the strategic concept.
c. Support the war-making capacity of our forces in all areas, with first priority given to those forces in or designated for employment in combat areas in the war against Japan.	Delete c. and substitute the following as b:—
	b. Support the war-making capacity of our forces in all areas, with first priority given to those forces in or destined for combat areas.
d. Maintain vital overseas lines of communication.	
5. In order to attain the over-all objective, first priority in the provision of forces and resources of the United States and Great Britain, including reorientation from the European Theater to the Pacific and Far East, will be given to meeting requirements of tasks necessary to the execution of the overall strategic concept and to the basic undertakings fundamental to the prosecution of the war.	

Appendix "A" to C.C.S. 900/2

TOP SECRET

| *U.S. Proposals* | *British Proposals* |

The invasion of Japan and operations directly connected therewith are the supreme operations in the war against Japan; forces and resources will be allocated on the required scale to assure that invasion can be accomplished at the earliest practicable date. No other operations will be undertaken which hazard the success of, or delay, these main operations.

6. The following additional tasks will be undertaken in order to assist in the execution of the over-all strategic concept:—

a. Encourage Russian entry into the war against Japan. Provide such aid to her war-making capacity as may be necessary and practicable in connection therewith.

b. Undertake such measures as may be necessary and practicable in order to aid the war effort of China as an effective ally against Japan.

c. Provide assistance to such of the forces of liberated areas as can fulfill an active and effective role in the present war. Within the limits of our available resources assist co-belligerents to the extent they are able to employ this assistance in the present war. Having regard to the successful accomplishment of basic undertakings, to provide such supplies to the liberated areas as will effectively contribute to the capacity of the United Nations to prosecute the war against Japan.

    Add at the end of the first sentence: "or are required to maintain world order in the interests of the war effort."

    Delete the last sentence of 6 *c.* because this is dealt with in paragraph 7 below.

Appendix "A" to C.C.S. 900/2

TOP SECRET

U.S. Proposals	British Proposals
d. In cooperation with other Allies conduct operations, if required, to liberate enemy-occupied areas.	
7. The inclusion under Basic Undertakings of terms concerning a specific resource such as cargo shipping is undesirable.	7. Present estimates of the requirements for cargo shipping indicate the position to be sufficiently manageable to provide for the maximum effort in the prosecution of the war against Japan, for the maintenance of the war-making capacity of the British Commonwealth of Nations and the Western Hemisphere in so far as it is connected with the prosecution of the war against Japan, for an additional amount for the reconstruction and rehabilitation of the United Kingdom, for supplies to liberated areas and for essential programmes of the Western Hemisphere.
It is agreeable, however, to include in the text of the report the following paragraph:—	
CARGO SHIPPING	
Present estimates of the requirements for cargo shipping indicate the position to be sufficiently manageable to provide for the maximum effort in the prosecution of the war against Japan, for the maintenance of the war-making capacity of the British Commonwealth of Nations and the Western Hemisphere, in so far as it is connected with the prosecution of the war against Japan, and for an additional amount for civilian requirements. Should a substantial conflict arise, the shipping situation will be a matter for examination by the two governments at the time and in the light of changed conditions.	Should substantial conflict arise, the shipping situation will be a matter for examination by the two governments at the time and in the light of changed conditions.

Appendix "A" to C.C.S. 900/2

TERMINAL CONFERENCE

MINUTES OF MEETINGS

OF THE

COMBINED CHIEFS OF STAFF

TOP SECRET

COMBINED CHIEFS OF STAFF

C.C.S. 193d Meeting

TERMINAL CONFERENCE

Minutes of Meeting Held in the Conference Room
at 25 Ringstrasse, Babelsberg, Germany,
on Monday, 16 July 1945, at 1430.

PRESENT

United States

Fleet Admiral W. D. Leahy, USN
General of the Army
  G. C. Marshall, USA
Fleet Admiral E. J. King, USN
General of the Army
  H. H. Arnold, USA

British

Field Marshal Sir Alan F. Brooke
Marshal of the Royal Air Force
  Sir Charles F. A. Portal
Admiral of the Fleet
  Sir Andrew B. Cunningham

ALSO PRESENT

General B. B. Somervell, USA
Lt. Gen. J. E. Hull, USA
Vice Adm. C. M. Cooke, Jr., USN
Maj. Gen. L. Norstad, USA
Captain A. S. McDill, USN
Captain H. R. Oster, USN

Field Marshal Sir H. M. Wilson
General Sir Hastings L. Ismay
Lt. Gen. Sir Gordon N. Macready
Maj. Gen. R. E. Laycock
Maj. Gen. L. C. Hollis

SECRETARIAT

Brig. Gen. A. J. McFarland, USA
Brigadier A. T. Cornwall-Jones
Captain C. J. Moore, USN
Lt. Col. T. Haddon

TOP SECRET

1. *PROGRAM AND PROCEDURE FOR THE CONFERENCE*
   (C.C.S. 880/9 and 880/10)

   THE COMBINED CHIEFS OF STAFF:—

   Approved C.C.S. 880/10.

2. *ESTIMATE OF THE ENEMY SITUATION*
   (C.C.S. 643/3)

   SIR ALAN BROOKE referred to the last sentence on page 10 of the paper* where the survival of the institution of the Emperor was mentioned. He asked whether the United States Chiefs of Staff had given any thought to the question of the interpretation of the term "unconditional surrender." From the military point of view it seemed to the British Chiefs of Staff that there might be some advantage in trying to explain this term to the Japanese in a manner which would ensure that the war was not unduly prolonged in outlying areas. If, for instance, an interpretation could be found and communicated to the Japanese which did not involve the dissolution of the Imperial institution, the Emperor would be in a position to order the cease-fire in outlying areas whereas, if the dynasty were destroyed, the outlying garrisons might continue to fight for many months or years. If an interpretation on these lines could be found an opportune moment to make it clear to the Japanese might be shortly after a Russian entry into the war.

   THE UNITED STATES CHIEFS OF STAFF explained that considerable thought had been given to this subject on the political level. One suggestion was that some form of agreed ultimatum might be issued at the correct psychological moment, for example, on Russian entry into the war, the idea being to explain what the term "unconditional surrender" did not mean rather than what it did mean.

   ADMIRAL LEAHY suggested that as the matter was clearly a political one primarily, it would be very useful if the Prime Minister put forward to the President his views and suggestions as to how the term "unconditional surrender" might be explained to the Japanese.

   THE COMBINED CHIEFS OF STAFF:—

   a. Took note of the estimate of the enemy situation in C.C.S. 643/3.

   b. Invited the British Chiefs of Staff to consider the possibility of asking the Prime Minister to raise with the President the matter of unconditional surrender of Japan.

---

* Page 19, paragraph 2.

TOP SECRET

3. *PROGRESS REPORTS ON OPERATIONS IN THE PACIFIC AND SOUTHEAST ASIA COMMAND*
(C.C.S. 892 and 893)

SIR ALAN BROOKE said that the only area not dealt with in these two reports was the China Theater. The British Chiefs of Staff would welcome a report of progress in this theater.

GENERAL MARSHALL described certain features of the operations in the China Theater, particularly as to the effectiveness of Chinese troops when properly equipped. He further stated that a report of operations in the China Theater would be prepared and presented to the Combined Chiefs of Staff.

THE COMBINED CHIEFS OF STAFF:—

Took note:—

a. Of the progress report on operations in the Pacific and Southeast Asia Command in C.C.S. 892 and C.C.S. 893.

b. That the United States Chiefs of Staff would submit later a report on operations in China.

4. *DEVELOPMENT OF OPERATIONS IN THE PACIFIC*
(C.C.S. 880/4)

THE COMBINED CHIEFS OF STAFF:—

Took note of the memorandum on the development of operations in the Pacific in C.C.S. 880/4.

5. *REPORT ON ARMY AIR OPERATIONS IN THE WAR AGAINST JAPAN*
(C.C.S. 894)

GENERAL ARNOLD commented in detail on certain aspects of the report.

THE COMBINED CHIEFS OF STAFF:—

Took note of the report on Army air operations in the war against Japan in C.C.S. 894, and of General Arnold's explanatory remarks.

TOP SECRET

COMBINED CHIEFS OF STAFF

C.C.S. 194th Meeting

TERMINAL CONFERENCE

MINUTES OF MEETING HELD IN THE CONFERENCE ROOM AT 25 RINGSTRASSE, BABELSBERG, GERMANY, ON TUESDAY, 17 JULY 1945, AT 1430.

PRESENT

United States

General of the Army
  G. C. Marshall, USA
Fleet Admiral E. J. King, USN
General of the Army
  H. H. Arnold, USA

British

Field Marshal Sir Alan F. Brooke
Marshal of the Royal Air Force
  Sir Charles F. A. Portal
Admiral of the Fleet
  Sir Andrew B. Cunningham

ALSO PRESENT

General B. B. Somervell, USA
Lt. Gen. J. E. Hull, USA
Vice Adm. C. M. Cooke, Jr., USN
Maj. Gen. L. Norstad, USA
Captain A. S. McDill, USN
Captain H. R. Oster, USN

Field Marshal Sir H. M. Wilson
General Sir Hastings L. Ismay
Lt. Gen. Sir Gordon N. Macready
Maj. Gen. R. E. Laycock
Maj. Gen. L. C. Hollis

SECRETARIAT

Brig. Gen. A. J. McFarland, USA
Brigadier A. T. Cornwall-Jones
Captain C. J. Moore, USN
Lt. Col. T. Haddon

TOP SECRET

1. *APPROVAL OF THE MINUTES OF THE C.C.S. 193D MEETING*

THE COMBINED CHIEFS OF STAFF:—

Approved the conclusions of the 193d Meeting and approved the detailed report of the meeting subject to any later minor amendments.

2. *BRITISH PARTICIPATION IN THE WAR AGAINST JAPAN*
(C.C.S. 889 and 889/1)

SIR ALAN BROOKE referred to a memorandum by the United States Chiefs of Staff containing their views on the proposals of the British Chiefs of Staff concerning British participation in the war against Japan. He said that the British Chiefs of Staff were very pleased to see that the United States Chiefs of Staff agreed in principle to the participation in the final phase of the war against Japan of a British Commonwealth land force, subject to the resolution of certain operational problems with the Commander in Chief, U.S. Army Forces, Pacific, and Commander in Chief, U.S. Pacific Fleet, and to the clarification of certain factors with which he then proposed to deal.

Considering each of the subparagraphs of paragraph 2 of C.C.S. 889/1, *SIR ALAN BROOKE* made the following points:—

a. The land forces which were being offered would not be involved in operations in Southeast Asia prior to *CORONET*. The force envisaged contained one Australian division which was now completing operation in Borneo; one New Zealand division which was reforming in Italy; a British division which had been already withdrawn from the fighting in Southeast Asia, and an Indian division probably from Italy. This Indian division had operated in conjunction with Allied troops in Italy for some time and had, on one occasion, been under command of General Clark. It was considered a first-class division, and he thought that the difficulties incident to its employment and due to language complications would not prove insurmountable. The division had already been acclimatized.

SIR ALAN BROOKE, continuing, said these forces might be used as three divisions in the initial assault with a follow-up of two divisions a good deal later on. This delay was necessitated by shipping limitations. The British Chiefs of Staff would very much like to participate in the assault as opposed to taking part only in the follow-up. The administrative factors could perhaps be discussed with General MacArthur.

b. This question had been dealt with in *a.* above and Sir Alan Brooke hoped that it would be found possible to overcome any difficulties in this connection.

c. When the question of British participation in the final assault had first been considered, the inclusion of Canadian forces had been envisaged. It had since been learned, however, that a Canadian division had been accepted by the United States Chiefs of Staff, to be equipped with American equipment, with a view to operating under American command. Although the British Chiefs of Staff would like to include a Canadian element in the Empire forces, it was not desired to upset these plans and he therefore suggested that the matter might be left open to discussion. The Canadian division might be used in a follow-up role. Detailed discussions on this matter could be carried out with General MacArthur.

d. It was hoped that answers would be received from the Dominions concerned in the near future.

e. It was entirely agreed that the inclusion of a British force in the final phase of the war against Japan would lead to complicated logistical problems. These problems could be considered in detail with commanders on the spot.

f. The question of where the forces should be concentrated prior to the operation would have to be carefully considered. The Australian division was at present well placed and it should be found possible to concentrate one or two additional divisions in a suitable area. This also could be discussed in detail with the force commanders.

g. It had always been the intention of the British Chiefs of Staff to provide, from British resources, sufficient assault lift for two divisions. The provision of certain close-support craft, was, however, likely to be most difficult owing to the distances involved.

h. SIR CHARLES PORTAL said that while it was realized that there would be adequate United States tactical air forces available, he very much hoped that the United States Chiefs of Staff would consider the inclusion of a small tactical air force consisting of about 15 squadrons (about 250 aircraft in all). He made this request as he felt that the Commonwealth forces would like to have supporting them some of their own tactical reconnaissance and fighter-bomber units. The forces he had in mind should not cause complications as they would be Mustangs similar to those operated by United States forces.

GENERAL ARNOLD undertook to investigate the possibility of the inclusion of a force as indicated by Sir Charles Portal, and asked to be supplied with the necessary details to carry out this investigation.

i. SIR ALAN BROOKE said that the effect of these proposals upon continued operations in the Southeast Asia Command would be to limit the capacity to undertake amphibious operations, as the proposals would necessitate the use of landing craft. It was proposed to submit to the Combined Chiefs of Staff a directive to the Supreme Commander, Southeast Asia, for land operations across the Thailand-Burmese frontier and small amphibious operations to Sumatra and Java with the object of establishing small bridgeheads on those islands which could be developed later as the opportunity arose. The provision of shipping and assault craft was the limiting factor.

SIR ALAN BROOKE explained further that in approaching this problem it had been the aim of the British Chiefs of Staff to produce the maximum effort against Japan, continuing meanwhile such operations in Southeast Asia Command as could be conducted without detracting from the effort against Japan. The limiting factors affecting the British proposals were the provision of shipping and administrative troops. Hence three alternative suggestions had been included in C.C.S. 889.

As the United States Chiefs of Staff were prepared to accept the proposals in principle, it was suggested that a force commander and his staff (of the nature of a corps commander and staff) should be appointed and sent out to discuss details with General MacArthur and to draw up concrete proposals for submission to the Combined Chiefs of Staff.

GENERAL MARSHALL said that the dispatch of a corps commander and staff to the Pacific was acceptable to the United States Chiefs of Staff and General MacArthur would be informed accordingly.

GENERAL MARSHALL then read extracts from a dispatch from General MacArthur on the subject of the participation of a Commonwealth force in the final phase of the war against Japan.* He undertook to make available to the British Chiefs of Staff suitable extracts from the dispatch.

GENERAL HULL said that tentative proposals had been made by the Australian Government to the United States Chiefs of Staff for the inclusion

---

* C.C.S. 889/2

of an Australian force in the operation against Japan and for the inclusion of a small token force in Southeast Asia Command under Admiral Mountbatten. The proposal had merely expressed the desire of the Australian Government to participate in these operations and no details had as yet been discussed.

ADMIRAL KING said that there were two factors concerning the employment of Australian forces with which he presumed the British Chiefs of Staff were familiar. The first was that the Australian military establishment was being reduced to approximately three divisions. The second was the question of the possible return to New Zealand of the New Zealand division concerned.

SIR ALAN BROOKE said that while it had at one time been suggested that the New Zealand division should be returned to New Zealand, it had subsequently been agreed that the division consisting of two brigades would be available for operations in Southeast Asia Command. Arrangements had been made to send replacements to Italy and it would therefore not be necessary for the New Zealand division to return to New Zealand for rehabilitation. The views of the New Zealand Government on the present proposal had, however, not yet been received.

SIR ALAN BROOKE said that the British Chiefs of Staff fully recognized that the participation of British troops in the final phase of the war against Japan would lead to certain complications and he expressed sincere gratitude on behalf of the British Chiefs of Staff for the way in which the proposal had been received by the United States Chiefs of Staff.

GENERAL MARSHALL said that the United States Chiefs of Staff welcomed the proposals and would be pleased to make room for the employment of British forces, within the limitations of shipping and logistic support.

THE COMBINED CHIEFS OF STAFF:—

a. Agreed in principle to the participation of a British Commonwealth land force in the final phase of the war against Japan, subject to the satisfactory resolution of operational problems and to the clarification of certain factors which the United States Chiefs of Staff believe will be controlling.

b. Agreed that the British Chiefs of Staff should send out appropriate commanders and staff to visit General MacArthur and Admiral

TOP SECRET

Nimitz and draw up with them a plan for submission to the Combined Chiefs of Staff.

c. Took note that the British Chiefs of Staff would keep the United States Chiefs of Staff informed of the reactions of the Dominions to the proposals.

d. Took note that the United States Chiefs of Staff would take up with the appropriate theater commanders the possibility of establishing a small British tactical air force in support of the proposed Commonwealth land force.

TOP SECRET

COMBINED CHIEFS OF STAFF

C.C.S. 195th Meeting

TERMINAL CONFERENCE

MINUTES OF MEETING HELD IN THE CONFERENCE ROOM
AT 25 RINGSTRASSE, BABELSBERG, GERMANY,
ON WEDNESDAY, 18 JULY 1945, AT 1430.

PRESENT

United States

General of the Army
  G. C. Marshall, USA
Fleet Admiral E. J. King, USN
General of the Army
  H. H. Arnold, USA

British

Field Marshal Sir Alan F. Brooke
Marshal of the Royal Air Force
  Sir Charles F. A. Portal
Admiral of the Fleet
  Sir Andrew B. Cunningham

ALSO PRESENT

General B. B. Somervell, USA
Lt. Gen. J. E. Hull, USA
Vice Adm. C. M. Cooke, Jr., USN
Maj. Gen. L. Norstad, USA
Captain H. R. Oster, USN
Captain A. S. McDill, USN

Field Marshal Sir H. M. Wilson
General Sir Hastings L. Ismay
Lt. Gen. Sir Gordon N. Macready
Maj. Gen. R. E. Laycock
Maj. Gen. L. C. Hollis

SECRETARIAT

Brig. Gen. A. J. McFarland, USA
Brigadier A. T. Cornwall-Jones
Captain C. J. Moore, USN
Lt. Col. T. Haddon

TOP SECRET

1. *APPROVAL OF THE MINUTES OF THE C.C.S. 194TH MEETING*

   THE COMBINED CHIEFS OF STAFF:—

   Approved the conclusions of the C.C.S. 194th Meeting and approved the detailed report of the meeting subject to the substitution in the first paragraph on page 3 of the words "dispatch of a corps commander and staff to the Pacific" for "above" and subject to any later minor amendments.

2. *FRENCH AND DUTCH PARTICIPATION IN THE WAR AGAINST JAPAN*
   (C.C.S. 842, 842/1, and 842/2)

   THE COMBINED CHIEFS OF STAFF:—

   Approved the memorandum in the enclosure to C.C.S. 842/2 and directed the Secretaries to forward it separately to the French and Netherlands Representatives to the Combined Chiefs of Staff.

3. *STAFF CONVERSATIONS WITH PORTUGAL*
   (C.C.S. 462/25 and 462/26)

   THE COMBINED CHIEFS OF STAFF:—

   Approved the letter to the Department of State and Foreign Office in the Enclosure to C.C.S. 462/25, as amended in C.C.S. 462/26.

4. *SOUTHEAST ASIA AND SOUTHWEST PACIFIC AREA*
   (C.C.S. 890/2)

   The Combined Chiefs of Staff considered paragraphs 2, 3, and 4 of C.C.S. 890/2.

   In regard to paragraph 2, *GENERAL MARSHALL* asked the British Chiefs of Staff if they would express their reaction to dividing Indo-China into two parts, leaving the northern part in the China Theater.

   ADMIRAL CUNNINGHAM pointed out that the line dividing Indo-China would be dependent to some extent on contemplated operations through Thailand.

TOP SECRET

ADMIRAL KING stated that the division of Indo-China along the latitude of 15 degrees north was an arbitrary division and might be changed to suit contemplated operational requirements.

The British Chiefs of Staff expressed the view that they should like to study the question of the dividing line before making any proposals in regard to the matter.

The proposals contained in paragraph 3 were accepted by the Combined Chiefs of Staff without discussion.

In the discussion of paragraph 4, *SIR ALAN BROOKE* explained that the British Chiefs of Staff were in doubt as to the commitment which they would be undertaking if they agreed to the transfer on a particular date. They did not know when the operations in Borneo were scheduled to be completed nor what sort of liability they would be accepting in the form of maintenance and support for those operations.

In reply, *GENERAL MARSHALL* referred to the United States Chiefs of Staff reply to the questionnaire which the British Chiefs of Staff had submitted (C.C.S. 852 and 852/1),* and described the extent to which the United States Chiefs of Staff were proposing to support operations in the new British command. He said that most of the U.S. troops had been withdrawing from the area of the proposed new British command and that no further operations were scheduled in Borneo. He added that in any event there would be no question of "leaving the Borneo operations in the lurch."

GENERAL MARSHALL then went on to point out that it would be a great advantage to the United States Chiefs of Staff if the transfer of the area to Admiral Mountbatten could take place at an early date. General MacArthur is fully occupied with operations to the northward and it would be a considerable benefit to him if he could be relieved of these responsibilities as soon as possible.

SIR CHARLES PORTAL said that Admiral Mountbatten also was fully occupied in his present and contemplated operations in the Southeast Asia Command, and since General MacArthur was familiar with and is dealing with the Australians at the present, it might be best to continue that procedure until Admiral Mountbatten was in a better position to undertake these new responsibilities.

The British Chiefs of Staff agreed that it was desirable to effect a transfer of command in the Southwest Pacific Area at an early date, but considered

---

* Not published herein.

that it would be necessary for them to study the matter before a definite time could be agreed upon.

GENERAL MARSHALL suggested that as Admiral Mountbatten was about to visit General MacArthur in Manila, that he and General MacArthur might discuss the timing of the transfer of command.

THE COMBINED CHIEFS OF STAFF:—

a. Agreed in principle that that part of the present Southwest Pacific Area lying south of the boundary proposed in paragraph 2 of C.C.S. 852/1,* should pass from United States to British command as soon as possible.

b. Took note that the British Chiefs of Staff would investigate and report to the Combined Chiefs of Staff the earliest possible date on which the transfer of the above area could be effected.

c. Took note that the British Chiefs of Staff would consider where the dividing line might lie in the event that approximately half of French Indo-China should be included in the new British command.

(At this point the Combined Chiefs of Staff went into closed session.)

5. *COMMAND AND CONTROL IN THE WAR AGAINST JAPAN*
(Paragraphs 5 and 6, C.C.S. 890/2)

GENERAL MARSHALL said that he wished to explain the point of view of the United States Chiefs of Staff.

He pointed out that the general concept of operations in the Pacific had been approved by the Combined Chiefs of Staff and that the control of operational strategy lay with the United States Chiefs of Staff. He recognized that in the past the British Chiefs of Staff had not had all the information that they wanted and assured them that this would be remedied in the future. He felt, however, that the operational strategy in the Pacific must remain the responsibility of the United States Chiefs of Staff. He explained the extensive difficulties in the conduct of the strategy of the Pacific arising from the great distances involved and the enormous land, sea, and air forces employed. He said that the United States Chiefs of Staff felt that they could not, in addition to

---

* See paragraph 13, CCS 900/3.

TOP SECRET

these problems, shoulder the burden of debating the "pros" and "cons" of operational strategy with the British Chiefs of Staff.

The United States Chiefs of Staff would be glad to give the British Chiefs of Staff timely information of U.S. plans and intentions and to hear their comments. But they felt bound to retain freedom to decide ultimately what should be done. If then the British Chiefs of Staff felt that they could not commit British troops to the operations decided upon, then they would of course be at liberty to withdraw British forces from those operations; but he desired to make it clear that if this were done, it would be necessary for the United States Chiefs of Staff to be given ample warning of British intentions so that plans of United States Chiefs of Staff could be adjusted accordingly.

SIR ALAN BROOKE said that the British Chiefs of Staff had felt that they had been rather left out of the picture but confirmed that the British Chiefs of Staff entirely supported the strategy which the United States Chiefs of Staff had so far developed. For the future, they hoped that they would be consulted on the further development of strategy but had no wish to suggest that they should interfere in any way with the operational strategy.

ADMIRAL CUNNINGHAM asked if the British Chiefs of Staff would be consulted in regard to the strategy that would be adopted in the event of the Russians coming into the war.

GENERAL MARSHALL said that the strategy to be adopted in these circumstances would be considered on a tripartite basis.

ADMIRAL KING said that the United States Chiefs of Staff would consult with the British Chiefs of Staff, of course, but must reserve the final decision to themselves.

GENERAL MARSHALL said that in the event of any disagreement, the British Chiefs of Staff would certainly be given the opportunity of convincing the United States Chiefs of Staff that they were wrong.

THE COMBINED CHIEFS OF STAFF:—

Agreed that with respect to the strategic control of the war against Japan:—

   a. The control of operational strategy in the Pacific Theater will remain in the hands of the United States Chiefs of Staff.

TOP SECRET

b. The United States Chiefs of Staff will provide the British Chiefs of Staff with full and timely information as to their future plans and intentions.

c. The United States Chiefs of Staff will consult the British Chiefs of Staff on matters of general strategy, on the understanding that in the event of disagreement, the final decision on the action to be taken will lie with the United States Chiefs of Staff.

d. In the event the British Chiefs of Staff should decide that they cannot commit British troops in support of a decision made by the United States Chiefs of Staff as indicated in c. above, the British Chiefs of Staff will give to the United States Chiefs of Staff such advance notice of their decision as will permit them to make timely rearrangements.

e. In the event the U.S.S.R. enters the war against Japan, the strategy to be pursued should be discussed between the parties concerned.

TOP SECRET

COMBINED CHIEFS OF STAFF

C.C.S. 196th Meeting

TERMINAL CONFERENCE

Minutes of Meeting Held in the Conference Room
at 25 Ringstrasse, Babelsberg, Germany,
on Thursday, 19 July 1945, at 1430.

PRESENT

United States

General of the Army
  G. C. Marshall, USA
Fleet Admiral E. J. King, USN
General of the Army
  H. H. Arnold, USA

British

Field Marshal Sir Alan F. Brooke
Marshal of the Royal Air Force
  Sir Charles F. A. Portal
Admiral of the Fleet
  Sir Andrew B. Cunningham

ALSO PRESENT

General B. B. Somervell, USA
Lt. Gen. J. E. Hull, USA
Vice Adm. C. M. Cooke, Jr., USN
Maj. Gen. L. Norstad, USA
Captain H. R. Oster, USN
Captain A. S. McDill, USN

Field Marshal Sir H. M. Wilson
General Sir Hastings L. Ismay
Maj. Gen. R. E. Laycock
Maj. Gen. L. C. Hollis

SECRETARIAT

Brig. Gen. A. J. McFarland, USA
Brigadier A. T. Cornwall-Jones
Captain C. J. Moore, USN
Lt. Col. T. Haddon

TOP SECRET

1. *APPROVAL OF THE MINUTES OF THE C.C.S. 195TH MEETING, 18 JULY 1945*

   THE COMBINED CHIEFS OF STAFF:—

   a. Approved the conclusions of the C.C.S. 195th Meeting subject to the following amendments:

   (1) Change item 4 a. to read:

   "Agreed in principle that that part of the present Southwest Pacific Area lying south of the boundary proposed in paragraph 2 of C.C.S. 852/1, should pass from United States to British command as soon as possible."

   (2) Change item 5 e. to read as follows:

   "In the event the U.S.S.R. enters the war against Japan, the strategy to be pursued should be discussed between the parties concerned."

   b. Approved the detailed report of the meeting subject to later minor amendments.

2. *PARTICIPATION OF TWO FRENCH COLONIAL INFANTRY DIVISIONS IN FAR EASTERN OPERATIONS*
   (C.C.S. 895, 895/1, and 895/2)

   THE COMBINED CHIEFS OF STAFF:—

   Approved the reply to the Chief of the French Military Mission in the United States in the Enclosure to C.C.S. 895/2.

3. *COMBINED CHIEFS OF STAFF MACHINERY AFTER THE WAR WITH JAPAN*
   (C.C.S. 891 and 891/1)

SIR ALAN BROOKE said that the British Chiefs of Staff had considered the memorandum by the United States Chiefs of Staff in C.C.S. 891/1. The British Chiefs of Staff were prepared to discuss the matter or to take note of the views of the United States Chiefs of Staff as the latter desired.

GENERAL MARSHALL said that the United States Chiefs of Staff were not in a position to discuss at this date the post-war relationship between the respective military staffs.

TOP SECRET

ADMIRAL KING said that the second paragraph of C.C.S. 891/1 was meant to refer to the procedure envisaged in the changed conclusion under 5 *e.* of the minutes of the Combined Chiefs of Staff 195th Meeting.

THE COMBINED CHIEFS OF STAFF:—

Took note of C.C.S. 891 and 891/1.

4. *INFORMATION FOR THE RUSSIANS CONCERNING THE JAPANESE WAR*
(C.C.S. 884, 884/1, and 884/2)

SIR ALAN BROOKE said that the British Chiefs of Staff felt that it was desirable that the policy adopted in imparting information concerning the Japanese war to the Russians should be coordinated with the policy of the United States Chiefs of Staff.

GENERAL MARSHALL said that the United States Chiefs of Staff had considered the matter raised in the memorandum by the British Chiefs of Staff and had come to the following conclusion:—

a. The United States Chiefs of Staff desired to retain freedom of action regarding the passing of purely operational information and intelligence to the Russians.

b. On matters of information and intelligence which were not purely operational, the United States Chiefs of Staff would agree not to pass such information to the Russians without consulting the British Chiefs of Staff.

c. As regards information and intelligence from purely British sources, this would not be passed without permission of the British Chiefs of Staff.

SIR CHARLES PORTAL said that there was considerable technical information which had been developed by joint effort, and he asked whether this information would be handled the same as operational information.

ADMIRAL KING said that information on technical equipment was not included in purely operational information. Operational information or intelligence included information on such matters as weather and the composition and disposition of enemy forces. The technical information referred to by Sir Charles Portal would not, therefore, be handled under *a.* above.

TOP SECRET

GENERAL MARSHALL said that it was the policy of the United States Chiefs of Staff to pass purely operational information and intelligence freely to the Russians and not to withhold it for bargaining purposes. If such information contributed to the efficiency of the Russian armies or aided in the prosecution of the war the United States Chiefs felt that it should be given to the Russians regardless of whether or not the Russians reciprocated.

SIR ALAN BROOKE said that this policy would be agreeable to the British Chiefs of Staff as they felt that it would be better for the British and United States Chiefs of Staff to pursue the same policy in this matter since both countries have military missions in Moscow.

THE COMBINED CHIEFS OF STAFF:—

Agreed:

a. *Operational Information and Intelligence*

That the U.S. and British Chiefs of Staff will pass to the Russians such operational information and intelligence regarding the theatres in which they are respectively responsible as either may wish and without bargaining.

b. *Information and Intelligence Other than Operational*

The United States and British Chiefs of Staff will consult together before passing to the Russians any information and intelligence other than operational. Neither party will pass to the Russians information or intelligence derived wholly or in part from the other party's sources without their consent.

5. *PLANNING DATE FOR THE END OF ORGANIZED RESISTANCE BY JAPAN*
(C.C.S. 880/8)

THE COMBINED CHIEFS OF STAFF:—

Agreed that for the purpose of planning production and the allocation of manpower, the planning date for the end of organized resistance by Japan be 15 November 1946; that this date be adjusted periodically to conform to the course of the war.

6. *APPOINTMENT OF COLONEL DOUGLAS TO ALLIED COMMISSION IN ITALY*

FIELD MARSHAL WILSON reported that he had attended that afternoon a meeting between the U.S. Secretary of War, the U.S. Assistant Secretary

TOP SECRET

of War, and Field Marshal Alexander at which the appointment of Colonel Douglas as Chief Commissioner to the Allied Commission in Italy had been discussed.

It was proposed at that meeting that Colonel Douglas should visit Italy for a month or so to examine the situation on the spot. He could then take over the appointment from Admiral Stone in September, when all Italian territory, excluding Venezia Giulia, would have been handed back to the Italian Government and a change in the status of the Control Commission to more of a civilian basis would take place.

This proposal had been accepted by the United States and British representatives present at the meeting, and subject to approval by Colonel Douglas which was being requested from Washington, it was decided to adopt the above suggestions provided the Department of State and the Foreign Office agreed.

THE COMBINED CHIEFS OF STAFF:—

Took note of Field Marshal Wilson's statement.

TOP SECRET

COMBINED CHIEFS OF STAFF

C.C.S. 197th Meeting

TERMINAL CONFERENCE

Minutes of Meeting Held in the Conference Room at 25 Ringstrasse, Babelsberg, Germany, on Friday, 20 July 1945, at 1430.

PRESENT

United States

General of the Army
  G. C. Marshall, USA
Fleet Admiral E. J. King, USN
General of the Army
  H. H. Arnold, USA

British

Field Marshal Sir Alan F. Brooke
Marshal of the Royal Air Force
  Sir Charles F. A. Portal
Admiral of the Fleet
  Sir Andrew B. Cunningham

ALSO PRESENT

General B. B. Somervell, USA
Lt. Gen. J. E. Hull, USA
Vice Adm. C. M. Cooke, Jr., USN
Maj. Gen. L. Norstad, USA
Rear Adm. H. A. Flanigan, USN
Captain A. S. McDill, USN

Field Marshal Sir H. M. Wilson
General Sir Hastings L. Ismay
Lt. Gen. Sir Gordon N. Macready
Maj. Gen. R. E. Laycock
Maj. Gen. L. C. Hollis

SECRETARIAT

Brig. Gen. A. J. McFarland, USA
Brigadier A. T. Cornwall-Jones
Captain C. J. Moore, USN
Lt. Col. T. Haddon

TOP SECRET

1. *APPROVAL OF THE MINUTES OF THE C.C.S. 196TH MEETING, 19 JULY 1945*

   THE COMBINED CHIEFS OF STAFF:—

   a. Approved the conclusions of the C.C.S. 196th Meeting subject to the amendment of the conclusions under item 4 to read as follows:—

   "*a. Operational Information and Intelligence*

   That the United States and British Chiefs of Staff will pass to the Russians such operational information and intelligence regarding the theatres in which they are respectively responsible as either may wish and without bargaining.

   "*b. Information and Intelligence Other than Operational*

   The United States and British Chiefs of Staff will consult together before passing to the Russians any information and intelligence other than operational. Neither party will pass to the Russians information or intelligence derived wholly or in part from the other party's sources without their consent."

   b. Approved the detailed report of the meeting, subject to any later minor amendments.

2. *DIRECTIVE TO THE SUPREME ALLIED COMMANDER, SOUTHEAST ASIA* (C.C.S. 892/1)

   THE COMBINED CHIEFS OF STAFF had before them a draft directive to the Supreme Allied Commander, Southeast Asia, proposed by the British Chiefs of Staff.

   THE UNITED STATES CHIEFS OF STAFF proposed a few amendments to the text of the directive.

   GENERAL MARSHALL said that the United States Chiefs of Staff were prepared to accept the directive on the understanding that the British Chiefs of Staff would be responsible for obtaining the approval of the Australian, New Zealand and Dutch Governments to the proposed reallocation of areas and command set-up in Southwest Pacific and Southeast Asia, since these governments had been party to the original arrangements.

TOP SECRET

THE COMBINED CHIEFS OF STAFF:—

a. Approved the directive to the Supreme Allied Commander, Southeast Asia, in C.C.S. 892/1 as amended during the discussion. (Subsequently circulated as C.C.S. 892/2.)

b. Took note that the British Chiefs of Staff would take steps to obtain the agreement of the Australian, New Zealand, and Dutch Governments to the proposed reallocation of areas and command set-up in Southwest Pacific and Southeast Asia.

3. *DISPOSAL OF ENEMY WAR MATÉRIEL IN GERMANY AND AUSTRIA*
(C.C.S. 706/11 and 706/14)

THE COMBINED CHIEFS OF STAFF:—

Approved Appendices "A" and "B" to C.C.S. 706/11, as amended in C.C.S. 706/14. (Subsequently dispatched to SACMED as FAN 603.)

TOP SECRET

COMBINED CHIEFS OF STAFF

C.C.S. 198th Meeting

TERMINAL CONFERENCE

MINUTES OF MEETING HELD IN THE CONFERENCE ROOM AT 25 RINGSTRASSE, BABELSBERG, GERMANY, ON SATURDAY, 21 JULY 1945, AT 1530.

PRESENT

United States

Fleet Admiral W. D. Leahy, USN
General of the Army
  G. C. Marshall, USA
Fleet Admiral E. J. King, USN
General of the Army
  H. H. Arnold, USA

British

Field Marshal Sir Alan F. Brooke
Marshal of the Royal Air Force
  Sir Charles F. A. Portal
Admiral of the Fleet
  Sir Andrew B. Cunningham

ALSO PRESENT

General B. B. Somervell, USA
Lt. Gen. J. E. Hull, USA
Vice Adm. C. M. Cooke, Jr., USN
Maj. Gen. L. Norstad, USA
Rear Adm. H. A. Flanigan, USN
Captain A. S. McDill, USN

General Sir Hastings L. Ismay
Lt. Gen. Sir Gordon N. Macready
Maj. Gen. L. C. Hollis

SECRETARIAT

Brig. Gen. A. J. McFarland, USA
Brigadier A. T. Cornwall-Jones
Captain C. J. Moore, USN
Lt. Col. T. Haddon

TOP SECRET

1. *APPROVAL OF THE MINUTES OF THE 197TH MEETING OF THE COMBINED CHIEFS OF STAFF, 20 JULY 1945*

   THE COMBINED CHIEFS OF STAFF:—

   a. Approved the conclusions of the C.C.S. 197th Meeting subject to the amendment of conclusion b. under item 2 to read as follows:

   "Took note that the British Chiefs of Staff would take steps to obtain the agreement of the Australian, New Zealand, and Dutch Governments to the proposed reallocation of areas and command set-up in Southwest Pacific and Southeast Asia."

   b. Approved the detailed report of the meeting, subject to:

   (1) The amendment of the 3d paragraph under item 2 to read as follows:

   "*GENERAL MARSHALL* said that the United States Chiefs of Staff were prepared to accept the directive on the understanding that the British Chiefs of Staff would be responsible for obtaining the approval of the Australian, New Zealand, and Dutch Governments to the proposed reallocation of areas and command set-up in Southwest Pacific and Southeast Asia, since these governments had been party to the original arrangements."

   (2) Any later minor amendments.

2. *BASIC OBJECTIVES, STRATEGY, AND POLICIES*
   (C.C.S. 877, 877/1, 877/2, 877/4, and 877/5)

   SIR ALAN BROOKE said that the British Chiefs of Staff had considered C.C.S. 877/5 and had come to the conclusion that the matter had now reached a stage which was outside the scope of the British Chiefs of Staff. He said that the hands of the British Chiefs of Staff were bound just as were those of the United States Chiefs of Staff. He regretted, therefore, that nothing further could be done in the matter until a decision had been reached on a higher level. He requested that the matter be deferred until such time as a decision on a higher level was forthcoming.

   THE COMBINED CHIEFS OF STAFF:—

   Agreed to defer consideration of C.C.S. 877/5.

TOP SECRET

3. *BRITISH TROOPSHIP EMPLOYMENT IN U.S. TRANS-ATLANTIC PROGRAMS, FIRST HALF OF 1946*
   (C.C.S. 679/7)

   THE COMBINED CHIEFS OF STAFF:—

   Agreed to defer consideration of this matter.

4. *DISPOSITION OF CAPTURED GERMAN PASSENGER SHIPS*
   (C.C.S. 679/6)

   THE COMBINED CHIEFS OF STAFF:—

   Agreed to defer consideration of this matter.

TOP SECRET

COMBINED CHIEFS OF STAFF

C.C.S. 199th Meeting

TERMINAL CONFERENCE

MINUTES OF MEETING HELD IN THE CONFERENCE ROOM
AT 25 RINGSTRASSE, BABELSBERG, GERMANY,
ON MONDAY, 23 JULY 1945, AT 1130.

PRESENT

United States

Fleet Admiral W. D. Leahy, USN
General of the Army
  G. C. Marshall, USA
Fleet Admiral E. J. King, USN
General of the Army
  H. H. Arnold, USA

British

Field Marshal Sir Alan F. Brooke
Marshal of the Royal Air Force
  Sir Charles F. A. Portal
Admiral of the Fleet
  Sir Andrew B. Cunningham

ALSO PRESENT

General B. B. Somervell, USA
Lt. Gen. J. E. Hull, USA
Vice Adm. C. M. Cooke, Jr., USN
Maj. Gen. L. Norstad, USA
Rear Adm. H. A. Flanigan, USN
Captain A. S. McDill, USN

Field Marshal Sir H. M. Wilson
General Sir Hastings L. Ismay
Lt. Gen. Sir Gordon N. Macready
Maj. Gen. R. E. Laycock
Maj. Gen. N. G. Holmes
Maj. Gen. L. C. Hollis

SECRETARIAT

Brig. Gen. A. J. McFarland, USA
Brigadier A. T. Cornwall-Jones
Captain C. J. Moore, USN
Lt. Col. T. Haddon

TOP SECRET

1. *APPROVAL OF THE MINUTES OF THE 198TH MEETING OF THE COMBINED CHIEFS OF STAFF, 21 JULY 1945*

    THE COMBINED CHIEFS OF STAFF:—

    Approved the conclusions of the 198th Meeting and approved the detailed report, subject to any later minor amendments.

2. *EMPLOYMENT OF CAPTURED ENEMY OCEAN-GOING PASSENGER SHIPPING AND BRITISH TROOPSHIP EMPLOYMENT IN U.S. TRANS-ATLANTIC PROGRAMS IN THE FIRST HALF OF 1946*
    (C.C.S. 679/6, 679/7, 679/8, and 679/9)

    SIR ALAN BROOKE said that the British Chiefs of Staff had considered C.C.S. 679/9 and regretted that the amendments proposed by the United States Chiefs of Staff were not acceptable to the British Chiefs of Staff. It appeared to be the view of the United States Chiefs of Staff that if the seven captured German ships were moved to the Pacific they would be unable to make more than one trip before the 31st of December, 1945. If then, as a result of the review of the combined requirements and combined resources for the first half of 1946, it was decided that these seven captured ships should no longer be allocated to the United States, their initial assignment to the Pacific in 1945 would prove uneconomical. He said he appreciated the point of view of the United States Chiefs of Staff.

    SIR ALAN BROOKE pointed out, however, that the very fact that these ships had been moved to the Pacific would be a strong argument for retaining them there. This argument would be weighed with all the other arguments when it came to the combined review which the British Chiefs of Staff had proposed in paragraph 6 of C.C.S. 679/8. To exclude these ships from the review at this stage seemed to the British Chiefs of Staff to be wrong.

    ADMIRAL KING proposed that the Combined Chiefs of Staff accept C.C.S. 679/8, provided that the combined study on the lines suggested by the British Chiefs of Staff be undertaken as a firm commitment to be completed by mid-September.

    THE COMBINED CHIEFS OF STAFF:—

    a. Agreed to allocate the total lift of the seven ships listed in C.C.S. 679/6 for United States employment up to 31 December 1945.

    b. Took note that the United States Chiefs of Staff would allocate to the United Kingdom a lift of 16,000 during the remainder of 1945 for the movement of Canadians.

TOP SECRET

    c. Directed the Combined Military Transportation Committee, in collaboration with the Combined Shipping Adjustment Board, to submit by 15 September 1945 a report, on the lines of C.C.S. 679/1, of the combined requirements and combined resources (including captured enemy trooplift) for the first half of 1946, the study to cover the recommendation in paragraph 7 of C.C.S. 679/7 and the employment during the first half of 1946 of the seven ships listed in C.C.S. 679/6.

3. *PROVISION OF PERSONNEL SHIPS FOR THE REQUIREMENTS OF ALLIED GOVERNMENTS*
(C.C.S. 897)

THE COMBINED CHIEFS OF STAFF:—

Approved the memorandum in Enclosure "A" to C.C.S. 897, subject to amendments agreed in discussion, and directed that it be dispatched to the Combined Shipping Adjustment Board.

4. *COMMAND IN FRENCH INDO-CHINA*
(C.C.S. 890/3)

THE COMBINED CHIEFS OF STAFF:—

Approved the recommendation in paragraph 3 of C.C.S. 890/3, and directed that the statement contained in that paragraph, as amended in discussion, be included in their final report to the President and Prime Minister.

5. *REPORT TO THE PRESIDENT AND PRIME MINISTER*
(C.C.S. 900)

THE COMBINED CHIEFS OF STAFF:—

Approved C.C.S. 900, as amended in discussion.

6. *CONTROL OF ALLIED NAVAL UNITS OTHER THAN U.S. AT PRESENT UNDER COMMAND OF SEVENTH U.S. FLEET*

THE COMBINED CHIEFS OF STAFF:—

Took note that upon the dissolution of the U.S. Seventh Fleet pursuant to the reallocation of areas and change in command in the Southwest Pacific, as proposed in C.C.S. 890/1, it was the intention of the Commander in Chief of the United States Fleet to release to British control those Allied naval units other than U.S. at present incorporated in the U.S. Seventh Fleet.

TOP SECRET

COMBINED CHIEFS OF STAFF

C.C.S. 200th Meeting

TERMINAL CONFERENCE

MINUTES OF MEETING HELD IN THE CONFERENCE ROOM AT 25 RINGSTRASSE, BABELSBERG, GERMANY, ON TUESDAY, 24 JULY 1945, AT 1730.

PRESENT

United States

General of the Army
  G. C. Marshall, USA
Fleet Admiral E. J. King, USN
General of the Army
  H. H. Arnold, USA

British

Field Marshal Sir Alan F. Brooke
Marshal of the Royal Air Force
  Sir Charles F. A. Portal
Admiral of the Fleet
  Sir Andrew B. Cunningham

ALSO PRESENT

General B. B. Somervell, USA
Lt. Gen. J. E. Hull, USA
Vice Adm. C. M. Cooke, Jr., USN
Maj. Gen. L. Norstad, USA
Captain A. S. McDill, USN
Captain H. R. Oster, USN

Admiral The Lord Louis Mountbatten
Field Marshal Sir H. M. Wilson
General Sir Hastings L. Ismay
Lt. Gen. Sir Gordon N. Macready

SECRETARIAT

Maj. Gen. L. C. Hollis
Brig. Gen. A. J. McFarland, USA
Brigadier A. T. Cornwall-Jones
Lt. Col. G. Mallaby

TOP SECRET

1. 200TH MEETING OF THE COMBINED CHIEFS OF STAFF

The Combined Chiefs of Staff took note that this was their 200th Meeting.

2. OPERATIONS IN SOUTHEAST ASIA COMMAND

GENERAL MARSHALL said that the United States Chiefs of Staff would like to extend a welcome to Admiral Mountbatten and take this opportunity of congratulating him personally on the conclusion of his great campaign in Burma.

ADMIRAL MOUNTBATTEN thanked the United States Chiefs of Staff and then proceeded to give an account of past, present, and future operations in his command.

In recounting the broad tale of events in Southeast Asia from the SEXTANT Conference in 1943 to the capture of Rangoon in May, 1945, he emphasized two points of importance:—

a. Air transport was the lifeblood of all operations in his command. They had saved the day when things looked black in the spring of 1944 and had enabled him to complete successfully the great overland campaign to recapture Burma which had previously been thought impracticable. The Dakota was far and away the best transport aircraft for his purposes.

b. The tremendous steps in the reduction of casualties made possible by preventive medicine.

In describing the current situation in Burma, ADMIRAL MOUNTBATTEN explained that:—

a. He had some 56,000 Japs still to destroy. At the moment seven divisions were employed on the job, three of which would soon be withdrawn to take part in forthcoming operations. Considerable fighting was still going on.

b. He had a big problem in getting supplies through to the native population in the face of one of the worst monsoons in history. He was being forced to use some air transport for this as well as for the maintenance of the troops.

c. His air transport squadrons were some 20 percent under strength.

TOP SECRET

As regards future operations, the Supreme Commander paid tribute to the immense effort being put forward by the India Command to organize India as a base for these operations which were the largest that had ever been undertaken from the country. He drew a picture of the problem of mounting operation ZIPPER; the vast distances over which the forces would have to converge on the objective; the fact that they would have to rely on carrier-borne air support for the landing; and the degree of opposition they were likely to meet. Risks were involved but these were calculated risks which he was prepared to accept.

Finally, he paid tribute to the morale of the troops and the high degree of inter-Allied cooperation that had been built up in the past two years. This spirit, he felt, would carry the command through forthcoming operations in spite of the disappointments inevitably involved in the acceptance of a second priority in the war as a whole.

SIR ALAN BROOKE then invited the United States Chiefs of Staff to put any questions they would like to Admiral Mountbatten, observing that the British Chiefs of Staff would have the opportunity at subsequent discussions in London.

GENERAL MARSHALL suggested that it might be possible to use more submarines to prevent the infiltration into Malaya of further Japanese reinforcements.

SIR ANDREW CUNNINGHAM said that no specific demand for further submarines for this purpose had been made from the theater and that within reason there was no limitation on the number that might be employed. There were, however, very few worthwhile targets left in the area.

ADMIRAL MOUNTBATTEN said that he felt that the present distribution of submarines, balanced as it was to meet the various tasks to be carried out, was satisfactory.

GENERAL MARSHALL asked the Supreme Commander how soon he thought he would be able to take over the new command, explaining that the United States Chiefs of Staff were very anxious to relieve United States commanders in the Pacific of their responsibilities for the area at the earliest possible moment.

ADMIRAL MOUNTBATTEN said that he had not expected to be called upon to assume these new responsibilities until MAILFIST had been

TOP SECRET

completed. He would like a little further time to consider the idea of taking them on earlier, but assured the United States Chiefs of Staff that he would do his best to meet them. When assured by General Marshall that the forces now in the area would be left there, he said that this certainly made things easier. It appeared that the problem would be merely a matter of assuming the higher direction of operations in the area.

GENERAL MARSHALL asked what Admiral Mountbatten thought of the idea of splitting French Indo-China into two and placing the southern half, south of 16°N, in the Southeast Asia Command.

ADMIRAL MOUNTBATTEN said that he had just heard of the proposition and that his first reactions were favorable. He would have liked some latitude in the actual northern limit of the area in case his operations were to develop either to the north or to the south of the degree of latitude suggested, but did not feel very strongly on the point. He thought the French might find the proposition a little less agreeable.

GENERAL MARSHALL explained the background to the French offer of two French divisions for operations in the war against Japan, and said that the Combined Chiefs of Staff were agreed that the best place to employ these divisions would probably be in French Indo-China. One of these two divisions had had battle experience and had done well. Both were composed of white men and the French proposal specifically provided that they would arrive with corps-supporting and service units. He asked Admiral Mountbatten's opinion as to the acceptance of these two divisions in Southeast Asia Command. They could not be moved out for several months and it would probably be the late spring of 1946 before he could expect to get them.

ADMIRAL MOUNTBATTEN said that, subject to the views of the British Chiefs of Staff, he would certainly welcome these two French divisions provided they came with a proper proportion of service and supporting units. The obvious place to employ them would be in French Indo-China where he would be relieved of the necessity of dealing with a problem which could be satisfactorily handled only by Frenchmen.

GENERAL HULL said that General MacArthur had drawn up a list of the supporting and service units which these two divisions would require if they came out to the Pacific, and this list has been communicated to the French. He undertook to provide Admiral Mountbatten with this list.

MINUTES OF THE

PLENARY MEETING

(BETWEEN THE UNITED STATES AND GREAT BRITAIN)

These Minutes were transcribed from notes taken by the United States Secretaries, Combined Chiefs of Staff.

TOP SECRET

TERMINAL CONFERENCE

MINUTES OF THE PLENARY MEETING BETWEEN THE UNITED STATES AND GREAT BRITAIN, HELD AT 2 KAISERSTRASSE, BABELSBERG, GERMANY, ON TUESDAY, 24 JULY 1945, AT 1130.

PRESENT

United States	British
The President	The Prime Minister
Fleet Admiral William D. Leahy	Lord Leathers
General of the Army G. C. Marshall	Field Marshal Sir Alan F. Brooke
Fleet Admiral E. J. King	Marshal of the Royal Air Force Sir Charles F. A. Portal
General of the Army H. H. Arnold	Admiral of the Fleet Sir Andrew B. Cunningham
General B. B. Somervell	General Sir Hastings L. Ismay
	Field Marshal Sir H. M. Wilson
	Maj. Gen. R. E. Laycock

SECRETARIAT

Major Gen. L. C. Hollis
Brig. Gen. A. J. McFarland
Brigadier A. T. Cornwall-Jones

TOP SECRET

FINAL REPORT TO THE PRESIDENT AND PRIME MINISTER
(C.C.S. 900/2)

THE MEETING had before them C.C.S. 900/2, the draft of the final report of the Combined Chiefs of Staff to the President and the Prime Minister on the results of the *TERMINAL* Conference.

THE PRESIDENT and *THE PRIME MINISTER* proceeded to examine the report paragraph by paragraph.

With respect to paragraph 4, *ADMIRAL LEAHY* explained that there was a divergence of opinion on two or three points in connection with the basic undertakings and policies for the prosecution of the war and that the respective views of the United States and British Chiefs of Staff were set out in Appendix "A."

Appendix "A," paragraph 4.

ADMIRAL LEAHY said that the United States Chiefs of Staff proposed to include the following:—

"*a*. Maintain the security of the Western Hemisphere and the British Commonwealth.

"*b*. Maintain the war-making capacity of the United States and the British Commonwealth in so far as it is connected with the prosecution of the war against Japan."

THE BRITISH CHIEFS OF STAFF on the other hand wished to combine these two paragraphs into the following:—

"Maintain the security and war-making capacity of the Western Hemisphere and the British Commonwealth as necessary for the fulfillment of the strategic concept."

The view of the United States Chiefs of Staff was that the basic commitment in this respect should be confined to the maintenance of war-making capacity in so far as it was connected with the prosecution of the war against Japan, whereas the British Chiefs of Staff felt that it should be extended to include the occupation of Germany and Austria, as provided in the strategic concept.

THE PRIME MINISTER said that he supported the British Chiefs of Staff and suggested that the holding down of Germany and Austria was certainly a very vital matter. He felt therefore that this commitment should be embraced in this particular section of the basic undertakings.

He called attention to the extent to which the British industrial effort had been interwoven with that of the United States by reason of agreements reached earlier in the war and his own discussions with President Roosevelt at Quebec. As a result of these agreements many British units were equipped with U.S. equipment and no provision had been made to replace this equipment from British sources. To make such provision would take time and he hoped very much that the President would be able to make it possible for him to pass smoothly from this position of dependence on the United States to one in which British forces could be independent. He feared that a rigid interpretation of an undertaking to maintain the British war-making capacity only in so far as it was connected with the prosecution of the war against Japan, would place him in great difficulties. He hoped also that the rules applied to the supply of lend-lease equipment would not be held to limit British sovereign rights over British equipment. He must be free to give British equipment, for example, to the Belgians, if His Majesty's Government felt that this was desirable, and he hoped that this would not result in the drying up of equivalent supplies from the United States.

THE PRESIDENT explained that he was handicapped in his approach to this matter by the latest renewal of the Lend-Lease Act. As Vice President, he had worked out its clauses together with Senator George, who had explained to the Congress that the Act was intended to be a weapon of war only. The President was now striving to give to the Act the broadest interpretation possible and he had no intention of causing the British any embarrassment in the matter of furnishing supplies to the British troops or the maintenance thereof. However, he must ask the Prime Minister to be patient as he wished to avoid any embarrassment with Congress over the interpretation of the Act and it might be necessary for him to ask for additional legislation in order to clear the matter up.

With respect to the basic undertaking under discussion, *THE PRESIDENT* said that he thought that the holding down of Germany and Austria was quite definitely a part of war. After all, we were technically still at war with Germany and Austria.

TOP SECRET

GENERAL MARSHALL said in view of the foregoing that the United States Chiefs of Staff accepted the paragraph proposed by the British Chiefs of Staff.

THE PRESIDENT agreed.

Appendix "A," paragraph 4 c.

THE PRIME MINISTER said that he could not see very much difference between the two subparagraphs proposed. He suggested that the proposal of the United States Chiefs of Staff should be accepted.

THE PRESIDENT agreed.

Appendix "A," first sentence of paragraph 6 c.

ADMIRAL LEAHY explained that the British Chiefs of Staff were anxious to add a clause at the end of the first sentence of this paragraph which would extend the combined liability to provide assistance not only to such of the forces of the liberated areas as could fulfill an active and effective role in the present war but also to such of those forces as were "required to maintain world order in the interests of the war effort." In his view, therefore, the issue before the meeting was whether or not the United States was prepared to undertake a commitment to equip and supply forces of occupation other than American.

THE PRIME MINISTER asked what the British Chiefs of Staff had in mind in proposing this clause.

FIELD MARSHAL BROOKE instanced the Belgian and Dutch forces and *ADMIRAL CUNNINGHAM* suggested that such French divisions as were not going to the Far East would also fall into this category.

In the light of this explanation, *THE PRIME MINISTER* felt that the point had already been covered under paragraphs 4 *a.* and *b.* above, where it had already been agreed that occupational forces should be included in that particular basic undertaking.

It was agreed that the point would be adequately covered if the words "in accordance with the over-all strategic concept," were added to the first sentence of paragraph 6 *c*, in lieu of the clause proposed by the British Chiefs of Staff.

Appendix "A," paragraph 7.

At this point Lord Leathers entered the meeting.

THE PRIME MINISTER said that he attached great importance to the United Kingdom import program and would not wish to see it lose its status in a document of this nature.

THE PRESIDENT said that he was not quite clear how far he could accept liability for reconstruction and rehabilitation of the United Kingdom under existing United States law. Therefore, if this paragraph were intended to indicate any such liability his acceptance of it would have to be on the understanding that the necessary authority did exist.

ADMIRAL KING and *GENERAL MARSHALL* said that the United States Chiefs of Staff felt that the matter contained in this paragraph was out of place among the basic undertakings. *GENERAL MARSHALL* drew attention to paragraphs 20, 21, and 22 at the end of the report and pointed out that there was no more reason for including cargo shipping among the basic undertakings than the similar matters dealt with in these paragraphs. He suggested that this paragraph should also be placed at the end of the report under the heading "Miscellaneous."

LORD LEATHERS pointed out that the inclusion of the United Kingdom import program had been implicit in the basic undertakings at previous conferences. In consonance with the changed situation, a major change was now being made in the presentation of the basic undertakings. As shipping requirements for military and civilian needs were closely interlocked, his view was that the United Kingdom import program would be more properly associated with military requirements if it were linked to them in the basic undertakings.

GENERAL MARSHALL said that he did not consider that any great change had been made in the presentation of the basic undertakings. He still felt that the matter would be more appropriately placed at the end of the report under the heading "Miscellaneous."

THE PRIME MINISTER inquired whether this would result in the sweeping aside of the United Kingdom import program.

THE PRESIDENT said the Prime Minister could take his word for it that the United Kingdom import program would not suffer from this change. He suggested that General Marshall's proposal be accepted and the paragraph incorporated at the end of the report.

THE PRIME MINISTER said that on this undertaking he would certainly agree that the paragraph should be included at the end of the report.

Appendix "A," last sentence of paragraph 6 c.

LORD LEATHERS suggested that as it had now been agreed that paragraph 7 should be removed from the basic undertakings and placed at the end of the report, the last sentence of paragraph 6 c. would more properly be deleted. However, if it were held that this sentence merely referred to supplies and not to shipping, he thought it might remain.

THE PRESIDENT and *THE PRIME MINISTER* agreed that the last sentence of paragraph 6 c. should stand.

THE PRIME MINISTER referred to paragraph 8 d. of the report in which it had been agreed that "In the event the British Chiefs of Staff should decide that they cannot commit British troops in support of a decision made by the United States Chiefs of Staff, the British Chiefs of Staff will give to the United States Chiefs of Staff such advance notice of their decision as would permit them to make timely rearrangements." *THE PRIME MINISTER* said that he hoped it would not be thought the British Chiefs of Staff would wish to take advantage of this arrangement. What was good enough for the United States would certainly be good enough for the British.

ADMIRAL KING said that the United States Chiefs of Staff did not expect the British Chiefs of Staff to invoke this paragraph and *GENERAL MARSHALL* explained that it had been put in at his suggestion. After OLYMPIC for example, if the British Chiefs of Staff did not agree with the action proposed by the United States Chiefs of Staff, they would, under this paragraph, be free to take such action as they thought fit. The paragraph was a result of an attempt on his part to cover both sides.

THE PRIME MINISTER thanked the United States Chiefs of Staff for their explanation and the spirit in which this provision had been made.

THE PRESIDENT and *THE PRIME MINISTER* accepted and approved the report as amended in the above discussion and directed the copies of the revised version be submitted to them for signature. (The report in its approved form was subsequently circulated as C.C.S. 900/3.)

MINUTES OF THE

TRIPARTITE

MILITARY MEETING

*These Minutes were transcribed from notes taken by
the United States Secretaries, Combined Chiefs of Staff.*

TOP SECRET

TERMINAL CONFERENCE

MINUTES OF THE TRIPARTITE MILITARY MEETING HELD IN CECILIENHOF PALACE, BABELSBERG, GERMANY, ON TUESDAY, 24 JULY 1945, AT 1430.

PRESENT

United States

Fleet Admiral W. D. Leahy, USN
General of the Army
  G. C. Marshall, USA
Fleet Admiral E. J. King, USN
General of the Army
  H. H. Arnold, USA
Lt. Gen. J. E. Hull, USA
Vice Adm. C. M. Cooke, Jr., USN
Maj. Gen. L. Norstad, USA
Maj. Gen. J. R. Deane, USA

British

Field Marshal Sir Alan F. Brooke
Marshal of the Royal Air Force
  Sir Charles F. A. Portal
Admiral of the Fleet
  Sir Andrew B. Cunningham
Field Marshal Sir H. M. Wilson
General Sir Hastings L. Ismay

U.S.S.R.

Army General Antonov
  Chief of Staff, Red Army
Admiral of the Fleet Kuznetsov
  Peoples Commissariat for the Navy
Marshal of Aviation Fallalev
  Chief of Soviet Air Staff
Lt. Gen. Slavin
  Assistant to the Chief of Staff, Red Army

SECRETARIAT

Brig. Gen. A. J. McFarland, USA
Captain C. J. Moore, USN
Lt. Col. G. Mallaby

INTERPRETERS

Major Hill Lunghi
Major Evsekov
Lieutenant Joseph Chase, USNR

TOP SECRET

GENERAL OF THE ARMY ANTONOV asked Fleet Admiral Leahy to preside at this, the first tripartite meeting of the Chiefs of Staff at *TERMINAL*.

ADMIRAL LEAHY said that he was glad to accept the duties of presiding officer at this session.

ADMIRAL LEAHY then asked that General Antonov outline the intentions and plans of the U.S.S.R. with reference to the Japanese.

GENERAL ANTONOV said that Soviet troops were now being concentrated in the Far East and would be ready to commence operations in the last half of August. The actual date, however, would depend upon the result of conferences with Chinese representatives which had not yet been completed. The objective of the U.S.S.R. in the Far East was the destruction of the Japanese troops in Manchuria and the occupation of the Liaotung Peninsula. After the defeat of Japan in combination with the Allied armies it was the Russian intention to withdraw their troops from Manchuria.

GENERAL ANTONOV said that at the present time the Japanese have in Manchuria approximately 20 infantry divisions, two tank divisions, and a sufficient number of depot divisions, separate brigades and separate battalions to bring the total Japanese forces up to a strength of approximately 30 divisions. In addition to these there were approximately 20 divisions of Manchurian troops, making an aggregate of approximately 50 divisions in all on the Russian front.

If the Russian operations were to be successful it was important to prevent the Japanese from strengthening their Manchurian front by reinforcements from China and the Japanese Islands. It was estimated that the Japanese might bring for this purpose 10 divisions from China and 7 from the Japanese Islands. If, therefore, the U.S.S.R. was to be able to carry out its operations successfully it was necessary to prevent any such reinforcement.

GENERAL ANTONOV said he wished to call attention to the fact that there was only a single railroad line connecting central Russia with the Far East; the effect of this was to limit rail movements of all kinds and effectively prevent any rapid movement of troops.

ADMIRAL LEAHY then asked General Marshall to outline the situation of the Japanese with respect to ground troops.

TOP SECRET

GENERAL MARSHALL said that it is estimated that the Japanese have at present approximately 1,800,000 Japanese troops in Japan proper; there are approximately 500,000 troops in Kyushu and a fairly large garrison in the Ryukyus outside of Okinawa. The Japanese garrison in Formosa has recently been increased to about 260,000 men.

In the Philippines there are now about 12,000 to 14,000 Japanese survivors collected in the mountains of northern Luzon for the final death struggle. In Mindanao there are about 20,000 troops scattered throughout the central plateau, all of the coastline positions having now been lost. In the remainder of the Philippines there are approximately 25,000 troops who are widely scattered.

There are, throughout the Pacific islands, isolated garrisons who are under constant surveillance and periodic bombing and whose presence cause no inconvenience to United States forces. There are a considerable number of isolated Japanese troops in Borneo, in New Guinea and the Celebes, in Bougainville in the Solomons group and in the Bismarck Archipelago. The Japanese troops in the Solomons and the Bismarck Archipelago are confronted by the Australians, who are also taking care of a considerable force in the north central part of New Guinea. All of these island garrisons are suffering from gradual exhaustion of their military supplies. In New Guinea they are suffering, in addition, from malaria and other tropical diseases. The remaining garrisons in Java and Sumatra have been reduced by movements to the Malay Peninsula.

The United States Chiefs of Staff estimate that there are about a million Japanese in China. At the present time the most noticeable movements of Japanese troops have been towards Kyushu. In the last three months two divisions from Manchuria had been identified there and it is understood that these divisions have left in Manchuria the cadres for two additional divisions. Two divisions have recently been moved from Korea to the Japanese homeland. One of these is composed of depot troops and the composition of the other is unknown. In the recent past deceptive measures instituted by U.S. forces have resulted in the concentration of Japanese troops in the Kuriles north of Hokkaido. It is known now, however, that the Japanese are moving troops out of the Kuriles and a division of these troops has recently been identified in Kyushu.

U.S. troops now have firm control of Okinawa where they are busy improving harbors and developing numerous airfields. It is expected that in addition to the naval and Marine Corps planes now on Okinawa that General

MacArthur's air force will have 2,000 planes there before the end of the summer. On Luzon strenuous efforts are being made to develop the necessary base facilities for incoming troops. Because of harbor destruction and the sinking of 500 ships in Manila Bay this has been a difficult task but satisfactory progress is being made.

With reference to General Antonov's remark regarding the severing of Japanese communications with Manchuria, *GENERAL MARSHALL* said it is the present understanding the Japanese communications have been seriously interfered with by U.S. submarine action in the Sea of Japan, and by the continued laying of submarine mines by B-29's at the western entrance of the Inland Sea near Shiminoseki and the blockade of such harbors on the west coast of Honshu as Niigata.

The ferry service between Japan and Fusan and shipping in the Yellow Sea has been terminated. Ferry service to Fusan has been moved to the ports further north in Korea. Mine laying by B-29's has extended north along the Korean coast from Fusan to Ginzan. Mines have also been laid in the Inland Sea in the Bungo Channel and in the Bay of Tokyo. Naval air action has extended to northern Honshu and Hokkaido and numerous coastal ports have been attacked by naval aircraft and by direct bombardment. In recent months aircraft based in the Philippines have reduced the normal traffic from ports as far south as Indo-China to Japan from forty convoys a day to none whatever at the present time. By these various actions the Japanese have been compelled to stop all operations at sea except minor operations in the Sea of Japan and coastal lugger traffic in the Java Sea and along the coasts of Malaysia. As a result of increased naval action and mining by super-bombers, there is little likelihood of any Japanese troop movements between Japan and Manchuria. By September or October we expect it to be impossible for the Japanese to move any cargo over this route. It is believed that Japanese operational shipping of one thousand tons and over has been reduced from seven or eight million tons at the beginning of the war to 1¼ million tons at the present time.

In referring to General Antonov's remarks relating to the movement of Japanese reinforcements from China to Manchuria, *GENERAL MARSHALL* said that the general movement of Japanese troops in China indicates a withdrawal from the south. Garrisons in Indo-China and to the southward have been cut off by Chinese forces. It appears that the Japanese are establishing a fortress garrison of about 150,000 men for the defense of Hong Kong and Canton. A similar garrison is being established in Shanghai, including Chusan Island. An inland fortress garrison is being established in Hankow. Our evidence indicates that in spite of their efforts to withdraw their forces to the northward, the continued air attacks on the single-track railroad and sabotage by Chinese guerrillas will prevent the Japanese from moving more than a trickle of troops to the north. Not only is the rail route interrupted, but the rolling stock is in bad condition. They are, therefore, dependent largely on water transportation. In the course of time the Japanese could move troops from North China to Manchuria through the Peking-Kalgan and the Tientsin regions.

The redeployment of troops from the European Theater to the Pacific is now well underway. The first troops have reached Manila. Our first requirement is for engineering and similar troops to restore the harbors and prepare cantonments. Six divisions from Germany with the attached corps and army troops are now in the United States. They will be moved from the west coast of the United States as rapidly as shipping is available.

In the Pacific at the present time the principal difficulty is to find ground room for troops and aircraft we wish to deploy there. The early requirement for engineering troops in the Philippines is thus apparent.

The divisions already in the Pacific have largely been withdrawn from combat and are now being reconditioned and trained for the next operation.

The next most important difficulty in the Pacific is the provision of shipping. By the improvement of harbors, by decreasing the turnaround of our vessels and by making all possible air transport available we hope to overcome the shipping shortage.

In closing, *GENERAL MARSHALL* said that attacks upon Japan from the air and the sea are now proceeding in tremendous volume, but the intensity of these attacks would increase each week.

ADMIRAL KING said that he would briefly supplement General Marshall's remarks. He said that since Yalta the United States Navy had participated in the complete conquest of the Philippine Islands. Commencing in April the conquest of Okinawa and adjacent islands had been accomplished, and bases for land, sea, and air forces were being developed preparatory to the next move against the Japanese homeland. In addition to the Okinawa operation, carrier task forces had attacked air and naval bases in Japan proper. Recently the Third Fleet, under Admiral Halsey, had bombarded the Tokyo area and northern Honshu and Hokkaido. Commencing with the Ryukyus

TOP SECRET

campaign a part of the British Fleet had operated as a task force of the U.S. naval forces. The Japanese navy is now only one-third of its maximum strength and most of the remaining units are of questionable military value, except perhaps for suicide purposes. Naval reconnaissance aircraft now range to the Shantung Peninsula, Korea and the Sea of Japan. Our submarines are operating against the sea communications between Japan and Korea, in Japanese home waters and in the Sea of Japan. We have developed naval bases in Guam and Saipan, in the Marianas group, and are now developing a base in Okinawa.

GENERAL ARNOLD said that he would furnish some additional details regarding the matters discussed by General Marshall. The limited land areas in the Pacific Theater make it impossible to utilize at present all of the large number of airplanes which had been used in the European Theater. When commencing the air campaign against Japan proper we were limited in operations by the airfields we could develop in the Marianas. From these islands the B-29's performance enabled us to carry out attacks against the Japanese industrial areas in Honshu. During the first part of the campaign Japanese air opposition, as well as anti-aircraft fire, was intense. Navigation problems were most difficult. The weather through which we had to fly had an effect on the ability of the plane crews to carry the maximum weight in bombs. With the increase in the strength of our attacks the opposition by the enemy decreased. After the capture of Iwo Jima we were able to base fighter planes there which were able to accompany the B-29's on their attacks on Japanese Islands. Not long after the employment of long-range accompanying fighters was initiated the Japanese Air Force assumed a condition of impotency and we have records of many instances when B-29's reached their objectives without encountering any enemy air opposition. We have learned more about Japanese weather and this and experience gained enabled us to add 30 percent to the bomb load of our B-29's. With fields established on Okinawa B-24's will be able to operate to the north of Port Arthur and B-29's to a range of 200 miles north of Harbin. We will be able to carry maximum bomb loads against Japanese industries and lines of communication in Manchuria. The B-29's operating from Okinawa will carry a bomb load of 20,000 pounds. The difficulty of operating air units from Okinawa will be appreciated when it is realized that the island is only 80 miles long and that only 48 miles of its length can be used for airfields. This usable part of the island is only six or seven miles wide at the widest part. We expect to operate between 2,000 and 3,500 planes from the fields we are building there.

GENERAL ARNOLD said that the exact proportion of Japanese industry now operating in Manchuria was not known but it was estimated to be about twenty percent.

TOP SECRET

He said that the Japanese Air Forces now have some 5,000 planes, a larger number than they have ever had before, but their air force is at its weakest point operationally.

The 5,000 planes referred to above include all types of planes—operational and non-operational—reconnaissance, photographic and combat. Of these the Japanese have set aside about 1,200 for suicide operations. These are now concentrated largely in northern Honshu where the crews are being given special training in suicide technique against airplanes both on the ground and in the air and against ships—warships as well as cargo ships unloading at our ports such as Okinawa.

The Japanese have lost many of their best air leaders—most of their experienced pilots and large numbers of their maintenance crews. They are also very short of gasoline and oil. As a result, Army and Navy planes operating over Hokkaido, Honshu, and the Ryukyus rarely encounter more than 70 or 80 planes.

GENERAL ANTONOV asked General Marshall if he thought it would be possible for the Japanese to move large forces from Japan to Manchuria and from China to Manchuria.

In reply, GENERAL MARSHALL said that he believed no troops could be moved from Japan to Manchuria. He thought the Japanese would be unable to move a large number of troops from China to Manchuria by rail but, given time, they could increase their forces in Manchuria from Central China via the Peking-Kalgan route or via Tientsin. The rail line south of Shantung is susceptible to air attack and sabotage. For this reason it would be a slow process to move large numbers of troops over this route.

General Wedemeyer, the United States Commander in China, has 1,000 planes of the Tenth and Fourteenth Air Forces under his command to operate against this railroad.

Continuing, GENERAL MARSHALL said that at the present time 100,000 tons of supplies a month are being moved into China by air over the mountains and via the old Burma Road. Over this route heavy movements of Chinese troops have been made from Burma to China. The movement of troops and supplies to China has been undertaken in order to have ready by August, 15 Chinese divisions of 10,000 men each equipped with American arms, trained by American officers and enlisted men, and directed under American guidance. He said he mentioned this movement of troops and their equipment from Burma since these movements had prevented an increase in the gasoline supply to China. As the equipping of these divisions is completed and the operations to be undertaken succeed, a greatly increased gasoline supply will be available which will enable heavy attacks to be made on the railroad to North China.

Chinese troops in August will attack Fort Bayard, a port on the China Sea north of Hainan and south of Canton. This port is within 150 miles of the area from which the American-trained Chinese troops will advance on Canton and Hong Kong. It had been estimated that one Liberty ship in Fort Bayard was the equivalent of three or four in Calcutta; one transport plane in Fort Bayard was the equivalent of ten or more in Burma, and 20,000 men in Fort Bayard was the equivalent of 150,000 in Burma. All of these advantages would be reflected in the air operations against the railroad in China.

GENERAL MARSHALL said that the Chinese troops had given a good account of themselves in Burma and their effectiveness was encouraging beyond expectations. He thought that with heavy air support the Chinese troops would operate with considerable success against a Japanese withdrawal to the northward.

With support of the Chinese forces by ship rather than through Burma he thought that the air forces would be able to completely destroy the Chinese railroad, and although the railroad could be attacked from Okinawa it would not be a profitable target for aircraft based there.

GENERAL ANTONOV asked if the United States would operate against the Kuriles in order to open the line of communications to Siberia. He said that they had some strength in Kamchatka and would like to assist with some forces, and that he considered opening this sea route to be most important. He also asked if it would be possible for the United States forces to operate against the shores of Korea in coordination with the Russian forces which would be making an offensive against the peninsula.

ADMIRAL KING said that it would not be possible to operate against the Kuriles and that he saw no reason why a line of communications could not be maintained through the Kuriles as the passages were wide and deep. In reply to the question in regard to operations against Korea, *GENERAL MARSHALL* said that such amphibious operations had not been contemplated, and particularly not in the near future. To undertake amphibious operations against Korea would seriously expose our shipping to Japanese suicide attack by air and surface vessels until we had completely destroyed enemy air strength in southern Korea and until certain portions of the Japanese homeland had been brought completely under our control. To stage such an operation would require a great number of assault ships which would be engaged in three landings on Kyushu. There were no additional assault ships which would permit a landing in Korea. With only a small amphibious force landings could be made on the China coast south of Shanghai which would be of great assistance to General Wedemeyer. He realized the importance of Korea to the Russian operations but said that the possibility of an attack on Korea would have to be determined after the landings on Kyushu. He thought that Korea could be controlled from airfields that would be established in Kyushu.

ADMIRAL KING said that he hoped and expected that after the Kyushu operation we would have such control over the waters of Japan and Korea that we could establish a line of sea communications through those waters to Vladivostok and the Maritime Provinces.

GENERAL MARSHALL pointed out that we had already severed the line of communications between Korea and the main islands of Japan.

GENERAL MARSHALL said that he had with him some questions which he would leave with General Antonov to be answered at his convenience since he did not think that he would be prepared to give the answers at the present time.

ADMIRAL KING said that he would like to call the attention of the Russian Chiefs of Staff to the conversation that took place at Yalta regarding La Perousse Strait, the control of which, we understood, would be undertaken by the Russians by capturing the southern end of Sakhalin Island at as early a time as the Russian Chiefs of Staff thought practicable.

GENERAL ANTONOV said that the first task facing the Russians would be the destruction of the Japanese troops in Manchuria. Because of the distance of Sakhalin, additional troop movements would be required in order to complete its capture in time to be of value in opening La Perousse Strait. Therefore, the attack on southern Sakhalin would be undertaken as a second offensive.

GENERAL MARSHALL then gave General Antonov a book explaining the experiences of our forces in fighting the Japanese which he thought might be of value to him. He also gave him an estimate of the situation in the Far East.

TOP SECRET

GENERAL ANTONOV said that he was grateful for the very valuable information which General Marshall had given him and said that it would be truly exploited.

In regard to operations in Southeast Asia under Admiral Mountbatten, SIR ALAN BROOKE said that the reconquest of Burma had recently been completed but that some Japanese still remained in Burma where they had been cut off by the advance on Rangoon. These Japanese had been making an attempt to join other enemy forces in Siam and five hundred of them had been killed in the last two days. Operations in Burma were being interfered with by the monsoon which was still continuing. When the weather clears, SIR ALAN BROOKE said that Admiral Mountbatten would continue on towards Siam. In Burma there were the remnants of nine enemy divisions facing the British and behind these remnants was one division in Siam and four in Indo-China.

SIR ALAN BROOKE said that they were preparing for an operation to secure Malaya and Singapore and to open the Straits of Malacca. The opening of these straits would shorten the line of communications for the support of British forces operating in the Pacific Theater against the main islands of Japan.

In Malaya there were little more than two divisions of Japanese troops which were being reinforced from Java and Sumatra.

Plans were being prepared for a small expeditionary force to cooperate with the United States forces in the attack on Japan. The limiting factor for operations in this area was shipping.

ADMIRAL CUNNINGHAM said that only remnants of the Japanese Fleet in the Southeast Asia area remained and that within the last two months the two efficient Japanese cruisers had been sunk. Only two damaged ones remained in Singapore. The British East Indies Fleet was unrestricted in its movements except in the very narrow parts of Malacca Strait.

SIR CHARLES PORTAL said that the British and United States air forces in Southeast Asia maintained complete supremacy over the Japanese air forces in that area. His estimate of the strength of enemy air forces in Burma, Siam, Malaya, Sumatra, and Indo-China on 15 July was 260 operating aircraft plus 150 training units. He said he considered any substantial increase in air strength most unlikely and that Admiral Mountbatten had ample aircraft for his future operations.

TOP SECRET

ADMIRAL LEAHY asked General Antonov if he desired to ask the British Chiefs of Staff any questions, to which *GENERAL ANTONOV* replied that he did not.

GENERAL ANTONOV said, however, that he would require some time to consider the questions which had been presented to him by General Marshall and that when he was prepared he would like to arrange another meeting. He said he was very grateful for the information that had been furnished him by the United States and the British Chiefs of Staff.

ADMIRAL LEAHY expressed the appreciation of both the United States and the British Chiefs of Staff for the information given to them by the Russian Chiefs of Staff.

MINUTES OF THE MEETING

OF THE CHIEFS OF STAFF

OF

THE UNITED STATES AND THE SOVIET UNION

These minutes were transcribed from notes taken by the United States Secretaries.

TOP SECRET

TERMINAL CONFERENCE

MINUTES OF THE MEETING OF THE CHIEFS OF STAFF OF THE UNITED STATES AND OF THE SOVIET UNION HELD IN CECILIENHOF PALACE, BABELSBERG, GERMANY, ON THURSDAY, 26 JULY 1945, AT 1500.

PRESENT

United States

General of the Army
  G. C. Marshall, USA
Fleet Admiral E. J. King, USN
General of the Army
  H. H. Arnold, USA
Lt. Gen. J. E. Hull, USA
Vice Adm. C. M. Cooke, Jr., USN
Maj. Gen. L. Norstad, USA
Maj. Gen. J. R. Deane, USA
Rear Adm. M. B. Gardner, USN
Rear Adm. J. B. Maples, USN
Captain A. S. McDill, USN

U.S.S.R.

Army General Antonov
  Chief of Staff, Red Army
Admiral of the Fleet Kuznetsov
  Peoples Commissariat for the Navy
Marshal of Aviation Fallalev
  Chief of the Soviet Air Staff
Lt. General Slavin
  Assistant to the Chiefs of Staff,
  Red Army
Admiral Kucherov

SECRETARIAT

Brig. Gen. A. J. McFarland, USA
Captain C. J. Moore, USN

INTERPRETERS

Major Evsekov
Lieutenant Joseph Chase, USNR

TOP SECRET

GENERAL ANTONOV asked General Marshall if he would preside at the meeting.

GENERAL MARSHALL said that he appreciated the honor but under the circumstances he suggested General Antonov preside and he hoped that he would accept.

GENERAL ANTONOV asked if General Marshall had had an opportunity to become acquainted with the answers to the five questions General Marshall had given him at the meeting on 24 July (See Annex to these minutes). He said that Generalissimo Stalin had handed the written answers to President Truman yesterday at eleven o'clock a.m.

GENERAL MARSHALL said that he was sorry that he had not seen the answers which had been prepared by General Antonov.

GENERAL ANTONOV then read the answer to the first question as follows:—

The Soviet Command agrees to establish in Petropavlovsk and Khabarovsk radio stations for transmitting weather data in accordance with the request made in a letter from President Truman delivered on 23 July 1945. The Soviet Command is ready to accept and use the radio stations and equipment proposed in that letter for the above purpose.

As regards the personnel for maintaining and operating the stations, we consider it wiser to use Soviet personnel which already has a great deal of experience in working with American radio stations.

In addition to these two stations we shall increase the network of local stations in order to give better information on weather.

When the reading of the answer to the first question was completed, GENERAL ANTONOV asked if he should proceed to read the answers to the remaining questions. GENERAL MARSHALL replied that the United States Chiefs of Staff would prefer to discuss the answer to each question as it was read.

ADMIRAL KING said that the United States Chiefs of Staff were disappointed that American personnel was not acceptable for liaison purposes at the central weather stations, since they felt that it would increase the efficiency of the Russian effort as well as our own. He thought, therefore, that we should request reconsideration of this point. If American personnel were used, he said that it was the intention to have 18 officers and 42 enlisted men at Khabarovsk and 9 officers and 24 enlisted men at Petropavlovsk. He had a memorandum relating to the details of equipment and personnel which he thought the Russian High Command should have for use in connection with the reconsideration requested.

GENERAL ANTONOV said that Russian personnel had had experience in the use of the equipment and in the communication procedure in the vicinity of Sevastopol and Odessa as well as near Murmansk. The proposal to use Russian personnel had been made because it had been considered that the operation of these stations would then be more simple. However, if the United States Chiefs of Staff insisted on American personnel at these stations, there would be no objection to employing them.

ADMIRAL KING then gave General Antonov the memorandum he had previously mentioned.

GENERAL ANTONOV pointed out that he had not received an answer as to whether the United States Chiefs of Staff insisted on the use of American personnel.

GENERAL MARSHALL said that the United States Chiefs of Staff would prefer to use American personnel and pointed out that the major service rendered by this personnel would be to U.S. naval forces and to the strategic air forces. For this reason he thought that American personnel would be more satisfactory.

GENERAL ANTONOV said that the first question could then be considered solved and American liaison personnel would be employed at the stations under discussion.

GENERAL ANTONOV then read the answer to the second question as follows:—

Separate zones of naval and air operations are to be set up for the United States and the U.S.S.R. in the Sea of Japan. The boundary between these zones will be along the lines connecting Cape Boltina on the coast of Korea to point 40° north 135° east to point 45° 45′ north 140° east thence along the parallel 45° 45′ north to the line connecting Cape Crillon (Kondo) (on the southern tip of southern Sakhalin) with Cape Soya Missaki (Soyasaki) (on the northern tip of Hokkaido).

The U.S.S.R. naval and air forces will operate north of this line. United States naval and air forces will operate to the south of this line. This line shall be the limiting line of operations for surface and submarine craft and for aviation.

Depending upon circumstances in the future, this boundary line may be subject to change.

United States naval and air operations north of this boundary line and Soviet naval and air operations south of this boundary line will be subject to coordination.

In the Sea of Okhotsk there shall be a zone of mutual operations for the naval and air forces of the United States and the Soviet Union. Operations in the Okhotsk Sea will take place in accordance with mutual agreements.

In the Bering Sea there shall be a zone of mutual operations of our Pacific Fleet and aviation and the United States Fleet and aviation bounded on the north, east and south by a line going from Cape Dezhnev to Diomede Island and thence along the boundary of the territorial waters of the U.S.S.R. and the United States to parallel 51° 30′ north and thence through 50° 35′ north 157° east; thence to 49° 50′ north 156° 20′ east and thence along the parallel 49° 50′ north to the Fourth Kurile Strait.

The remainder of the Bering Sea as well as bordering regions of the Pacific Ocean shall be the zone of operations of the United States Fleet.

GENERAL MARSHALL said that the line of demarcation for sea and air operations in the Sea of Japan was acceptable.

ADMIRAL KING said that he desired to confirm the proposed conditions in the Sea of Okhotsk. He said he understood that this sea would be free for operations of both the United States Navy and the Navy of the Soviet Union and that coordination would be arranged through mutual understanding and cooperation. He asked also if the area to the north of the red line shown on the chart prepared by the Russian Chiefs of Staff, and described in the answer to the second question, was subject to joint control by the United States and the Soviet Navies, in the same manner as in the Sea of Okhotsk.

Admiral King's understanding was confirmed by Admiral Kuznetsov.

GENERAL MARSHALL said that with this understanding, the proposals by the Russian Chiefs of Staff were acceptable.

TOP SECRET

GENERAL ANTONOV repeated that the areas as set forth in answer to the second question were for both sea and air operations, and there was agreement on this answer.

GENERAL ANTONOV then read the answer to the third question as follows:—

The boundary line between operational zones of the United States and Soviet air forces in Korea and Manchuria shall be as follows: Cape Boltina, Changchun, Liaoyuan, Kailu, Chihfeng, Peking, Tatung and thence along the southern boundary of Inner Mongolia.

United States aviation will operate south of this line including all the above-named points. U.S.S.R. aviation will operate north of this line. Depending upon future conditions this line is subject to change. United States air operations north of this line and Soviet air operations south of this line must be coordinated.

GENERAL ARNOLD said he would like to call attention to the fact that the boundary line as proposed by the Russian Chiefs of Staff would deprive the United States air forces of certain railroad centers and lines of communication north of the line as targets unless each individual mission were arranged for separately. He asked if the United States air forces could send missions north of the boundary line within 24 hours after application had been made to the local Russian authorities. He thought that if his understanding as to local coordination was correct, the desired operations of the United States air forces could be worked out satisfactorily. He called the attention of the Russian Chiefs of Staff to the range of the heavy bombers, medium bombers, and light bombers, as indicated on a map which he presented, and pointed out where the United States bombing effort could be made effective to the north of the boundary line.

AIR MARSHAL FALLALEV said that the boundary line suggested by the Russian Chiefs of Staff was to the northward of the principal railroad junctions. These junctions would therefore be available to attack by the United States air forces. If it became necessary to attack targets to the north of the line, reliable communications would permit arrangements to be made within 24 hours. Since, however, the communication might not always be reliable, this question might involve some difficulties.

GENERAL MARSHALL said that with the understanding that if the means of communication for coordinating attacks north of the boundary line were too slow, the question of its position would be discussed again, the proposals made by the Russian Chiefs of Staff were acceptable. However, he said, there was an additional matter he would like to raise in regard to both the second and third questions previously discussed. This concerned the flight of individual reconnaissance aircraft, and he asked that the Russian Chiefs of Staff comment on this point.

AIR MARSHAL FALLALEV said that it was considered that as a general rule, the boundary proposed should apply to reconnaissance aircraft as well as to bombing flights. When necessary to fly reconnaissance aircraft beyond the boundary line, the flight should be coordinated through the liaison officers.

GENERAL ANTONOV then read the answer to the fourth question as follows:—

> The Soviet Command agrees that beginning with military operations of the Soviet Union against Japan, to establish liaison groups between the American and Soviet commanders in the Far East. To accomplish this liaison it is suggested that there be Soviet liaison groups with General MacArthur, with Admiral Nimitz, and in addition, in Washington, to have a Soviet Military Mission.
>
> American liaison groups will be located with the Soviet High Commander in the Far East, Marshal Vassilievski, in Khabarovsk; and with the commander of the Soviet Pacific Fleet, Admiral Yemashev, in Vladivostok.
>
> The Soviet Command is ready to accept the radio-teletype equipment for installation at the indicated points.

GENERAL MARSHALL said that the proposal of the Russian Chiefs of Staff appeared entirely acceptable, but he wished to ask if it was the intention that the liaison groups to be provided should make it possible for immediate coordination of operations. He asked if operations in the Sea of Okhotsk, for example, or in any other special area, would normally be referred to Washington and Moscow, or whether the necessary decisions would be made in the field with the minimum delay.

GENERAL ANTONOV replied that Marshal Vassilievski is the commander in chief of all forces of the Soviet Union in the Far East. Marshal Vassilievski had authority to solve all questions of local coordination which were included in the tasks assigned him by the High Command of the Soviet Union. He said that similarly Admiral Yemashev is the commander in chief of all Russian naval forces in the Pacific. He said that these two officers would be able to solve the questions of coordination of action within the limits of the questions and answers which were being discussed here.

GENERAL MARSHALL said that the statement of General Antonov made the answer to the fourth question entirely acceptable.

GENERAL ANTONOV then referred back to the third answer and asked if the question of liaison was now clear.

GENERAL MARSHALL replied that his question had concerned the employment of reconnaissance aircraft and that he considered the question of liaison as provided for in the fourth answer entirely satisfactory. He said, moreover, that as the operations proceeded he hoped that there would develop such an intimacy in liaison that we would find later that the commanders in the field would develop an even greater intimacy. This would of course depend on them.

GENERAL ANTONOV read the answer to the fifth question as follows:—

The Soviet Command agrees to select ports and airfields for ships and planes in need of repairs and to make available, as far as possible, repair facilities and medical assistance to the personnel of the above-mentioned ships and planes.

For this purpose we can designate:—

a. *Naval ports:*

In the Japanese Sea, Port Nahodka (America Strait); in the Okhotsk and Bearing Sea regions—Nikolaevsk, on the Amur, and Petropavlovsk, on Kamchatka.

b. *Airfields:*

In the region of Vladivostok, in the region of Alexandrovsk on Sakhalin Island and in the region of Petropavlovsk on Kamchatka.

GENERAL MARSHALL said that the proposals of the Russian Chiefs of Staff were entirely acceptable.

GENERAL ARNOLD asked if the matter of identification of aircraft at the Russian airbases which would be available to United States aircraft would be handled as a local matter. He said that sometimes a plane was so disabled that it was necessary to come into a landing field from any direction, identifying itself by radio signal only.

AIR MARSHAL FALLALEV said that the names of airfields, methods of approach, corridors and other details would be furnished and that the requirements of the aircraft and personnel upon landing would be provided. He said that a disabled aircraft, after making a certain signal, could land from any direction without other formality. Aircraft crews should be instructed, however, not to fly over such ports as Vladivostok, because of the danger of being fired upon by anti-aircraft batteries.

GENERAL ARNOLD pointed out that his inquiry was in regard to whether arrangements of this nature would be made locally, to which Air Marshal Fallalev replied that the principle was being established here, and that the details would be determined on the spot by the commanders in the field.

GENERAL ANTONOV said that he now considered that the five questions given him by General Marshall on 24 July had been answered. He wished, however, to make an additional statement in regard to them. He said that he considered that all of the arrangements provided for under the five questions would come into being on the entry of Russia into the war against Japan.

GENERAL MARSHALL asked if it would be possible to get the communication equipment discussed in the first question into Siberia before that date, or if it would be necessary to wait until after Russia had entered the war.

GENERAL ANTONOV said that preliminary arrangements for the liaison wireless stations could be made beforehand, and that agreements could be reached with reference to each particular question raised.

GENERAL ANTONOV said that at the meeting on 24 July, Admiral King had pointed out that after the seizure of Kyushu communications might be opened from Kyushu to Vladivostok. This line of communications was very important, since the Straits of Tsushima could be used throughout the year, whereas the route through the Kuriles and through La Perousse Strait was closed during part of the year by ice. He asked General Marshall when the invasion of Kyushu would take place and when the opening of the sea route from the south could be expected.

GENERAL MARSHALL said that the occupation of Kyushu depended on three factors. The first was the movement of troops from Europe. This was

TOP SECRET

being done as rapidly as possible, and engineering troops were being moved first in order to prepare the way for the full application of air power. The movement involved two oceans and one continent, and although we could not be certain of carrying out the entire movement on schedule, and were now somewhat behind on both personnel and cargo, he hoped that all difficulties would be overcome. The second factor was the movement of large amounts of supplies from the Solomons, New Guinea, and Halmahera, north to the Philippines and Okinawa, to be loaded on assault ships for the tremendous amphibious effort against Kyushu. The third factor was the recent withdrawal of our divisions engaged in the Philippines and Okinawa from heavy fighting, and the problem of rehabilitation and training for the next operation.

Finally, he said, the weather conditions in the area made landings in September and early October too hazardous to undertake, although this was not a controlling factor as to date. At the present time he expected the landing on Kyushu to take place the last part of October.

GENERAL MARSHALL said further that the assault on Japan by naval and air forces which would extend also to Korea and the Liaotung Peninsula would be continued and increased. By these means he anticipated that by the time of the landing on Kyushu we will have destroyed Japanese oil, other material production, and communications, and will have virtually destroyed the Japanese air force. He said that Admiral King has added that the Japanese Navy would be destroyed as well. He said that all plans for the operation against Kyushu were complete, shipping was being assembled, the construction of bases was proceeding at top speed, and the operations of the United States Fleet and all air forces would proceed with increased vigor from now on. He thought, however, that the Tsushima Strait could not be opened before the end of October. The difficulties of opening Tsushima Strait would involve the sweeping of the passage for mines. The most serious threat to these operations would be from Japanese suicide planes which had caused us so much difficulty in previous operations.

GENERAL ANTONOV said that he would be much pleased if the route to Vladivostok via Tsushima Strait could be opened in October since by that time communications through the Kuriles and La Perousse Strait would be closed by ice.

GENERAL MARSHALL said he understood and appreciated the urgent necessity to the Russian Chiefs of Staff of opening the southern route and said that we would do all in our power to clear the straits as early as possible. General Marshall said that Admiral King had pointed out that the operations to open Tsushima Strait could not take place until after the landing in Kyushu and until after our air forces were established in northwestern Kyushu. It would be necessary, of course, for our minesweepers to have adequate air cover during their operations in clearing the straits of mines. The time required to establish the necessary airfields would depend to a large degree on Japanese resistance in Kyushu and the straits might not be opened until the middle of December or about six weeks after the first landing on Kyushu. He pointed out that we would make every effort to expedite the operation for the benefit of our forces as well as for the benefit to the Russians. He wanted to make this point clear since he desired to avoid any misunderstanding as to our capabilities in clearing Tsushima Strait for traffic to Vladivostok.

GENERAL MARSHALL then read a memorandum which he said related to this discussion and which gave the progress, from partial reports, covering the last ten days of naval and air action against Japan.

GENERAL ANTONOV expressed his appreciation for the information contained in the memorandum read by General Marshall.

GENERAL MARSHALL said that the United States Chiefs of Staff were prepared to furnish to the Russian Chiefs of Staff, until operations against Japan were commenced by the Soviet Union, a weekly report of operations similar to that contained in the memorandum, through General Deane or his naval associate. Thereafter, reports of such operations would be furnished through the commanders in the field.

GENERAL ANTONOV said that he would be glad to receive this information and asked if there were any other questions to be considered at this meeting.

GENERAL MARSHALL said that directions had been given to furnish the Russian Chiefs of Staff with copies of the minutes of this meeting in order to provide a means of determining if there was a mutual understanding of the conversations which had taken place. In the absence of comment by the Russian Chiefs of Staff, it would be assumed that the record was a correct basis for understanding and guidance.

GENERAL ANTONOV said that he would examine the minutes and if he had any comment he would inform the United States Chiefs of Staff thereof.

TOP SECRET

GENERAL MARSHALL said that it was planned that he, Admiral King and General Arnold would leave for the United States tomorrow. Admiral Leahy would remain until the conference was completed. He said that the principal assistants of the Chiefs of Staff, Admiral Cooke, General Hull and General Norstad would remain at the conference to handle any matters that might arise. He said that if he, Admiral King and General Arnold leave tomorrow as planned, he desired to take this occasion to express for the United States Chiefs of Staff their appreciation for the opportunity afforded to discuss these important matters with the Russian Chiefs of Staff. He was gratified that they had been able to reach decisions so satisfactory to all.

GENERAL ANTONOV also expressed his pleasure and satisfaction over the results of the conference and said that he hoped that his close contact with General Marshall would be continued in the future so that all questions that might arise might be settled promptly. He then gave General Marshall a map showing the areas which had been considered in the discussion.

GENERAL MARSHALL said that he regretted that through a misunderstanding the United States Chiefs of Staff had not received the answers to the five questions and were, therefore, not well prepared for the afternoon's discussion. He thanked General Antonov for his patience in reading the answers which he had presented.

TOP SECRET

ANNEX

First Question — Has the Soviet High Command received any instructions regarding the proposal to establish United States weather liaison groups in Petropavlovsk and Khabarovsk as presented to Generalissimo Stalin by President Truman on 23 July 1945?

Second Question — United States naval surface forces will operate without restriction in the Seas of Okhotsk and Japan. United States submarine forces will operate without restriction in the Seas of Okhotsk and Japan, south and east of a line established by connecting the following points: Coast of Korea at latitude 38° north, thence to latitude 40° north longitude 135° east, thence to latitude 45°45' north longitude 140° east, thence along the parallel of latitude 45°45' north. This boundary will be subject to later change as the situation may require. United States submarine operations north and west of this boundary and Soviet operations south and east of this boundary will be subject to coordination. Does the Soviet General Staff have any suggestions regarding further coordination of naval operations?

Third Question — United States air forces will operate without restriction south and east of the following line: Cape Lopatka, west to point at latitude 51°10' north longitude 147° east, thence to point at latitude 45°45' north longitude 144° 20' east, thence to point at latitude 45°45' north longitude 139°30' east, thence to point at latitude 41°20' north longitude 133°20' east, thence westward to Seishin, Korea, thence north to railroad at Korean border, thence westward along railroad to Yungki and Changchun, thence along the river to Liaoyuan, Kailu and Chihfeng, thence along the railroad through Tolun, Paochang, Wanchuan, Tatung, Fengchan, Tsining to Kweisui, thence northwest to the border of Outer Mongolia. This boundary will be subject to later change as the situation may require. United States air operations north and west of this boundary and Soviet operations south and east of this boundary will be subject to coordination. Does the Soviet General Staff have any suggestions regarding further coordination of air operations?

Fourth Question — Does the Soviet High Command agree to the proposal for the immediate establishment of operational coordination and liaison as proposed by the United States Chiefs of Staff in the letter sent by the Commanding General, United States Military Mission, to General Antonov on 5 July 1945?

TOP SECRET

Fifth Question — It is assumed that, after D-day, Soviet or United States air and naval craft in emergencies will have access to the nearest Soviet or United States ports or airfields where they may obtain repairs, servicing, medical care and otherwise be assisted in making a speedy return to combat. Although in extreme emergency the nearest friendly facility would be sought, it is considered desirable to designate certain ports, airfields or areas where maximum facilities would be available. Will the Soviet Government designate such ports, airfields or areas furnishing information necessary for proper location, identification and approach together with information on recognition signals, corridors of approach and exit for general use in any emergency, landing or coastal approach? The United States is prepared to take corresponding action in the case of Soviet aircraft.

Annex

INDEX

A

ADMIRALTY ISLANDS

Control of the Admiralty Islands, 153, 157

AGENDA FOR "TERMINAL" CONFERENCE

102, 105, 107, 109, 111
Program and procedure for the conference, 124, 127, *270*

AIR OPERATIONS

Admiral Mountbatten's statements regarding air transport operations in the Southeast Asia Command, *304*
Boundary line between operational zones of the U.S. and Soviet air forces in Korea and Manchuria, *329*
Concentration of Japanese industrial targets, 207
Efforts to sever the Japanese line of communications between Japan proper and Manchuria, *316*
Establishment of liaison groups between the American and Soviet commanders in the Far East for coordination of air operations, *330*
General Arnold's statements regarding Army air operations against Japan and her lines of communication in Manchuria, *318*
Over-all strategic concept for the prosecution of the war, 249
Planned deployment for tactical and strategic air operations against the Japanese mainland, 215
Rate of Hump tonnage delivery to China, 192
Report on Army air operations in the war against Japan, 206
Sir Charles Portal's statement regarding strength of the Japanese air forces in Southeast Asia, *322*
Tactical air operations in the war against Japan, 211
U.S. and U.S.S.R. zones of naval and air operations in the Sea of Japan, *327*
U.S. concept of strategy and operations for the main effort in the Pacific, 118

AIR TRANSPORT COMMAND

Rate of Hump tonnage delivery to China, 192

AIRBASES (*See* Bases)

AIRCRAFT

Aircraft production in Japan, 22, 29

AIRFIELDS (*See* Bases)

AIR LIFT

U.S. action to augment trooplift situation in redeployment of forces from Europe to the Pacific, 46

ALEXANDROVSK, SIBERIA

Selection of ports and airfields for emergency purposes, *331*

ALLIED COMMISSION IN ITALY

Appointment of Colonel Douglas to the Allied Commission in Italy, *288*

ALLIED FORCE HEADQUARTERS, MEDITERRANEAN

Arrangements for restricting the activities of Allied Force Headquarters, Mediterranean, 77, 79

ANDAMAN ISLANDS

Japanese situation, capabilities and intentions in the southern areas, 38

ANTONOV, ARMY GENERAL

Statements with reference to:
Adjournment of conference, *335*
Boundary line between operational zones of the U.S. and Soviet air forces in Korea and Manchuria, *329*
Liaison groups between the American and Soviet commanders in the Far East, *330*
Line of communications from Kyushu to Vladivostok, *332*

Note: Italic numerals refer to pages in minutes of meeting.
Plain type numerals refer to pages in C.C.S. Papers.

INDEX

ANTONOV, ARMY GENERAL (Cont'd)

Operations against the Kuriles and Korea, *320*

Operations to control La Perousse Strait, *321*

Radio stations in Petropavlovsk and Khabarovsk for transmitting weather data, *326*

Russian intentions and plans for the war against Japan, *314*

Selection of emergency ports and airfields, *331*

Strength of the Japanese force in Manchuria and on the Russian front, *314*

U.S. and U.S.S.R. zones for naval and air operations in the Sea of Japan, *327*

Weekly report of operations for the Russian Chiefs of Staff, *334*

ARNOLD, GENERAL H. H.

Statements with reference to:

Army air operations against Japan and her lines of communication in Manchuria, *318*

Boundary line between operational zones of the U.S. and Soviet air forces in Korea and Manchuria, *329*

Estimate on the strength of the Japanese air force, *319*

Possibility of including a British tactical air force in operations against Japan proper, 276

Selection of emergency ports and airfields, *331*

ASIA, SOUTHEAST (See Southeast Asia)

ATLANTIC

Employment of British passenger liners in the North Atlantic, 50

AUSTRALIA

Australian participation in operations on Borneo, 185

CCS discussion regarding employment of Australian forces in the operation against Japan, 277

CCS note that British Chiefs of Staff will obtain agreement of Australian, New Zealand and Dutch Governments to proposed reallocation of areas and command set-up in Southwest Pacific and SEAC, *293*

Control and command in the war against Japan, 148, 153, 157, *282*

General MacArthur's comments regarding British participation in the assault against Japan proper, 141

AUSTRIA

Assignment of enemy war matériel in Germany and Austria, 56, 64, *293*

B

B-29

Effectiveness of B-29 operations in the war against Japan, 210

BALIKPAPAN (See Borneo)

BANDA SEA

Japanese situation, capabilities and intentions in the southern areas, 38

BASES

Construction of airbases in Cocos Islands, 172

Construction of airfields in SEAC, 173

Planned deployment of tactical and strategic air operations against the Japanese mainland, 215

Selection of emergency ports and airfields, *331*

Theater commander's decision with regard to strategic course of action in the China Theater, 197

BASIC UNDERTAKINGS

Statement of basic undertakings and policies for the prosecution of the war, 82, 249, *310*

Note: Italic numerals refer to pages in minutes of meeting.
Plain type numerals refer to pages in C.C.S. Papers.

INDEX

BERING SEA

Bering Sea shall be a zone of mutual operations of the U.S. and Soviet Navy and air units, *328*

Selection of emergency ports and airfields in the Bering Sea area, *331*

BISMARCK ARCHIPELAGO

Allied operations against by-passed enemy garrisons, 185

General Marshall's statement regarding Japanese garrisons in the Pacific islands, *315*

Japanese situation in the Bismarcks, 16, 40

BLOCKADE

Efforts to sever the Japanese line of communications between Japan proper and the China Coast, *315*

Over-all strategic concept for the prosecution of the war, 249

U.S. concept of strategy and operations for the main effort in the Pacific, 118

BONIN ISLANDS

Japanese situation in the Bonins, 40

Report on air operations from Okinawa and Iwo Jima bases, 184

Report on operations for the capture of Iwo Jima and Okinawa, 183

U.S. concept of strategy and operations for the main effort in the Pacific, 118, 251, 256

BORNEO

General Marshall's statement regarding extent to which the U.S. Chiefs of Staff were proposing to support operations in the new British command, *281*

General Marshall's statement regarding isolated Japanese garrisons in the Pacific islands, *315*

Japanese situation, capabilities and intentions in the southern areas, 17, 38

Report on operations in Borneo, 185

Target date for the seizure of Balikpapan, 119

U.S. concept of strategy and operations for the main effort in the Pacific, 118, 256

BOUGAINVILLE

General Marshall's statement regarding isolated Japanese garrisons in the Pacific islands, *315*

BOUNDARIES

Boundary line between operational zones of the U.S. and Soviet air forces in Korea and Manchuria, *329*

CCS agreement on change in command in the Southwest Pacific area, *282*

CCS note that British Chiefs of Staff will obtain agreement of Australian, New Zealand and Dutch Governments to the proposed reallocation of areas and command set-up in Southwest Pacific and SEAC, *293*

Command arrangements in Indo-China, 160, *301*

Directive to the Supreme Allied Commander, Southeast Asia, 176, 252, 258, *292*

Reallocation of areas and command in the Southwest Pacific and Southeast Asia areas, 252, *281*

U.S. and U.S.S.R. zones of naval and air operations in the Sea of Japan, *327*

BROOKE, FIELD MARSHAL SIR ALAN

Statements with reference to:

Allocation of seven captured German passenger ships for U.S. employment in the Pacific, *300*

British land forces for operation CORONET, *274*

British participation in the war against Japan, *274*

Combined Chiefs of Staff machinery after the war with Japan, *286*

Date of transfer of command in the Southwest Pacific, *281*

Employment of the New Zealand division in Southeast Asia, *277*

Operations in Southeast Asia and plans for participating in the operations against Japan proper, *322*

Policy for imparting information to the Russians concerning the Japanese war, *287*

Shipping and assault craft, a limiting factor in amphibious operations against Sumatra and Java, *276*

Strategic direction in the war against Japan, *283*

Note: Italic numerals refer to pages in minutes of meeting.
Plain type numerals refer to pages in C.C.S. Papers.

INDEX

BROOKE, FIELD MARSHAL SIR ALAN
(Cont'd)

    Survival of the institution of the Emperor, *270*
    U.S. equipping of forces of occupation other than American, *310*

BRUNEI BAY (*See* Borneo)

BURMA

    Admiral Mountbatten's statement regarding enemy strength in Burma, *304*
    Admiral Mountbatten's statements regarding operations in the Southeast Asia Command, *304*
    British contribution to the final phase of the war against Japan, 137
    Construction of airfields in SEAC, 171
    Directive to the Supreme Allied Commander, Southeast Asia, 176, 252, 258, 292
    Enemy capabilities in Southeast Asia, 169, 172
    Japanese situation, capabilities and intentions in the southern areas, 16, 38
    Progress report on operations in the Southeast Asia Command, 169
    Rate of Hump tonnage delivery to China, 192
    Rehabilitation of oil fields in Burma, 173
    Sir Alan Brooke's statement regarding operations in Southeast Asia and plans for participating in the operations against Japan proper, *322*
    Transportation facilities in Burma, 173

C

CANADA

    Allocation of U.S. trooplift for the repatriation of 16,000 Canadians during 1945, 254, *300*
    Arrangements for one Canadian division to operate as part of a U.S. corps, 139, 141, *275*
    General MacArthur's comments regarding British participation in the assault against Japan proper, 141

CANTON

    General Marshall's statement regarding Japanese establishing fortress garrisons for defense of strategic points in China, *316*

CANTON-HONG KONG AREA

    Securing a major port on the China Coast, 194
    Theater commander's decision with regard to strategic course of action in the China Theater, 197

CAPTURED ENEMY EQUIPMENT

    Assignment of enemy war matériel in Germany and Austria, 56, 64, *293*

CAPTURED ENEMY SHIPPING

    Use of captured German passenger ships for movement of U.S. troops in the Pacific, 46, 51, 53, 254, *300*

CARIBIA, MS

    Employment in the Pacific, 46, 254, *300*

CAROLINE ISLANDS

    Report on air operations from Okinawa and Iwo Jima bases, 184

CASUALTIES

    Air casualties in the Philippine campaign, 214

CELEBES ISLAND

    General Marshall's statement regarding isolated Japanese garrisons in the Pacific islands, *315*
    Japanese situation, capabilities, and intentions in the southern areas, 38

CHINA

    Basic undertakings and policies for the prosecution of the war, 249, *310*
    General Marshall's statements regarding:
        Effectiveness of Chinese troops, *271*

Note: Italic numerals refer to pages in minutes of meeting.
Plain type numerals refer to pages in C.C.S. Papers.

INDEX

CHINA *(Cont'd)*

Effectiveness of Chinese troops and their planned operations against the port of Fort Bayard, 320

Estimated strength of the Japanese forces, 315

Movement of Japanese reinforcements from China to Manchuria, 316, 319

Movement of supplies to China, 320

Japanese foreign policy in China, 18, 41

Japanese military situation, capabilities, and intentions in China, 15, 36

Progress report on operations in China, April 1944 through June 1945, 192

Rate of Hump tonnage delivery to China, 192

Relative strengths of Japanese and Chinese troops in China, 194

Theater commander's decision with regard to strategic course of action in the China Theater, 197

Theater commander's estimate of:
Enemy capabilities in China, 195
Enemy situation in China, 193

Training and equipping Chinese forces, 193

COCOS ISLANDS

Construction of airbase in the Cocos Islands, 171, 172

COMBINED CHIEFS OF STAFF

Continuation of the Combined Chiefs of Staff machinery after the war with Japan, 162, 165, *286*

COMBINED SHIPPING ADJUSTMENT BOARD

Provision of personnel shipping for the requirements of Allied governments, 236, 243, 254, *301*

COMMAND

Admiral King's statement regarding relationship between U.S. and U.K. in the strategic direction of the war, *312*

Admiral Mountbatten's statement regarding assumption of the new command in the Southwest Pacific, *305*

CCS agree to recommend that the President and Prime Minister approach the Generalissimo to secure his agreement to the division of Indo-China between the China Theater and SEAC, 160, *301*

CCS agreement on change in command in the Southwest Pacific Area, *282*

CCS agreement on control and command in the war against Japan, *283*

Command arrangements in Indo-China, 160, *301*

Dissolution of the U.S. Seventh Fleet, *301*

General MacArthur's comments regarding British participation in the assault against Japan proper, 141

Reallocation of areas and command in the Southwest Pacific and Southeast Asia areas, 252, *280*

Sir Alan Brooke's statement regarding date of transfer of command in the Southwest Pacific, *281*

Strategic direction in the war against Japan, 151, 153, 158, *250, 280, 282*

The Prime Minister's statement regarding strategic direction of the war, *312*

"CORONET"

British contribution to the final phase of the war against Japan, 136, 139, 141, 251, *274*

CUNNINGHAM, ADMIRAL OF THE FLEET SIR ANDREW B.

Statements with reference to:
Division of Indo-China along the latitude of 15 degrees north, *280*
Equipping of forces of occupation other than American, *310*
Paucity of submarine targets in SEAC, *305*
Remnants of the Japanese Fleet in Southeast Asia, *322*
Strategic direction in the war against Japan, *282*

D

DANUBE RIVER

Internationalization of the Danube River, 228, 233

Note: Italic numerals refer to pages in minutes of meeting.
Plain type numerals refer to pages in C.C.S. Papers.

INDEX

DECEPTION

General Marshall's statement regarding effect of deception measures to cause Japanese concentration in the Kuriles, *315*

DECISIONS

ALLIED FORCE HEADQUARTERS

Future of Allied Force Headquarters, Mediterranean, 77, 79

BRITISH PARTICIPATION

CCS agreed in principle on the participation of a British Commonwealth land force in the final phase of the war against Japan, *277*

CCS agreed that British commanders and staff shall visit General MacArthur and Adm. Nimitz and draw up a plan for submission to the CCS, *277*

CCS took note that possibility of establishing a small British tactical air force in support of the proposed Commonwealth land force would be studied, *278*

CAPTURED EQUIPMENT

CCS approve arrangements for the disposal of enemy war matériel in Germany and Austria, *293*

COMBINED CHIEFS OF STAFF

CCS took note of British and U.S. memoranda regarding CCS machinery after the war with Japan, *287*

COMMAND

CCS agree to recommend that the President and Prime Minister approach the Generalissimo to secure his agreement to the division of Indo-China between the China Theater and SEAC, 160, *301*

CCS agreement on control and command in the war against Japan, *283*

Control of Allied naval units other than U.S. at present under command of Seventh U.S. Fleet, *301*

DANUBE RIVER

Internationalization of the Danube River, 228, 233

FRENCH AND DUTCH PARTICIPATION

CCS approved memorandum to the French and Netherlands representatives to the CCS regarding their participation in the war against Japan, *280*

CCS approved a reply to the Chief of the French Military Mission in the U.S. regarding the participation of two French colonial infantry divisions in Far Eastern operations, *286*

OPERATIONS IN THE PACIFIC

CCS took note of a U.S. memorandum on the development of operations in the Pacific, *271*

PORTUGUESE PARTICIPATION

CCS approve letter to Department of State and Foreign Office with regard to Portuguese participation in operations against Timor, *280*

REPORTS

CCS took note of C.I.C. report on the estimate of the enemy situation, *270*

CCS took note of progress reports on operations in the Pacific and Southeast Asia Command, *271*

CCS took note of report on Army air operations in the war against Japan, *271*

Report to the President and Prime Minister, *301, 308*

SHIPPING

CCS approve procedure for allocation of personnel shipping to meet requirements of Allied governments, *301*

CCS decision regarding employment of captured enemy ocean-going passenger shipping and British troopship employment in U.S. trans-Atlantic programs during first half of 1946, *300*

SOUTHEAST ASIA COMMAND

CCS agreement on change in command in the Southwest Pacific Area, *282*

CCS approve the directive to the Supreme Allied Commander, Southeast Asia, *293*

CCS note that British Chiefs of Staff will obtain agreement of Australian, New Zealand and Dutch Governments to the proposed reallocation of areas and command setup in Southwest Pacific Area, *282*

Note: Italic numerals refer to pages in minutes of meeting.
Plain type numerals refer to pages in C.C.S. Papers.

INDEX

DECISIONS (Cont'd)

  SURRENDER

  Agreed planning date for the end of organized resistance by Japan, *288*

  CCS invite the British Chiefs of Staff to seek the opinion of the Prime Minister in the matter of unconditional surrender of Japan, *270*

  "TERMINAL" CONFERENCE

  CCS approve the program and procedure for the conference, *270*

  U.S.S.R.

  Boundary line between operational zones of the U.S. and Soviet air forces in Korea and Manchuria, *329*

  CCS decision regarding information for the Russians concerning the Japanese war, *288*

  Establishing radio stations in Petropavlovsk and Khabarovsk for transmitting weather data, *326*

  Establishment of liaison groups between the American and Soviet commanders in the Far East, *330*

  Selection of ports and airfields for ships and planes for emergency purposes, *331*

  Separate zones of naval and air operations to be set up for the U.S. and U.S.S.R. in the Sea of Japan, *327*

DOMINIONS

  British forces available for the invasion of Japan, 137, *251*

DOUGLAS, COLONEL J. H.

  Appointment of Colonel Douglas to the Allied Commission in Italy, *288*

E

ELECTRONICS (*See* Production)

EQUIPPING OF FORCES

  Basic undertakings and policies for the prosecution of the war, 249, *309*

  The Prime Minister's statement regarding need for U.S. assistance in equipping British forces, *309*

  Use of lend-lease for equipping occupational and post-war armies, 95

EUROPA, SS

  Employment of captured German passenger ships in the Pacific, 46, 254, *300*

F

FALLALEV, MARSHAL OF AVIATION

  Statements with reference to:
  Boundary line between operational zones of the U.S. and Soviet air forces in Korea and Manchuria, *329*
  Selection of ports and airfields for emergency docking and landing purposes, *332*

FAR EAST

  Establishment of liaison groups between the American and Soviet commanders in the Far East, *330*

  General Antonov's statement regarding Russian intentions and plans for the war against Japan, *314*

  Policy regarding French and Dutch participation in the war against Japan, 73, 252, *280*

FAR EAST AIR FORCES

  Tactical air operations in the war against Japan, 211

FOOD SUPPLY

  Economic situation in Japan, 13, 24

FORCES, ALLIED

  Admiral King's statement regarding employment of Australian forces in the operation against Japan, *277*

  Admiral Mountbatten's statement regarding employment of two French divisions in Indo-China, *306*

  Disposition of Allied forces in Southeast Asia, 170

  Equipping and employment of two French colonial infantry divisions in Far Eastern operations, 218, 223, 225, 253, *286*

Note: Italic numerals refer to pages in minutes of meeting.
Plain type numerals refer to pages in C.C.S. Papers.

INDEX

FORCES, ALLIED *(Cont'd)*
    General MacArthur's comments regarding British participation in the assault against Japan proper, 141
    General Marshall's statement regarding employment of two French divisions for operations in the war against Japan, *306*
    Participation of a British Commonwealth force in the final phase of the war against Japan, 137, 251, *277*
    Relative strengths of Japanese and Chinese troops in China, 195
    Sir Alan Brooke's statement regarding the British land forces for operation CORONET, *274*
    Size of Portuguese forces acceptable for training and operations in Timor, 5

FORCES, ENEMY
    Admiral Cunningham's statement regarding remnants of the Japanese Fleet in Southeast Asia, *322*
    Admiral Mountbatten's statement regarding enemy strength in Burma, *304*
    Capabilities of the Japanese air forces, 30, 39
    Capabilities of the Japanese Navy, 12, 31
    Effectiveness of the Japanese air forces, 210
    Enemy capabilities in Southeast Asia, 169, 172
    General Antonov's statement regarding strength of the Japanese forces in Manchuria and on the Russian front, *314*
    General Arnold's statement regarding estimate of the strength of the Japanese air force, *319*
    General Marshall's statement regarding the estimated strength of the Japanese forces, *315*
    Map showing disposition of the Japanese ground forces, 32
    Strength of the Japanese Armed Forces:
        Air, 14, 28
        Ground, 14, 27, 33
        National Volunteer Army, 28
        Naval, 15, 30

FORCES, NAVAL
    Admiral King's statement regarding naval operations against Japan and the development of bases in the Pacific, *317*

FORMOSA
    General Marshall's statement regarding the estimated strength of the Japanese forces, *315*
    Japanese military situation, capabilities and intentions in, 15, 37

FORT BAYARD
    General Marshall's statement regarding effectiveness of Chinese troops and their planned operations against the port of Fort Bayard, *320*
    Securing a major port on the China Coast, 194
    Theater commander's decision with regard to his strategic course of action in the China Theater, 197

FOURTEENTH AIR FORCE
    Progress report on operations in China, April 1944 through June 1945, 192

FRANCE
    Admiral Mountbatten's statement regarding employment of two French divisions in Indo-China, *306*
    Equipping and employment of two French colonial infantry divisions in Far Eastern operations, 218, 223, 225, 253, *286*
    General Marshall's statement regarding employment of two French divisions in operations against the Japanese, *306*
    Policy regarding French and Dutch participation in the war against Japan, 73, 252, *280*

G

GERMANY
    Assignment of enemy war matériel in Germany and Austria, 56, 64, *293*
    Use of captured German passenger ships for movement of U.S. troops in the Pacific, 46, 52, 53, 254, *300*

GUAM
    Admiral King's statement regarding naval operations against Japan and the development of bases in the Pacific, *317*

Note: Italic numerals refer to pages in minutes of meeting.
Plain type numerals refer to pages in C.C.S. Papers.

INDEX

H

HALMAHERA

Japanese situation, capabilities and intentions in the southern areas, 16, 38

HONG KONG

British contribution to the final phase of the war against Japan, 136, 139, 141, 178, 250, *274*

General Marshall's statement regarding Japanese establishing fortress garrisons for defense of strategic points in China, *316*

HONSHU

(*See also* Japan)

Report on air operations from Okinawa and Iwo Jima bases, 184

U.S. concept of strategy and operations for the main effort in the Pacific, 118, 250, 256

HULL, LT. GEN. J. E.

Statements with reference to:
Inclusion of an Australian force in the operations against Japan, *276*
List of the supporting and service units required by the two French divisions to be employed in the Far East, *306*

I

INDIA

Admiral Mountbatten's statements regarding operations in the Southeast Asia Command, *304*

British forces available for the invasion of Japan, 137

INDO-CHINA

Admiral Mountbatten's statement regarding employment of two French divisions in Indo-China, *306*

Admiral Mountbatten's statement regarding division of French Indo-China, *306*

CCS agree to recommend that the President and Prime Minister approach the Generalissimo to secure his agreement to the division of Indo-China between the China Theater and SEAC, 160, *301*

CCS agreement on change in command in the Southwest Pacific Area, *282*

Command arrangements in Indo-China, 160, *301*

Equipping and employment of two French colonial infantry divisions in Far Eastern operations, 218, 223, 225, 253, *286*

General Marshall's statement regarding dividing Indo-China between the China Theater and SEAC, *280, 306*

Japanese situation, capabilities, and intentions in the southern areas, 16, 38

INLAND SEA

General Marshall's statement regarding U.S. submarine action to sever Japanese communications in the Sea of Japan; and B-29 mine-laying near Shimonoseki and Niigata, *316*

ITALY

Appointment of Colonel Douglas to the Allied Commission in Italy, *288*

Arrangements for restricting the activities of Allied Force Headquarters, Mediterranean, 77, 79

IWO JIMA (*See* Bonin Islands)

J

JAPAN

Admiral Mountbatten's statement regarding enemy strength in Burma, *304*

Aircraft production in Japan, 22, 29

British contribution to the final phase of the war against Japan, 136, 139, 141, 250, *274*

British forces available for the invasion of Japan, 137, 251

Note: Italic numerals refer to pages in minutes of meeting.
Plain type numerals refer to pages in C.C.S. Papers.

INDEX

JAPAN *(Cont'd)*

CCS agreement on the participation of a British Commonwealth land force in the final phase of the war against Japan, 277

CCS invite the British Chiefs of Staff to seek the opinion of the Prime Minister in the matter of unconditional surrender of Japan, 270

Capabilities of the Japanese Air Forces, 30, 33

Capabilities of the Japanese Navy, 12, 31, 33

Concentration of Japanese industrial targets, 207

Economic situation in Japan, 20

Effectiveness of Japanese air forces, 210

Efforts to sever the Japanese line of communications between Japan proper and the China Coast, 315

Enemy capabilities in Southeast Asia, 169, 172

Estimate of the enemy situation (6 July 1945), 8, 12, *270*

General Antonov's statement regarding strength of the Japanese force in Manchuria and on the Russian front, *314*

General Arnold's statement regarding estimate of the strength of the Japanese air force, *319*

General Marshall's statement regarding the estimated strength of the Japanese forces, *315*

Japanese foreign policy, 18, 41

Japanese military situation in:
  Central and South China and Formosa, 15, 37
  Korea, Manchuria and North China, 13, 36
  Pacific islands, 16, 40
  Southern areas, 16, 38

Map showing disposition of the Japanese ground forces, 32

Over-all strategic concept for the prosecution of the war, 249

Planned deployment of tactical and strategic air operations against the Japanese mainland, 214

Planning date for the end of organized resistance by Japan, 122, 254, *288*

Political situation in Japan, 17, 41

Possibility of Japanese surrender, 43

Preparation of plans for occupation of Japan proper, 119

Probable military strategy of Japan, 17

Relative strengths of Japanese and Chinese troops in China, 195

Report on Army air operations in the war against Japan, 206

Sir Alan Brooke's statement regarding survival of the institution of the Emperor, *270*

Strength of the Japanese armed forces:
  Air, 14, 28
  Ground, 27, 33
  National Volunteer Army, 28
  Naval, 15, 30

Tactical air operations in the war against Japan, 211

Target date for the invasion of the Tokyo Plain, 119

Theater commander's estimate of the enemy capabilities in China, 195

U.S. concept of strategy and operations for the main effort in the Pacific, 118, 256

JAPAN, SEA OF

Discussion regarding selection of emergency ports and airfields in the North Pacific, *331*

Discussion regarding separate U.S.-U.S.S.R. zones of naval and air operations in the Sea of Japan, *327*

General Marshall's statement regarding U.S. submarine action to sever Japanese communications in the Sea of Japan, *316*

JAVA

Directive to the Supreme Allied Commander, Southeast Asia, 176, 252, 258, *292*

General Marshall's statement regarding isolated Japanese garrisons in the Pacific islands, *315*

Japanese situation, capabilities, and intentions in the southern areas, 17, 38

K

KHABAROVSK, SIBERIA

Establishing radio stations in Petropavlovsk and Khabarovsk for transmitting weather data, *326*

KIKAI JIMA (*See* Ryukyu Islands)

Note: Italic numerals refer to pages in minutes of meeting.
Plain type numerals refer to pages in C.C.S. Papers.

INDEX

KING, FLEET ADMIRAL E. J.

Statements with reference to:
Combined study on shipping resources and requirements, *300*
Division of Indo-China along the latitude 15 degrees north, *281*
Employment of Australian forces in the operation against Japan, *277*
Establishing radio stations in Siberia for transmitting weather data, *326*
Naval operations against Japan and the development of bases in the Pacific, *317*
Operations against the Kuriles and Korea, *320*
Operations to control La Perousse Strait, *321*
Policy for imparting information to the Russians concerning the Japanese war, *287*
Relationship between the U.S. and U.K. in the strategic direction of the war, *312*
Separate U.S.-U.S.S.R. zones for naval and air operations in the Sea of Japan, *327*

KOREA

Boundary line between operational zones of the U.S. and Soviet air forces in Korea and Manchuria, *329*
Japanese military situation, capabilities and intentions in Korea, 15, 36
Tripartite discussion regarding operations against the Kuriles and Korea, *320*

KURILE ISLANDS

General Marshall's statement regarding effect of deception measures to cause Japanese concentrations in the Kuriles, *315*
Line of communications from Kyushu to Vladivostok, *332*
Operations against the Kuriles and Korea, *320*
Report on operations in the North Pacific area, 184

KUZNETSOV, ADMIRAL OF THE FLEET

Statement with regard to separate U.S.-U.S.S.R. zones for naval and air operations in the Sea of Japan, *328*

KYUSHU (*See also* Japan)

Line of communications from Kyushu to Vladivostok, *332*
Report on air operations from Okinawa and Iwo Jima bases, 184
U.S. concept of strategy and operations for the main effort in the Pacific, 118, 250, 256

L

LABUAN ISLAND

Report on operations in Borneo, 185

LANDING SHIPS AND CRAFT

Sir Alan Brooke's statement regarding shipping and assault craft, a limiting factor in amphibious operations against Sumatra and Java, *276*

LA PEROUSSE STRAIT

Line of communications from Kyushu to Vladivostok, *332*
Operations to control La Perousse Strait, *321*

LEAHY, FLEET ADMIRAL WILLIAM D.

Statements with reference to:
Equipping of forces of occupation other than American, *310*
Explanation of differences of opinion which exist regarding the agreed "Basic Undertakings," *308*
Views of the Prime Minister on explaining to the Japanese the term "unconditional surrender," *270*

LEATHERS, LORD

Statement with regard to inclusion of the United Kingdom import program in the agreed "Basic Undertakings," *311*

Note: Italic numerals refer to pages in minutes of meeting.
Plain type numerals refer to pages in C.C.S. Papers.

INDEX

LEND-LEASE

The President's statement regarding furnishing supplies to the British troops, *309*

The Prime Minister's statement regarding need for U.S. assistance in equipping British forces, *309*

Use of lend-lease for equipping occupational and post-war armies, 95

LIAISON

Establishment of liaison groups between the American and Soviet commanders in the Far East, *330*

LIAOTUNG PENINSULA

General Antonov's statement regarding Russian intentions and plans for the war against Japan, *314*

LINES OF COMMUNICATION

Hump tonnage delivered to China, 192

Line of communications from Kyushu to Vladivostok, *332*

Preparation of plans for keeping open a sea route to Russian Pacific ports, 119

Transportation facilities in Burma, 173

Tripartite discussions regarding operations against the Kuriles and Korea, *320*

Securing a major port on the China Coast, 194

LOGISTICS

General MacArthur's comments with reference to logistical problems involved in British participation in the assault against Japan proper, 141

LONDON MUNITIONS ASSIGNMENT BOARD

Assignment of enemy war matériel in Germany and Austria, 56, 64, *293*

LUZON (See Philippine Islands)

M

MacARTHUR, GENERAL DOUGLAS

Comments regarding British participation in the assault against Japan proper, 141

MALACCA, STRAIT OF

British contribution to the final phase of the war against Japan, 137

Directive to the Supreme Allied Commander, Southeast Asia, 176, 252, 258, *292*

MALAY PENINSULA

Directive to the Supreme Allied Commander, Southeast Asia, 176, 252, 258, *292*

General Marshall's statement regarding isolated Japanese garrisons in the Pacific islands, *315*

General Marshall's statement regarding employment of submarines in SEAC to prevent infiltration of Japs into Malaya, *305*

Japanese situation, capabilities and intentions in the southern areas, 16, 38

Progress report on operations in the Southeast Asia Command, 168

MANCHURIA

Boundary line between operational zones of the U.S. and Soviet air forces in Korea and Manchuria, *329*

Estimate of the enemy situation in Manchuria, 194

General Antonov's statement regarding Russian intentions and plans for the war against Japan, *314*

General Antonov's statement regarding strength of the Japanese forces in Manchuria, *314*

General Marshall's statements regarding movement of Japanese reinforcements from China to Manchuria, *316*, *319*

Japanese foreign policy, 41

Japanese military situation, capabilities and intentions in Manchuria, 15, 36

Note: Italic numerals refer to pages in minutes of meeting.
Plain type numerals refer to pages in C.C.S. Papers.

INDEX

MANDATED ISLANDS

Japanese situation in the Japanese Mandated Islands, 16, 40

MANPOWER

Manpower situation in Japan, 13, 25

MAPS

Burma area, facing page 174
Disposition of the Japanese ground forces, 32
Ground situation, China, 6 June 1945, showing major U.S. airfields held by Japanese and Chinese, 203
Ground situation, China Theater, 1 April 1944, showing U.S. airfields that were subsequently overrun by Japanese drives, 199
Line showing maximum territory occupied by Japanese in South China during 1944-1945 including major U.S. airfields lost to the Japanese, 201
Review of Pacific situation, 1 February 1945, 189
Review of Pacific situation, 1 July 1945, 187

MARIANA ISLANDS

Admiral King's statement regarding naval operations against Japan and the development of bases in the Pacific, 317
U.S. concept of strategy and operations for the main effort in the Pacific, 118, 250, 256

MARSHALL, GENERAL OF THE ARMY G. C.

Statements with reference to:
Adjournment of the conference, 335
Australian, New Zealand and Dutch approval to the proposed reallocation of areas and command setup in the Southwest Pacific Area, 292
Boundary line between operational zones of the U.S. and Soviet air forces in Korea and Manchuria, 329
British proposals for participation in the war against Japan, 277
Combined Chiefs of Staff machinery after the war with Japan, 286
Dividing Indo-China into two parts to be included in the China Theater and SEAC, 280, 306
Effect of deception measures to cause Japanese concentrations in the Kuriles, 315
Effectiveness of Chinese troops and their planned operations against the port of Fort Bayard, 271, 320
Emergency ports and airfields in Siberia and the North Pacific, 331
Employment of submarines in SEAC to prevent infiltration of Japs into Malaya, 305
Employment of two French divisions for operations in the war against Japan, 306
Estimated strength of the Japanese forces, 314
Extent to which the U.S. Chiefs of Staff were proposing to support operations in the new British command, 281
Isolated Japanese garrisons in the Pacific islands, 315
Japanese establishing fortress garrisons for defense of strategic points in China, 316
Liaison groups between the American and Soviet commanders in the Far East, 329
Line of communications from Kyushu to Vladivostok, 332
Movement of Japanese reinforcements from China to Manchuria, 316, 319
Movement of supplies to China, 319
Offering U.S. Chiefs' congratulations to Admiral Mountbatten on the conclusion of his campaign in Burma, 304
Operations against the Kuriles and Korea, 320
Policy for imparting information to the Russians concerning the Japanese war, 288
Progress in redeploying U.S. troops from the European Theater to the Pacific, 317
Radio stations in Petropavlovsk and Khabarovsk for transmitting weather data, 326
Separate U.S.-U.S.S.R. zones for naval and air operations in the Sea of Japan, 327

Note: Italic numerals refer to pages in minutes of meeting.
Plain type numerals refer to pages in C.C.S. Papers.

INDEX

MARSHALL, GENERAL OF THE ARMY G. C. *(Cont'd)*

Shortages of shipping in the Pacific, *317*

Strategic direction in the war against Japan, *282*

Transfer of command in the Southwest Pacific, *281, 305*

U.S. submarine action to sever Japanese communications in the Sea of Japan and B-29 mine-laying near Shimonoseki and Niigata, *316*

U.S. position of control in Okinawa, *315*

Visit of a British corps commander and staff to the Pacific, *276*

Weekly report of operations for the Russian Chiefs of Staff, *334*

MATSUWA ISLANDS

Report on operations in the North Pacific area, 184

MEDITERRANEAN THEATER

Arrangements for restricting the activities of Allied Force Headquarters, Mediterranean, 77, 79

METEOROLOGY

Establishing radio stations in Petropavlovsk and Khabarovsk for transmitting weather data, *326*

General Arnold's statements regarding effect of weather on Army air operations against Japan and her lines of communication to Manchuria, *318*

MILWAUKEE, MS

Employment of captured German passenger ships for movement of U.S. troops in the Pacific, 46, 51, *300*

MINDANAO (*See* Philippine Islands)

MIYAKO JIMA (*See* Ryukyu Islands)

MOUNTBATTEN, ADMIRAL LORD LOUIS

Statements with reference to:
Assumption of the new command in the Southwest Pacific, *306*

Division of French Indo-China, *306*

Enemy strength in Burma, *304*

Employment of two French divisions in Indo-China, *306*

Operations in the Southeast Asia Command, *304*

N

NAURU ISLANDS

Operations against Nauru Islands, 153

NAVAL OPERATIONS

Admiral King's statement regarding naval operations against Japan and the development of bases in the Pacific, *317*

Line of communications from Kyushu to Vladivostok, *332*

Separate U.S.-U.S.S.R. zones for naval and air operations in the Sea of Japan, *327*

NETHERLANDS

British to obtain agreement to the proposed reallocation of areas and command in Southwest Pacific and SEAC, *293*

Policy regarding French and Dutch participation in the war against Japan, 73, *252, 280*

NEW GUINEA

Allied operations against by-passed enemy garrisons, 185

General Marshall's statement regarding isolated Japanese garrisons in the Pacific islands, *315*

Japanese situation, capabilities and intentions in the southern areas, 16, 38

Note: Italic numerals refer to pages in minutes of meeting.
Plain type numerals refer to pages in C.C.S. Papers.

INDEX

NEW ZEALAND

    British to obtain agreement on proposed reallocation of areas and command in Southwest Pacific and SEAC, *293*

    Sir Alan Brooke's statement regarding the employment of New Zealand division in Southeast Asia, *277*

NICOBAR ISLANDS

    Japanese situation, capabilities and intentions in the southern areas, 38

O

OCCUPATION OF JAPAN

    Basic undertakings and policies for the prosecution of the war, 249, *310*

    Over-all strategic concept for the prosecution of the war, 249

    Preparation of plans for occupation of Japan proper, 119

OKHOTSK SEA

    Selection of emergency ports and airfields, *331*

    Separate U.S.-U.S.S.R. zones for naval and air operations, *327*

OKINAWA (*See* Ryukyu Islands)

OVER-ALL OBJECTIVE, 249

OVER-ALL STRATEGIC CONCEPT, 249

P

PACIFIC OCEAN AREAS

    Admiral Mountbatten's statement regarding assumption of the new command in the Southwest Pacific, *305*

    Control and command in the war against Japan, 148, 153, 157, *282*

    General progress report on recent operations in the Pacific, 182

    Reallocation of areas and command in the Southwest Pacific and Southeast Asia areas, 252, *280*

    Report on operations for the capture of Iwo Jima and Okinawa, 183

    Report on operations in the North Pacific area, 184

    Report on operations in the Philippine Islands, 184

    Sir Alan Brooke's statement regarding date of transfer of command in the Southwest Pacific, *281*

    Strategy and plans for operations in the Pacific, 118, 250, 256

    U.S. Seventh Fleet, *301*

PARAMUSHIRU ISLANDS

    Report on operations in the North Pacific, 184

PATRIA, MS

    Employment of captured German passenger ships for movement of U.S. troops in the Pacific, 46, 51, 54, 254, *300*

PETROLEUM

    Petroleum situation in Japan, 23

    Rehabilitation of oilfields in Burma, 173

PETROPAVLOVSK, SIBERIA

    Establishing radio stations for transmitting weather data, *326*

    Selection of emergency ports and airfields, *331*

PHILIPPINE ISLANDS

    Air casualties in the Philippine campaign, 214

    General Marshall's statement regarding the estimated strength of the Japanese forces in the Philippines, *315*

    Japanese situation in the Philippines, 40

    Report on operations in the Philippine Islands, 184

    Tactical air operations in the war against Japan, 212

    U.S. concept of strategy and operations for the main effort in the Pacific, 118, 250, 256

Note: Italic numerals refer to pages in minutes of meeting.
Plain type numerals refer to pages in C.C.S. Papers.

INDEX

PLANNING

Planning date for the end of organized resistance by Japan, 122, 254, *288*

Preparation of plans for keeping open sea route to Russian Pacific ports, 119

Preparation of plans for occupation of Japan proper, 119

Visit of a British corps commander and accompanying officers with General MacArthur and Admiral Nimitz, 145, *251, 276*

PORTAL, SIR CHARLES F. A.

Statements in reference to:
Employment of a British tactical air force in operations against Japan proper, *275*
Policy for imparting information to the Russians concerning the Japanese war, *287*
SACSEA's assumption of command in the Southwest Pacific, *281*
Strength of the Japanese air forces in Southeast Asia, *322*

PORTS

Planned operations against the port of Fort Bayard, *320*

Selection of emergency ports and airfields in Siberia and the North Pacific, *331*

Securing a major port on the China Coast, 194

PORTUGAL

Portuguese participation in operations to expel the Japanese from Timor, 3, 5, *253, 280*

POST-WAR

Use of lend-lease for equipping occupational and post-war armies, 95, *309*

POTSDAM, SS

Employment of captured German passenger ships for movement of U.S. troops in the Pacific, 46, 51, 53, 254, *300*

PRESIDENT OF THE UNITED STATES

Reconstruction and rehabilitation of the United Kingdom, *311*

Supplies for British forces, *310*

PRETORIA, SS

Employment of captured German passenger ships for movement of U.S. troops in the Pacific, 46, *300*

PRIORITIES

Priorities for cargo shipping, 85, 88

PRIME MINISTER OF THE UNITED KINGDOM

Strategic direction of the war, *312*

U.S. assistance in equipping British forces, *309*

United Kingdom import program, *311*

PRODUCTION

Agreed planning date for the end of organized resistance by Japan, *288*

Aircraft production in Japan, 22, 29

Armament production in Japan, 22

Basic undertakings and policies for the prosecution of the war, *249, 309*

Industrial situation in Japan, 13, 21

PSYCHOLOGICAL WARFARE

Psychological effect of bombing Japanese cities, 13

Q

QUEENS

Employment of British passenger liners in the North Atlantic, 50

R

RAILROADS (*See* Transportation)

RAW MATERIALS

Economic situation in Japan, 23

Note: Italic numerals refer to pages in minutes of meeting.
Plain type numerals refer to pages in C.C.S. Papers.

INDEX

REDEPLOYMENT

Basic undertakings and policies for the prosecution of the war, 249, *310*

Employment of British passenger liners in the North Atlantic, 50

Employment of captured German passenger ships for movement of U.S. troops in the Pacific, 46, *300*

General Marshall's statement regarding progress in redeploying U.S. troops from the European Theater to the Pacific, *317*

U.S. efforts to assist trooplift situation in redeployment of forces from Europe to the Pacific, 46, 49

RELEASE OF INFORMATION

Policy for the release of information to the Russians concerning the Japanese war, 130, 131, 133, 253, *287*

REPORTS

Estimate of the enemy situation, 8

General progress report on recent operations in the Pacific, 182

Progress report on operations in China, April 1944 through June 1945, 192

Progress report on operations in the Southeast Asia Command, 168

Report on Army air operations in the war against Japan, 206

To the President and Prime Minister, 248

Weekly report of operations for the Russian Chiefs of Staff, *334*

RYUKYU ISLANDS

General Marshall's statement regarding the estimated strength of the Japanese forces, *315*

General Marshall's statement regarding the U.S. position of control in Okinawa, *315*

Report on air operations from Okinawa and Iwo Jima bases, 184

Report on operations for the capture of Okinawa, 183

U.S. concept of strategy and operations for the main effort in the Pacific, 118, 250, 256

S

SAIPAN

Admiral King's statement regarding naval operations against Japan and the development of bases in the Pacific, *317*

SAKHALIN ISLAND

Operations to control La Perouse Strait, *321*

SEVENTH U.S. FLEET

Change in command of elements of the U.S. Seventh Fleet, *301*

SHANGHAI

General Marshall's statement regarding Japanese establishing fortress garrisons for defense of strategic points in China, *316*

SHIPPING

Allocation of U.S. trooplift for the repatriation of 16,000 Canadians during 1945, 254, *300*

Authorized overloading of Victory and Liberty ships, 49

Combined shipping resources and requirement study to be completed by 15 September 1945, 254, *300*

Employment of British passenger liners in the North Atlantic, 50

Employment of captured German passenger ships for movement of U.S. troops in the Pacific, 46, *300*

Estimate of the cargo shipping situation, 255

General Marshall's statement regarding shortages of shipping in the Pacific, *317*

Lord Leathers' statement regarding inclusion of the United Kingdom import program in the "Basic Undertakings," *311*

Priorities for cargo shipping, 85, 88

Provision of personnel shipping for the requirements of Allied governments, 236, 243, 254, *301*

Note: Italic numerals refer to pages in minutes of meeting.
Plain type numerals refer to pages in C.C.S. Papers.

INDEX

SHIPPING *(Cont'd)*

Shipping position in Japan, 20
The Prime Minister's statement regarding the United Kingdom import program, *311*

SIAM (*See* Thailand)

SINGAPORE

British contribution to the final phase of the war against Japan, 137, 177, 251, 274
Directive to the Supreme Allied Commander, Southeast Asia, 176, 252, 258, 292

SOLOMON ISLANDS

Allied operations against by-passed enemy garrisons, 185, *315*
Japanese situation in the Solomons, 16, 40

SOUTHEAST ASIA

Admiral Cunningham's statement regarding remnants of the Japanese Fleet in Southeast Asia, *322*
Admiral Cunningham's statement regarding the paucity of submarine targets in SEAC, *305*
Control and command in the war against Japan, 148, 153, 157, *282*
Directive to the Supreme Allied Commander, Southeast Asia, 176, 252, 258, 292
Disposition of Allied forces in Southeast Asia, 170
Enemy capabilities in Southeast Asia, 169, 172
General Marshall's statement regarding employment of submarines in SEAC to prevent infiltration of Japs into Malaya, *305*
Japanese foreign policy, 18, 41
Progress report on operations in SEAC, 169
Reallocation of areas and command in the Southwest Pacific and Southeast Asia areas, 252, *280*

Sir Alan Brooke's statement regarding operations in Southeast Asia and plans for participating in the operations against Japan proper, *322*
Sir Charles Portal's statement regarding strength of Japanese air forces in Southeast Asia, *322*

STRATEGY

Admiral King's statement regarding relationship between the U.S. and U.K. in the strategic direction of the war, *312*
Basic undertakings and policies for the prosecution of the war, 249, *309*
Directive to the Supreme Allied Commander, Southeast Asia, 176, 252, 258
General Antonov's statement regarding Russian intentions and plans for the war against Japan, *314*
Over-all objective in the prosecution of the war, 249
Over-all strategic concept for the prosecution of the war, 249
Strategic direction in the war against Japan, 151, 153, 158, 250, *280, 282*
The Prime Minister's statement regarding strategic direction of the war, *312*
Theater commander's decision with regard to strategic course of action in the China Theater, 197
U.S. concept of strategy and operations for the main effort in the Pacific, 118, 250, 256

SUBMARINE WARFARE

Admiral Cunningham's statement regarding the paucity of submarine targets in SEAC, *305*
Admiral King's statement regarding naval operations against Japan and the development of bases in the Pacific, *317*
General Marshall's statement regarding employment of submarines in SEAC to prevent infiltration of Japs into Malaya, *305*
General Marshall's statements regarding U.S. submarine action to sever Japanese communications in the Sea of Japan and B-29 mine-laying near Shimonoseki and Niigata, *316*
Report on submarine campaign in the Western Pacific, 184

Note: Italic numerals refer to pages in minutes of meeting.
Plain type numerals refer to pages in C.C.S. Papers.

INDEX

SUMATRA

Directive to the Supreme Allied Commander, Southeast Asia, 252, 259
General Marshall's statement regarding isolated Japanese garrisons in the Pacific islands, *315*
Japanese situation, capabilities, and intentions in the southern areas, 16, 38

SURRENDER

CCS invite the British Chiefs of Staff to seek the opinion of the Prime Minister in the matter of unconditional surrender of Japan, *270*
Possibility of Japanese surrender, 43
Sir Alan Brooke's statement regarding survival of the institution of the Emperor, *270*

T

TARAKAN ISLAND

Report on operations in Borneo, 185

TARGET DATE

Planning date for the end of organized resistance by Japan, 122, 254, *288*
Target date for the invasion of the Tokyo Plain, 119
Target date for the seizure of Balikpapan, 119

TENTH AIR FORCE

Progress report on operations in China, April 1944 through June 1945, 193

"TERMINAL" CONFERENCE

Agenda for the conference, 102, 105, 107, 109, 111
Program and procedure for the conference, 124, 127, *270*
Size of military staffs for *TERMINAL*, 114, 115
Statements regarding adjournment of the conference, *335*

THAILAND

Directive to the Supreme Allied Commander, Southeast Asia, 176, 252, 258, *292*
Japanese situation, capabilities, and intentions in the southern areas, 16, 38
Progress report on operations in the Southeast Asia Command, 169

TIMOR

Portuguese participation in operations to expel the Japanese from Portuguese Timor, 3, 5, 253, *280*

TOKYO PLAIN (See Japan)

TRAINING

Training and equipping Chinese forces, 193
Size of Portuguese forces acceptable for training and operations in Timor, 5

TRANSPORTATION

Admiral Mountbatten's statements regarding operations in the Southeast Asia Command, *304*
Internationalization of the Danube River, 228
Transportation facilities in Burma, 173
Transportation position in Japan, 20

TRINCOMALEE

Preparation of base for support of naval operations in SEAC, 173

TROOPSHIPS (See Shipping)

TSUSHIMA, STRAIT OF

Line of communications from Kyushu to Vladivostok, *332*

XX BOMBER COMMAND

Progress report on operations in China, April 1944 through June 1945, 191

Note: Italic numerals refer to pages in minutes of meeting.
Plain type numerals refer to pages in C.C.S. Papers.

INDEX

U

U.S.S.R.

Basic undertakings and policies for the prosecution of the war, 249, *309*

Boundary line between operational zones of the U.S. and Soviet air forces in Korea and Manchuria, *329*

Japanese foreign policy, 18, 41

Liaison groups between the American and Soviet commanders in the Far East, *330*

Policy for the release of information to the Russians concerning the Japanese war, 130, 131, 133, 253, *287*

Preparation of plans for keeping open sea route to Russian Pacific ports, 119

Radio stations in Petropavlovsk and Khabarovsk for transmitting weather data, *326*

Selection of emergency ports and airfields, *331*

Separate U.S.-U.S.S.R. zones for naval and air operations in the Sea of Japan, *327*

UNITED KINGDOM

British contribution to the final phase of the war against Japan, 136, 139, 141, 177, 251, *274*

British forces available for the invasion of Japan, 137, 251

General MacArthur's comments regarding British participation in the assault against Japan proper, 141

The President's statement regarding reconstruction and rehabilitation of the United Kingdom, *311*

The Prime Minister's statement regarding United Kingdom import program, *311*

Visit of a British corps commander and accompanying officers with General MacArthur and Admiral Nimitz, 145, 251, *276*

UNITED MARITIME AUTHORITY

Provision of personnel shipping for the requirements of Allied governments, 236, 243, 254, *301*

V

VLADIVOSTOK, SIBERIA

Line of communications from Kyushu to Vladivostok, *332*

Selection of emergency ports and airfields, *331*

VULCANIA, MS

Use of captured German passenger ships for movement of U.S. troops in the Pacific, 46, *300*

W

WEATHER (*See* Meteorology)

WILSON, FIELD MARSHAL SIR H. M.

Field Marshal Wilson's statement regarding the appointment of Colonel Douglas as Chief Commissioner to the Allied Commission in Italy, *288*

Y

YELLOW SEA

Efforts to sever the Japanese line of communications between Japan proper and the China Coast, *315*

Report on air operations from Okinawa and Iwo Jima bases, 184

Z

"ZIPPER"

Progress report on operations in the Southeast Asia Command, 169

Note: Italic numerals refer to pages in minutes of meeting.
Plain type numerals refer to pages in C.C.S. Papers.

www.ingramcontent.com/pod-product-compliance
Lightning Source LLC
Chambersburg PA
CBHW060454300426
44113CB00016B/2585